Anonymous is one of porn directors in the ... lives in London with his girlfriend.

TOUCH WOOD

CONFESSIONS OF AN ACCIDENTAL PORN DIRECTOR

Anonymous

sphere

SPHERE

First published in Great Britain in 2007 by Sphere
This paperback edition published in 2008 by Sphere
Reprinted 2008 (twice)

A CIP catalogue record for this book
is available from the British Library.

ISBN 978-0-7515-3774-1

Typeset in Fairfield by M Rules
Printed and bound in Great Britain by Clays Ltd, St Ives plc

Papers used by Sphere are natural, renewable and recyclable
products made from wood grown in sustainable forests and certified
in accordance with the rules of the Forest Stewardship Council.

Mixed Sources
Product group from well-managed
forests and other controlled sources
www.fsc.org Cert no. SGS-COC-004081
© 1996 Forest Stewardship Council

Sphere
An imprint of
Little, Brown Book Group
100 Victoria Embankment
London EC4Y 0DY

An Hachette Livre UK Company
www.hachettelivre.co.uk

www.littlebrown.co.uk

For all the wankers in the world and the kind
souls who take their clothes off for a living

This is a work of non-fiction. However, the names and identities of some of the people and places in the book have been disguised to respect and protect their privacy

TOUCH WOOD

One

It's 8 a.m. and I'm standing outside Super Sex Lady in Pigalle, Paris, when it dawns on me. I'm not sure if it's the hundred porn films I've just watched on fast forward that get me thinking. Or if it's the collection of whips, vibrators and chains stuck underneath my plastic seat in the plywood booth that swings it. Or indeed the over-enthusiastic shouts of the next-door businessman. Whichever way, I can't help thinking: I could do better than this. I am an intelligent, educated man; I could do way better than this.

It's time I got into the porn business.

To be honest, my other career isn't exactly on fire. I have been playing shitty bass guitar for shittier bands for the last fifteen years. I'm only here in Paris because they promised me a first-class return on the Eurostar and two hundred quid in cash. Quite frankly something's got to give. I am hardly rolling in it. I am also not making my dad terribly proud. But then he is a vicar. Nothing short of beatification would get his attention. So porn it is.

And why not? People always say you should do what you know and love, and I know and love porn. While most men have a few dodgy old copies of *Clitty Cats* in among their box sets of *The West Wing*, or a *Cocks and Throbbers* left over from a stag weekend in Amsterdam, I have walls and walls of the stuff. In fact I used to have a top cupboard so crammed with magazines that when my girlfriend opened it, she was engulfed by the river of porn that poured out and very nearly drowned.

But these days porn doesn't hurt anyone. It's a perfectly legitimate business and has been since the summer of 2000. It's consenting adults screwing consenting adults, being filmed by consenting adults and watched by drunk and horny bastards alike. It is an interesting industry and I have been thinking about it for a while. Well, sitting around backstage, waiting for the star to turn up, you have plenty of time to contemplate your navel and come up with a change of career. The difference being that this plan is actually going to make it off the beer mat it was written on. I've even done a bit of research. I've quietly asked around. Sought the opinion of the occasional roadie. Chatted to a video director who has a mate who has a mate. I've read the business reports in the pink pages. I've cut articles from lad mags. I've made attempts to surf the net. And the figures and the statistics all seem to add up. Unlike in the States, where every year they make around eleven thousand hardcore movies and porn purveyors like Vivid Entertainment have an estimated revenue of $100 million, the industry in the UK is tiny. Just a few blokes with punning names and handicams. It is ripe and ready for the picking. And I'm the man to do it.

I can't see anything wrong with that. I celebrate my brave decision with a couple of miniature bottles of white wine on the train on the way back from Paris and fall asleep with my mouth open, thinking I can't wait to share my idea with my girlfriend, Ana.

*

'Hi honey,' she shouts from the sitting room, as soon as I get through the door. 'How was it?'

I find her all clean and soft and curled up on the cream sofa drinking a cup of tea. The cat is next to her, as are a pile of socially acceptable girls' magazines.

'Not bad,' I say, plucking up the courage.

'Good,' she replies. 'There is some food in the fridge, if you fancy.'

It is on the tip of my tongue. But she looks so sweet and happy, with her blonde hair wet, straight from the shower. Why bother to upset the status quo, I think? It could jeopardise our relationship. I'll tell her when I've got the company started. When I am up and running. In fact what is the point of telling anyone at all? If there's anything worse than a porn director, then it's a wannabe porn director with no film credits to his name. I'll stay schtum while I sort things out. Keep them all wondering, especially my dad.

Two days into my porn career and it has already become clear that this is not going to be an easy industry to crack. For a start there is no obvious person to call to ask what to do and no manual to consult. I mean, if I want to know about the music industry there are endless magazines and companies and TV programmes to watch to help you get started. However with the porn industry, how do you know where to start? If I'm going to make a film, I think, the first thing I need is girls. But where do you find them? And how would they know that I am legit? How would I know that they are? Can I be legit even if I haven't made a film yet? I spend most of my first day in porn at home in my apartment in north London leafing through the back pages of the *Stage* newspaper, looking for glamour models. All I find is advert after advert of girl groups gagging to be the new Spice Girls.

I have to say, I'm tempted to call up and offer them a career. Although then I think it is probably better to go for professionals on my first shoot. After all one of us has to know what we are doing.

My next port of call is the net. Having spent the best part of my twenties and thirties either in the pub, on tour or hanging out in nightclubs, I am the first to admit I'm not the most computer literate of people. I know how to send an email and write a letter but that is about it. I waste a lot of my time looking at sites for adult models who turn out to be just that: models who are adults, as opposed to children, and there is not a pussy or an arse shot between them. Then after a few hours flirting with the letter 'X' and 'X-rated', I stumble across something that looks hopeful. So I call.

'Hello Top Drawer Models,' comes this jaded, nasal male voice down the phone.

'Oh hi, hello,' I say, suddenly sounding stammeringly posh. 'Um, I wonder if you can help me?' There is silence down the other end of the phone. 'Hello?'

'Yes?' comes the voice.

'I am looking for some girls for a porn shoot,' I enquire, like I'm sourcing a new sofa.

'Yes.'

'So I was wondering if you could talk me a through a few things?'

'Like what?'

I can hear him put something in his mouth. He starts to crunch into my ear.

'Like, um, are you legitimate?' I ask.

'Legitimate?'

'Yeah, you know, like legal?'

'If you mean are all our girls tax-paying citizens with up-to-date VAT payments, then the answer is probably no. But if you mean have they been dragged kicking and screaming from the bosom of their family in Eastern Europe and packed off into the white slave trade, then the answer is also no. Everyone we have on our books wants to be on our books and they earn good money doing it.'

'Good, great,' I say. 'That's very good news.'

'For you or them?'

'Both of us.' I try and laugh, but it comes out like a gagging cough. There is another silence down the phone. 'So,' I say. 'I'm looking for girls for a film.'

'Well, you've come to the right place,' he says.

'I have plenty of money,' I hear myself saying. Why I feel the need to impress this man I have no idea. 'So I am looking to invest in something really special.'

'That's good,' he replies. His interest is only mildly piqued.

'I have only just started,' I confess. 'But give me a year and I shall be huge. One of the biggest pornographers in the industry.'

'Of course you will,' he says.

'I am the director of Touch Wood Films,' I say. 'I have a feeling that we shall be doing a lot of business.' There is another long silence. 'Anyway, I've had a look at your website and I am not quite sure what some of these terms mean.'

'Right?'

'So if I could just go through them one by one then I would be absolutely sure about what I am after? Do you mind?'

There is a long sigh down the end of the phone. 'Go on then.'

'Thanks, what's your name?'

'Derek,' he says.

'Thanks, Derek.' I reply. 'So, um, implied nude?'

'Oh, that's your usual *FHM*, *Loaded* sort of stuff: see-through bra, panties or, you know, topless with a see-through scarf.'

'Oh, OK,' I say. 'Artistic nude?'

'Naked but tasteful.'

'UK mag naked?'

'Oh, that's naked, bending over or with your legs open. Pink.'

'Continental? Or US mag?'

'That's legs open with a finger or a dildo.'

'Right. Bondage soft and hard is fairly self-explanatory.'

'Yes,' he yawns. 'Fetish is whips, water sports is pissing. Spanking is spanking. Then you've got your girl-girl, your boy-girl soft and hard, i.e. with cocks and not with cocks. Your DP – double penetration.'

'I know that.'

'One up each hole,' he continues. 'And then your multiple.'

'Multiple?' I ask.

'As many cocks and toys up the hole as you can get,' he replies.

'Oh.'

'And obviously the more you want, the more you pay,' he says.

'Fine,' I say.

'So what are you after?'

'Um,' I say. 'Would you mind if I called you back?'

Fucking hell, I think, as I sit back on the sofa. I knew there were different degrees of dirty; I knew about DP, G-G and B-G, I couldn't fail to with a porn habit like mine, but I didn't know it was all so ordered and categorised and priced accordingly. I was just sort of under the impression that when you made a porn film you simply got people into a room, asked them to fuck and filmed it. Apparently not. According to this Top Drawer website, some girls will only do certain things, like be spanked and snogged by other girls, whereas others will have three dildos shoved up their backside. I take out my notebook, turn down *Richard & Judy* on the TV, and conclude that if I am going to make it in this industry I am going to need the spankers, and quite possible the three-dildo girls, plus a shed-load of money.

Fortunately Ana is out on a job when I dress up to see the bank manager. She is a fashion stylist and has been working in the industry for about fifteen years; she does anything from the *Guardian*, *The Times*, *Vogue*, *Cosmo* through to *Elle*, and the occasional advertising shoot. Ana is usually rung up at a moment's notice for her jobs and it was touch and go this morning as to whether she was going to leave the house at all. Then *Elle* confirmed at the last minute and she was gone by 8 a.m. Having said that, I think she is already beginning to suspect something is going on. I am not being my usual depressed lazy self so her antennae are on full alert. Well, when your life is spent playing sessions in other people's rock bands, there tends not to be any great need to get up early. Most days I slob around until eleven, before I drag myself out from under the duvet to shovel in some cornflakes. However, since I have decided to become the richest pornographer in the UK, I have been a whole lot more motivated. Still, not even I could explain away a suit at ten in the morning.

I think the only reason the manager of my local bank agreed to see me was because I have £20k sitting in my deposit account and have done for the last eight years. It is the spoils of a more successful stint at the bass in the late eighties, when I toured with some household names and drank my bodyweight in expensive champagne. I always vowed that I would spend it on a house or a wedding or something useful; I wouldn't piss it against the wall like I had with almost everything else.

Andrew greets me at the door. Grey suit, grey tie, grey shoes, grey hair. I am a little worried how this meeting is going to go.

'So,' he rubs his hands before indicating for me to sit opposite him, 'how can I help you today?'

I look across his desk. There is nothing but his computer, some pens, a pad, a photo of his two buck-toothed children in a brown card frame and another shot of him skydiving on the back of someone else. He doesn't strike me as a man with a massive porn collection, but then again first impressions and all that.

'I want to start up my own business,' I say. 'I need a business account and that stuff.'

'Great.' Andrew rubs his hands again. 'What sort of a business?'

'The adult entertainment business,' I continue.

'Ah,' he replies.

'I thought that I would be very straight with you from the off,' I say. 'My father's a vicar. I find it quite hard to lie to people in authority.' What the hell am I saying? I should shut up now. But instead I carry on. 'I want to make porn films.'

'Porn films?' He looks shocked. He stops rubbing his hands. His ears are going red. Shit. He's a one-copy-of-*Clitty Cats* kind of guy.

'Very respectable porn films,' I hear myself saying. 'It's a legitimate business, all above board. You can make lots of money doing it.' The blood is leaving his ears. I get out pages of A4 from my black leather wallet and start trying to win him over with statistics. I hit him with the Vivid

Entertainment profits. I mention the eleven thousand films made every year in the US. I add that porn has an annual turnover of $13.5 billion in the States alone. There are 4.2 million sites on the web. Some sixty-eight million porn search engine requests every day. Of which 28 per cent are made by women. 'So we're all at it,' I conclude, giving him my best Brixton Academy smile.

'Well, not quite all of us,' he replies.

'Yes, but enough to make it a viable business, don't you think?'

He looks at me and I can tell he knows that I'm right. 'What were you thinking of calling it?' he ventures.

'Well, not Big Anal Dildos, if that's what you're thinking,' I laugh. He doesn't. 'Something along the lines of Touch Wood?' I suggest.

'That smacks of porn to me,' he says.

That is the idea, I think. 'What sort of thing do you have in mind?' I ask.

'Something innocent. Not mucky. Like a meadow?' he replies.

'A spring meadow?' I say.

'Fine,' he replies. 'Spring meadows are nice and respectable things. That could be the name of the holding company.'

'Absolutely. Spring Meadow.'

'And write me a letter promising not to bring the bank into disrepute or involve yourself with anything that might come back on us and I say we have a deal.'

'Really?'

'Why not,' says Andrew. 'And don't tell me anything more about the business. I don't want to know.'

'Of course,' I say.

'To Spring Meadow!' He stands up to shake my hand.

'Good luck. And oh,' he adds, 'make sure you never get into debt.'

I leave Andrew's office all fired up and excited. I am on a roll. It is all I can do to stop myself from going to my local, the Water Rat, to celebrate. Instead I stride home to my flat off St John's Wood High Street and get back on the phone. If I am going to have a proper porn company that makes films, I am also going to need a website where I can sell things, like dildos. I have heard that this market's massive and I could do with a piece of it to finance the more creative parts of my business. But in order to have a website, I need to be able to take payment from credit cards like Visa and MasterCard. I call the Royal Bank of Scotland to ask them about opening a Spring Meadow account.

'Sorry,' says Shelly, after I have given her the spiel and my statistics. 'We don't do anything below the waist.'

'What, nothing?' I say.

'No.'

'No willies?' I ask.

'No willies,' she replies.

'Let me get this right,' I say. 'Credit card companies are happy to make tens of millions in profit from all the porn on the net just so long as you don't know about it?'

'I couldn't possibly comment,' she says, before hanging up.

Time to go down to the Water Rat to commiserate.

I am three pints in when my mate Seb and his girlfriend Antonia walk in. She is a posh, Home Counties girl with a love of horses and a hefty serving of Catholic guilt. He is an eighties adman who is not doing so well in the noughties. Well, why else would they be coming for a swift half on a Tuesday afternoon? They buy a drink. I buy them another. And soon I am sharing with them my secret that I haven't even told the woman I've been living with for the past eight and a half years.

'Porn!' squeals Antonia in the sort of loud voice that only pertains to certain girls of her class. 'What a fucking scream!'

Seb is a little more reticent. 'Honestly, do you really think that you can make it?'

'It's ripe and ready for the taking,' I say. 'It is like the music industry was twenty years ago. And I know that like the back of my hand.'

'Hey,' says Antonia. 'Why don't you do one at our house? We've a leather sofa and a shag pile rug. What more do you want? And Seb can shoot it!' She beams with excitement and alcohol. 'Think about it, Seb. What a laugh! You will pay, won't you?' she asks. 'Cash?'

'Um, I don't know,' says Seb, sipping his lager top. 'I'm not sure.'

'He's not sure,' I say to Toni.

'What's not to be sure about?' she says. 'You used to shoot commercials. What's the difference between a beaver and a can of beer?'

'Well, er—' mumbles Seb.

'You would pay, wouldn't you?' she checks again.

'Yes, of course,' I say. 'This is a proper business.'

'How much?' she asks.

'Seven hundred?' I suggest.

'Make it a grand a day and you're on.' Toni whips out her slim hand. 'Shake,' she commands. I do. 'Done!' she declares and sits back on the banquette. 'Seb, darling,' she adds. 'Get us a V and T.'

By the time I leave the pub at around 8 p.m. with a skinful of eight pints I have agreed to meet up with Seb the next day to try to sort out the shoot in their expensive Maida Vale pad. Needless to say, Seb and Antonia have been sworn to secrecy. Ana can't find out. Ana can never find out. She is a nice girl from Norway. If she ever knew what I was about to do, I'm sure she would leave me. And I couldn't cope with that.

Amazingly, Seb knocks on my door at 10 a.m. Tall with dark hair and a straight nose, he is looking the worse for wear this morning, but he is holding a bag full of croissants and a couple of cups of latte coffees to compensate. I have to say I wasn't expecting him to turn up.

'Toni sent me,' he declares, as he walks in. 'She is very keen for this project to work.'

I knew he was hard up. But I didn't realise things were bad enough for him to start looking to me for a job. In the old days it was always me asking him for money, a job, a bed for the night. The first night I met him in Henry J Beans on the King's Road in the late eighties, he bought me a cocktail. However, what is even more extraordinary than Seb's arrival is the fact that he actually has a contact who works in the porn industry.

'When I say works,' he clarifies, 'he officially edits wedding videos. But in his spare time he edits porn. I have known him for years. I met him through my first business partner who used to snap weddings back in the eighties. We had this office in west London. I was trying to break into adverts; I was photographing lots of things on the side, as was my mate. Anyway, he hooked up with a porn photographer working over the road. Then he jacked in weddings, cut his hair and changed his name to something ridiculous. We went bust and I haven't seen him since. Before he left, though, he introduced me to this bloke Dave, who may, or may not, be useful. Do you want his number?'

Dave may be useful but he is certainly not busy. He

agrees to meet us that afternoon in his studio just outside Reigate. Seb puts a whole can of oil into his old BMW and we set off down the A3. It turns out, as we sit in a jam at some traffic lights, that he already has some ideas for the film.

'I tell you what will sell,' Seb says. 'Girls with red hair.'

'Really,' I reply, staring out of the window. 'Why do you say that?'

'Well, girls with red hair are sort of exotic, but not the usual Asian exotic, and they've got this amazing skin and freckles everywhere.'

'Right,' I say, turning to look at him. He is staring ahead clearly lost in thought. 'Well, maybe.' I smile as I remember Antonia's younger sister is a ginga with great tits.

We spend about an hour driving around the backstreets of Reigate trying to find Dave's studio. Eventually we find him the other side of a chipped white wooden door above a garage.

'Mate,' he says to Seb, although they are obviously not. 'Good to see you.'

He is quite a vision as he walks towards us. Legs like a Peperami, a thin moustache, a few wisps of hair pulled across the top of his pasty head, Dave unfortunately looks like the sort of bloke who's been banned from walking within a hundred yards of every primary school in the area.

'Hello,' he says to me. I shake his hot hand. 'Nice to meet you. Come in. Come in.' He beckons, ushering us past him. 'Come in to mission control.'

After a cursory look around the place, it is apparent that this mission control could barely send a letter, let alone a rocket into space. There are mountains of videos gathering dust all over the floor. A couple of orange leather chairs that are bleeding foam at the seams sit in front of an editing suite, itself peppered with empty Styrofoam cups and half-squashed Coke cans. Seb and Dave take the orange chairs and chat about the good old days when Seb was young and Dave had hair. Meanwhile I find myself sinking slowly into the bowels of the brown sofa that is shoved up against the opposite wall. On the screen in front of me is the frozen face of a bride. Her cheeks are flushed, her mouth is wide open, she is about to drink a glass of champagne.

'So you guys are getting into porn,' says Dave eventually, running his thumb and forefinger over his moustache.

'That's right,' I say from the sofa.

'Well, I edit a shitload here,' he says. 'You'll find plenty of us wedding video people do. There's a season for weddings. May to September. But porn is always in season. If you get my drift.' He laughs. Seb and I laugh along, too. 'I've got some great stuff here,' he says. 'Wanna take a look?'

Before either of us has a chance to nod, Dave's out of his chair, taking the bride off the screen and replacing her with a grainy close-up of a vagina. The camera pulls back to reveal a middle-aged bloke with a slack stomach and a hard cock. He takes the woman, turns her over and shoves his dick in from behind. The woman starts to shout, 'Fuck me, fuck me, fuck me', at the top of her voice and the man does just that to the accompaniment of some incidental music.

'Great, isn't it?' says Dave, a smile peeking out from under his 'tache. 'This is top of the range stuff.' Seb doesn't say a word. I smile at Dave. The shaking camera pulls back some more to reveal a heavily patterned carpet and a dark-red Draylon sofa.

'I'm thinking of shooting in glamorous surroundings,' I say. 'You know, upmarket sort of stuff?'

'Really?' says Dave, somewhat distracted by the increasingly vigorous doggy on the screen. 'Why?'

'You know, to make it more aspirational,' I say.

'Aspirational?' he repeats. 'Why the fuck would you want to do that?'

'To make it better to look at? Appeal to a broader, more sophisticated market?'

'We've always done it like this,' he says, picking up a packet of Embassy cigarettes. 'No point in reinventing the wheel.'

He turns back to look at the screen. The moaning and thrusting continue apace. We all fall silent and stare. 'Harder, harder,' screams the girl, her white blonde hair whipping around at the top of the screen. 'Yes, yes,' she yells. Seb shifts in his seat. Dave's mouth opens slightly. I cough. 'Yes, yes, yes,' she cries again. Seb scratches his nose. 'Yes, yes.' Suddenly the man pulls out and pushes his cock between her parted buttocks. There is some thrusting and wanking, and he comes all over her arse. The door opens. He rubs the sperm into her buttocks with his veined hands. Daylight pours into the studio. And we all turn to look.

'Oh hi,' says the silhouette of a young woman, backlit by sunlight. 'I was just—', her voice trails off as she takes in the scene: three slack-jawed blokes sitting in the dark, a large cum shot on the screen before them, '—seeing . . . how . . . you . . . were doing with my wedding . . . video.' She takes a step backwards towards the light. I recognise her as the blushing bride with the glass of champagne in her hand. 'But I can see you're busy.'

'Oh, don't worry about that, love,' says Dave, getting out of his seat. 'Come and sit yourself down. Do you want a tea? Coffee? A Bourbon biscuit? I can show you what I've done so far? It's coming along nicely. If you don't mind,' he says to Seb and me. 'Um,' he looks at the bride.

'Emily,' she says, sitting down in Dave's orange seat.

'Emily and I have a meeting?' he says, his eyes indicating the door.

'Of course,' I say. 'We'll call you?'

'Right you are,' he winks.

'Come on then, Seb,' I say.

'Good afternoon,' Seb nods to the bride as he passes. 'Ah, congratulations.'

'Thanks,' she mumbles.

'I hope you'll be very happy,' he adds, as we walk through the door.

Back at the flat Seb and I set about trying to get the film off the ground. I am thinking that the best way to raise money for Spring Meadow and to secure the future of Touch Wood Films is if I have something in my hands to show people. Otherwise I could spend endless hours in endless meetings and no one will take me seriously at all. We spend the next few days looking at potential porn stars on the net. Luckily Seb is much more computer literate than I am and seems to know his way around websites. Still, no matter how many pages of photos we look at, it is incredibly difficult to work out who the girls are and what they look like, they are all so covered in make-up. However, as well as their name or stage name, their age and how far they will go, there are other useful aesthetic pointers, such as 'no tattoos' or 'pierced navel and nose'. I can see it is going to be hard to find anyone who looks like the sort of girl I am after.

'How about her?' asks Seb. 'Poppy, twenty-three, no tattoos, no piercings.'

I lean in to take a closer look. She looks like a Bulgarian tart. 'No, for God's sake, look at her. She doesn't look twenty-three. She looks fifty-three.'

'How about her?'

'Angle?'

'I think she means Angel,' says Seb.

'Oh. She doesn't look too bad. But she's got tats, a pierced navel and fake tits.'

'They've nearly all got fake tits,' says Seb.

'And no pubic hair,' I complain. 'Wouldn't it be nice to a see a bit of minge?'

'I think that is a film thing,' opines Seb, knowledgeably. 'So you can see it go in and out.'

'I know that,' I say. 'But it would be nice to come across a full bush every so often. It would make things so much more interesting.'

'And seventies,' says Seb.

'I liked the seventies.'

'You were a teenager?'

'Doesn't mean I didn't have a laugh,' I protest.

'The pony club and the hunt balls rocked in the Cotswolds, then?' asks Seb.

'They had their moments.'

'Oh, here we go!' he says, suddenly. 'Total Babes. Now they look like they know what they are doing.'

They certainly do. They claim to be one of the largest glamour model agencies in the UK and they have an organised and packed website to prove it. Seb and I spend the rest of the day picking an A-list of girls we want and start planning what we should do scene by scene.

Almost every film that I have ever watched goes the same way. It is as if some bloke with an afro in Germany in the seventies set the rules down in stone and no one has ever really deviated from this. Your average porn movie has four scenes that go on for about half an hour each. You normally have more boys than girls, so that you have more pricks to play with, and plenty of holes to fill. There is always a foursome orgy scene, some deep penetration and very little subtlety. You open with the hardest scene that you have, which is usually some B-G with a bit of DP and then anal. It is the same the world over. The Italians and the Germans just have different locations and prettier girls. The Marbella swimming pool is a favourite. Eastern Europeans have stunning girls with a gas heater and dodgy curtains. And for all the glitz and money they have in the States, they can hardly be accused of pushing the imaginative boat out. They often don't even bother to pretend there is a story. They start with a stiffie and go straight to anal, and they are generally shot in some bland LA house where no one has ever touched the kitchen.

I want to be a little different. I want to put in more of a story, with outside shots and links and dialogue. Give the punter a little bit more than a quick bang in a bedsit. Play around with the rules more. Start the film with a slow and erotic lesbian scene to get the viewer in the mood. And I want more girls than boys on the shoot. I have to say that my idea of a good night is not going out with a mate and both of us screwing the same girl. I would love to be the one with two girls and me. It is surely a sexier fantasy than you and yer pal Steve and some girl in a crappy flat in Bolton?

We're halfway through planning the scenes and writing the script when Ana comes home early from work.

'What have you guys been up to?' she asks as soon as she comes through the door. Seb scrambles around gathering up the notes and papers while I try and head her off at the sitting-room door.

'How's your day been,' I ask, blocking the way.

'Fine,' she says, dropping her bags and flicking her long blonde hair. 'We finished early. I tried to call you for a drink but your mobile's off and the phone has been engaged all afternoon. What have you been doing?' She pushes past me. Her short, flowered summer dress brushes against my jeans. 'Oh, hi, Seb,' she says. 'Have you been here all afternoon?'

'Yes,' he says, his posh cheeks pinking. The poor bloke is giving the game away by just standing there.

'Nothing naughty?' she laughs.

'God no,' he says, letting off a rattle of laughter like a bloody machine gun.

'We've been on the net,' I say quickly.

'Oh yeah?' says Ana.

'Looking up advertising agencies for Seb.'

'Right,' she says. She has fortunately lost interest. 'D'you fancy a drink in the pub?'

At the Water Rat we bump into Antonia and an old banker friend of mine called Chris. He is a good-humoured sort of bloke with a wide girth, a fat wallet and a face florid from a decade of lunching at other people's expense. As soon as I walk up to the bar to get our round of drinks I can tell that Antonia has not kept her mouth shut. Chris has a large smirk across his face and a twinkle in his rheumy eyes. He comes up behind me at the bar, slaps my arse and whispers forcefully into my ear:

'I hear you've got a new line of business.'

'I'm working on it,' I say, shooting Toni a look out of the corner of my eye. She giggles into her bag of salt and vinegar crisps.

'Well, any time you want to use our place for a shoot you are more than welcome,' he says, giving my shoulder a squeeze. 'I'm sure Alice won't mind. In fact I reckon she'll think it's a huge laugh!' he sniggers.

'I might just take you up on your offer,' I say.

Chris and Alice have a large house in Notting Hill that

they have just done up. It is luxurious in the extreme, with modern furniture, smooth lines and crisp white sheets. Just the sort of thing I am looking for.

'I've spent £100k doing up the bathrooms,' he laughs. 'Someone better get laid in them because I'm sure as hell not.'

As I order the drinks at the bar I can't help but think that things are shaping up nicely. I have two sets of locations – Seb's cool place around the corner and now Chris and Alice's des res house – as well as an editor, a director and a list of models I want to book. All I need now is to get myself a cameraman, finalise my script and I will be in business. Oh, and book myself some stars.

The next day Seb and I call up Total Babes to run through the list of girls we want to see for a casting. I've been on enough music video shoots and listened to enough showbiz stories to know that casting is an important part of the business. Quite apart from the couch option, which I have made a very serious and conscious decision to stay well clear of, as I value my balls and my relationship with Ana, I also know that the camera does often lie and it is always better to see your models in the flesh. Especially as I am about to shell out something like seven grand of my wedding-day money on the shoot.

The bloke who answers the phone at the Total Babes office is charming and efficient. I give him the list of ten girls whom we are interested in. They are known mostly by their first names so he double-checks who we are after before completing the list.

'I'm organising a casting next week,' I say. 'Could you tell me who would be available, say, on the Wednesday?'

'A casting?' asks the bloke.

'That's right.'

'Um, I'm thinking you haven't been in this business long?'

'Er, no,' I say. 'You've got me there!'

'There is no such thing as a casting in the porn industry,' he says.

'There isn't?'

'I'm afraid not,' he says. 'There is such a demand out there; there are so many films being made and so few stars that they work every day if they want.'

'Oh.'

'They're not going to get the train in from Hastings to come and see you when they could be earning five hundred quid on a shoot.'

'I see.'

'So you choose who you want; we see if they are available, you pay us 20 per cent of what you're paying them and then we'll take it from there.'

'I pay you 20 per cent?'

'How else would we get any money?'

'Oh, OK,' I say. 'I'll call you back.'

I have to say that I am little wrong-footed by this. How can you work out which star would be good for which role if you can't see them on camera or listen to their voice? Fortunately Seb is having more luck on the cameraman front. He's had a chat with Dave, who has passed him on to a bloke going by the name of Mike Hunt.

'Mike Hunt?' I repeat.

'That's right,' he says.

'But that's the oldest joke in the book?'

'No older than Ben Dover,' says Seb. 'And he is one of the biggest stars in the business.'

'I think I have heard of Mike Hunt,' I say, trying to put a gloss on an increasingly lacklustre situation.

'You might have done,' says Seb. ' I understand he's made a lot of films. Quite a few with him in them.'

'So he's a lifestyle porner?'

'It seems that way. He'll shoot and join in at the end of the film. Or at least that's what Dave says.'

'Right,' I say. 'But he's good?'

'Apparently,' says Seb. 'Dave recommends him.'

'I'll give him a call, then.'

The shoot is set for next Tuesday. Mike Hunt is coming down from the North, where he is based, and I have got two blokes booked called Freddie and Big Stiff – they both sound very nice on the phone – and four girls from Total Babes. I have my two sumptuous locations; my script needs a bit of work but we are more or less there. All I need now is some lube and a few dildos.

Seb and I set off to the Ann Summers in Queensway as it is the only one I know the location of. For a man who is about to shoot a porn movie, Seb is remarkably squeamish. Firstly, he refuses to come into the shop. He says that it is embarrassing and asks to wait outside. He only enters after I loudly call him a 'stupid cunt' in the street. Embarrassed, he scurries in. And secondly, he refuses to play with the dildos.

'How else d'you think we can choose, if we don't look at them properly?' I ask, pulling a red rubber vibrator out of its packet.

'These aren't for us,' he mutters to the girl in the shop.

'No,' I say. 'We're making a porn film.'

Seb turns the colour of the dildo. 'Really?' she says, looking at us like we're a couple of losers who have no idea what we're doing. 'You'll be wanting this lube, then.' She points to a pink tube. 'It's much better than all the rest.'

'Thank you,' I say. 'You're very kind.'

'Are you Ben Dover?' she says.

'No,' I reply.

'No,' says Seb. 'I think *he* might know what sort of lube to buy.'

We go back to the flat and I shove all the toys and lube under the bed. Ana never looks under there. I mean, why would she? They should be safe for a couple of days. Seb and I retire to the sitting room to go through the final ideas for the script. I have tried not to be too ambitious with my first story and have kept things simple. Two students arrive in London. One is coming for an interview at a law firm and one from Brighton is to be interviewed by a professor. The Brighton girl arrives. The professor is fucking his secretary. The secretary fucks the student. The student meets the girl going to the law firm. They spend the night in a hotel room together. The room service guy arrives and sleeps with them both. They all go and meet the professor in a pub and come back and have an orgy in the hotel room. It doesn't take us too long to sort out. I reckon it should be a two-day shoot, starting in Seb's house and then moving on to Chris's place, which is going to double as the hotel room.

'Um, the thing is,' says Seb. He has been quite quiet all afternoon. I can sense something is wrong.

'What?'

'Toni says no.'

'What do you mean, Toni says no?'

'She says that she doesn't want people fucking in the house. We can't shoot there.' He is starting to stammer and looks at the floor. 'I'm sorry, man, I can't go against what she says. You know, what with all this lack of work stuff going on.'

'But I'm employing you!' I say. 'You're the director.'

'Nothing I can do,' he shrugs.

Bastard! I am so furious I can't be bothered to reason with him. The man is a pussy-whipped twat. Just because he is unemployed at the moment and she is being 'nice' about it doesn't mean he has to agree to everything she says. If I could get someone else for my shoot at this short notice I would. If I could shoot in my own flat I would. I just can't risk Ana finding out.

'Well, at least we still have Chris,' I say.

'Yeah,' he says. 'Thank God for that.'

The night before the shoot and I am not thanking God for Chris, I want to fucking kill him. He calls me on my mobile while I am in the pub and tells me there is no one at his Notting Hill palace who can let me in. He says he is away on business and that his wife is out of the country. The housekeeper is not well, either. 'So it's a no-go mate.' We both know that he is lying, but we are both too middle class to argue about it. I tell him not to worry. I sink back down in my seat. Ana returns from the loo and asks me what's wrong. It's nothing, I say. She seems to believe me and goes over to the other side of the bar to talk to a girlfriend, and I pull out my phone. I am on the verge of tears. My porn career is about to die on its arse. I am about to be made a laughing stock. I have porn stars travelling from all over the country. I have Mike Hunt getting the early morning train. This is a nightmare. I am going to have to call them all up and tell them the shoot is off. This has to be one of the worst nights of my life. I can see Ana laughing across the room. Thank God she doesn't know anything about this.

'All right,' sniffs this bloke standing next me.

'Hello.'

'Ian,' he says. 'We have met before. You came to my party a couple of weeks ago.'

'Of course! How are you? I am sorry, I'm a little bit all over the place. A few problems at work.'

'I heard,' he says.

'You did?' I say.

'Yeah, your voice is quite loud.'

'Oh right.'

'Don't worry,' he says. 'Your mate Chris let you down?'

'That's right,' I nod.

'You can use my place if you want?'

It is like he has been sent by God. 'Really?' I say. 'Are you sure?'

'Why not?'

'Is it big enough for all of us?'

'I'm sure I could squeeze you all in.'

'Thanks, mate.'

'Just be a bit careful of my neighbours.'

'Right. Of course. Whatever you say. Where is it?'

He gives me directions and tells me to arrive early-ish and not to make too much noise. I promise him money, beer, a knighthood, anything he wants. Ian smiles and says he'll see me tomorrow. I call Mike Hunt.

'Mike?' I say.

'Yeah?'

'There's been a change of plan.'

'Right.'

'The shoot's been moved to Battersea.'

Two

The day of my first-ever shoot – it's pissing with rain and I'm exhausted. I've been up half the night, drinking wine, smoking fags and whispering the change of location to porn stars down my mobile phone. What am I doing this for? This is not quite the golden start that I was after. Ana became increasingly annoyed with my furtive behaviour. I told her it was some music video shoot that someone was asking me to help out on and that things were going a little pear-shaped. She asked me three times if I was getting paid. After I reassured her yet again that I was, she sighed and sloped off to bed.

However, when she caught me stuffing sex toys into my bag this morning it was a different story. I can honestly say I have never seen a face like it. Her eyes were totally round and her mouth hung open. She was paralysed by shock and fear and was so appalled by my scrabbling around in the corner of the room with a collection of giant rubber cocks that she was silenced for a very helpful three seconds.

'It's a heavy metal shoot,' I lied. 'God knows what they're want with this shit.'

For some reason, she believed me. I think perhaps she

wanted to. The alternative explanations were too devastating to contemplate.

So for the moment I am in the clear, which is more than I can say for the traffic going over Albert Bridge. It's solid. I can't believe that this cab is taking so long. I'm supposed to be there at 9.30 a.m. and we are not moving. The windscreen wiper is rubbing against the glass. The loud squeaking is beginning to get on my nerves.

'Is there a short cut?' I ask, leaning over the ginger velour of the front seat.

'What?' mutters the driver.

'Can't you get me there any quicker?'

'I'm doing my best,' he replies, gesticulating towards the road in front of him.

I sigh and lean back into my seat. He does the same.

I'm really quite tense now. I'm supposed to be there first, if only to placate Ian. The man is a true saviour. I can't believe that both of my so-called mates pulled out at the last minute. Trying to get people to agree to let me film in their houses is the biggest and most unexpected headache of my porn career so far.

Finally the cab pulls up outside Ian's block of 1960's council flats. Low and long, made of red brick, with small windows, open walkways and poorly lit corners, they are a triumph of municipality over humanity. Not the sort of location I was after.

I pay the cabbie and take the dank, concrete stairs to the second floor. As I walk slowly along the corridor, buffeted by the wind and driving rain, I try to read the directions and remember the precise location of Ian's flat. I reach a junction. Should I turn left or right? Then suddenly I spot Ian. Dressed head to foot in black denim, he is standing outside his own flat, wringing his hands.

'Jesus Christ!' he announces, as I approach. 'There you fucking are!'

'Hi, everything all right?' I ask, trying to sound relaxed.

'They're here,' he whispers,

'Who are?'

'They're ALL here,' he says.

'Good,' I say.

'Yeah, well,' says Ian, his white sweaty face coming closer. 'I wasn't really expecting all this.'

'All what?'

'All this,' he says, slowly opening his front door.

Inside, Ian's small hall is chock-a-block with coats, suitcases and black boxes. Piled up high on top of each other, they lean precariously against the pale green, peeling walls. There is only the narrowest of routes to pick your way through to the sitting room. Standing at the entrance, I can see why Ian is so tense. Bathed in the bright, white, film lights are: a naked bloke pacing the room, tugging at his own penis; a naked girl horizontal on the sofa, her legs hooked behind her ears; a man with just his pants on reading *OK!* magazine; a bloke in black laying out cable; and sitting on the sofa a middle-aged man in a ginger leather jacket with lank Richard Madeley hair.

'Ah!' says the man in the ginger jacket, standing up. 'I'm Mike Hunt, and this', he indicates across the room, 'is my mate Pete.'

'Mike Hunt.' I shake his moisturised palm. He smells strongly of pine aftershave. 'Pete,' I nod. Pete nods back. I turn back to Mike. 'Lovely to meet you. You know, after talking so much on the phone.'

'Likewise,' he sniffs. 'Have you come far?'

'North London,' I hear myself saying, like I'm at some polite dinner party. 'You?'

'Leeds,' he says.

'Of course you have,' I reply. 'I'm glad you could make it.'

'Well, you booked me,' says Mike, raising his eyebrows, revealing a whole load of white crow's feet where he's missed with his fake tan.

'Yes, right, of course, but good to see you all the same,' I say, reaching for a dildo and a clipboard out of my bag. I really the wish the bloke in the corner would stop wanking. It's making it very hard to concentrate. 'So are you familiar with the script?' I riffle through my papers.

'Script?' snorts Mike. 'You haven't gone and written a bloody script?'

'Oh, no, not really.' I feel my heartbeat rising.

'What do you mean "not really"?' asks Mike, pulling his tight jeans out of his crotch.

'It's a sort of scene by scene breakdown, you know, what scenes we are doing today, etc. There's a bit of dialogue. But not much.'

'Well, you won't be wanting dialogue, mate. Take it from me as a bloke who has been in the business for nearly twenty years, you don't need the stuff. It only gets in the way. Punters want fucking not chatting.'

'Right.'

'Anyway,' he adds. 'I don't know what you mean by scenes. We only shoot a scene a day in the porn business.'

'That's old school,' I say. 'I'm doing at least four scenes a day.'

'Yeah, right,' laughs Mike like he knows so much better. 'Your star's not even turned up yet.'

I look up and realise that he is right. We're a porn star short. There are supposed to be four of them for the orgy scene and there only seem to be three, in various stages of masturbatory undress. And although it is difficult to tell exactly who's who from the quality of the headshots I received, the girl on the sofa, her head now seemingly buried between the thighs of one of the boys, resembles Helga, and not my leading lady, Shell.

'Hi guys,' I say, walking over to the first bloke, his thighs spread and Helga's head bouncing up and down between them. 'I'm the director/producer.'

'Hi, man, I'm Freddie,' says the man, his accent is French and his handshake as hard as his cock.

'Freddie,' I repeat.

'Helga,' says Helga, raising her head and drawing breath. She smiles and wipes her mouth on the back of her hand, extending it for me to shake. 'I do G-G, B-G, anal but not DP,' she lists in a thick Eastern European accent.

'Oh, OK.' I slowly shake her clammy hand. 'But your agent said—'

'Don't listen to that fucker bastard!' she laughs. 'He always says such things.'

'Ah,' I say.

'Big Stiff,' interjects the guy in the white jockey pants.

'Hello,' I say, noticing he looks anything but. 'Good morning.'

'All right?' he says. 'Any idea when we might be starting?'

'Um, just as soon as I have tracked down the other girl,' I say.

'Right,' he says. 'I do need to know, you see, as it depends when I start, you know,' he looks down at his crotch, 'pumping.'

'Of course,' I reply. 'Let me just make a couple of calls.'

I walk out of the sitting room, pick my way through the hall, out the front door and straight into the rain-soaked corridor outside. Jesus Christ! I throw myself flat against the wall. Jesus Christ! Where the fuck is Seb? What the hell is going on? This is not what I was expecting. My heart is really racing. I'm short of breath. I can feel dribbles of sweat snaking down my sides. I think I'm starting to panic. I never expected them all to be so bloody naked and so bloody up for it. What is that girl doing giving Freddie a blowjob? Is she doing it for fun? For free? I haven't asked her to do anything yet and she's already got her clothes off. And so's he! I never imagined the porn world would be like this. For some reason, like other performers I always thought that they would, well, fuck to order, turn it on when they have to, and then stop as soon as the director yells cut. It never occurred to me they might go off menu, or freelance, between takes. I've got to calm down. I'm the bloke who is supposed to be in control. The boss. I just wish it looked a bit more like I'd done this before. Confidence must be the key. I take a deep breath. Confidence.

I call up Total Babes to find out where the hell Shell is. Instead of the helpful bloke promising me the best girls this side of the Atlantic, I get someone who can hardly be bothered to form a sentence.

'She's on her way,' he mutters. 'Traffic.'

'Do you know how long she will be?'

'How long's a piece of string, mate? Ten minutes.'

'Could you ask her to call me?'

'Call her yourself,' he says. He hands over the number and hangs up.

I get through to Shell on the fourth attempt. She sounds half asleep and hungover when she answers. She promises to be here as soon as she can. Apparently, she is just having a little difficulty with her transport. I ask exactly how long she might be. She gets a bit cagey and, sounding increasingly like her agent, says something along the lines of ten minutes. I lean against the damp wall. Are those ten civilian minutes? Or ten porn minutes? I take out my clipboard again. I light a cigarette and try to work out how to shoot an orgy with only three people. Where's Seb when I need him?

By the time I come back into the sitting room, resolved to start with a straight boy-girl scene that takes in anal, there seems to be some sort of argument going on.

'I don't care what he says, I won't fuck him. I won't. Not ever.' Helga is not only sounding heated but appears to have found some standards since I left the room. 'I don't care,' she continues, pacing the room naked, her slim body totally devoid of hair. 'There are rules and regulations and I know my rights.'

'Calm down, baby,' says Mike Hunt, his soft hand resting on her buttocks.

'Don't you bloody "baby" me!' she huffs, pushing his hand off. 'I won't do it.'

'What's going on?' I ask.

'Oh, hello,' says Mike turning round. 'Back again?'

'Yes,' I nod.

'Good,' smiles Mike, running his hands through his long hair. 'Well, the thing is, Big Stiff here has forgotten his Aids certificate and Helga is refusing to go on with the shoot.'

'Oh,' I say.

'Yeah, "oh",' Mike mimics helpfully.

'I am up to date,' says Big Stiff from his chair. 'Promise. I've just forgotten it. I've got my two forms of ID if that's any help?'

'Yeah, well, I don't fucking care. No fucking certificate, no fucking fucking,' says Helga, her hands in the air. 'It is as simple as fucking that.'

The agency had warned me about all the paperwork to do with porn. Before any shoot can go ahead, they explained, you need photocopies of two forms of ID to make sure that the star is not under age, plus a copy of an HIV and STD certificate confirming that they are disease-free, and the certificates have to be less than a month old. The actors are then all required to sign a release form that allows me to use the footage before they leave.

Mike hands me all the papers and I look around the room. Freddie is pacing up and down playing with himself. Pete is organising lighting and Ian is sitting on his own sofa, his white face in his hands. In the space of twenty minutes the foursome orgy scene has deteriorated into a boy-on-boy gay sex scene and only the slim possibility of Helga joining in with one but certainly not the other guy.

'Um,' I say. Everyone stops what they are doing and stares at me. 'Surely there is a way around this?'

'Like fucking what?' asks Helga.

'Well . . .' I am thinking so damn fast here. 'Well . . .'

'Doesn't your clinic have a copy of your certificate?' Mike asks Big Stiff.

'Er,' he says.

'They must have,' says Mike. 'By law.'

'Great,' I say. 'Then let's get it faxed over.'

'Right,' nods Big Stiff. 'Good idea.'

'Good,' I smile. 'Ian, do you by any chance have a machine?'

'Yup,' says Ian, indicating towards his computer in the corner, 'if it's got some paper.'

'Great.' I pick up my clipboard and double-clicking my pen. 'So which clinic is it?'

'Oh, right,' says Big Stiff, like he has just been asked the most difficult question in the world.

'Where d'you go and get your tests done?' asks Mike.

'Hang on,' he says.

'Where do you live?' asks Mike.

'Hertfordshire,' he says.

'Hertfordshire.' I make a note. 'D'you get tested in the same area as you live?' He nods. 'Are you tested under your porn name or your real name?'

'Real name.'

'Which is?'

'I'd rather not say out loud.'

'You could whisper it to me?'

'OK,' he says, getting out of his chair. 'Lesley . . .' he mumbles very quietly in my ear.

'Thank you,' I say. 'I'll make a couple of calls and I'll be back in a second. Ian,' I ask, 'what's the fax number here?'

Armed with the number, Big Stiff's real name and my mobile, I go back outside to the rain-soaked passage to see if I can save the shoot from total collapse. His Hertfordshire clinic are helpful and understanding and amazingly agree to send over Lesley's Aids certificate within the hour. So now the only thing I have to sort out is the whereabouts of Shell.

I call and she picks up first time.

'All right?' she says.

'Hello,' I reply. 'Shell, I was just wondering where you are and exactly how much longer you will be?'

'Oh, right,' she says. 'Well, the thing is . . .'

'Yes?'

'I'm on my way . . .'

'Good.'

'But I'm coming from Birmingham.'

'Birmingham?'

'Yeah, Birmingham.'

'Right,' I say. 'I thought you were coming from London.'

'I was,' she says. 'But I went on a night out in town last night and I ended up here. I'm not really sure how I got here, or where exactly I was when I woke up. Anyway, I won't be long. It's not far.' She sounds optimistic.

'Great,' I say.

'Yeah,' she adds. 'I should be with you by dinnertime. I'm on the train.'

'Good,' I say.

'Won't be long, see ya,' she says and hangs up.

Porn stars, it seems, are not always the most professional of employees. Despite supposedly being in charge of this charade, there is no way I can get another star at such short notice, so I shall have to wait for Shell to wend her hungover way here from New Street Station. I lean against the wall, searching in my pocket for some fags. I've now got to rewrite the beginning of the film. I have to rejig the whole morning's shoot. Needless to say, the orgy is out of the window. We're going to have to do a threesome with two men, something that was never on the agenda, and I have two blokes and a porn star who won't do double penetration. Could things get any worse?

'Hi there,' comes a familiar voice from down the corridor. I look up. It's Seb. 'Sorry I am a bit late. Toni didn't really want me to come. We had a row. I said I couldn't let you down. So here I am.'

'Thank God,' I say. 'Everyone's already in there. We're a star short. But I'm sorting it.'

'Cool,' he says. 'Mike Hunt come with his equipment?'

'Looks like it.'

'Great,' he smiles, rubbing his hands together. 'Let's go and make some porn.'

I walk back into the room and try to exude control, coupled with enthusiasm.

'Right,' I say, looking round at everyone. 'I have made a few changes to the initial running order. This is Seb, the director.' They all smile and nod. 'He'll have a word in a minute but just to say Shell is on her way. In the meantime we'll work around her.'

'OK,' nods Mike from the sofa.

'All right then, Seb?' I turn and look at him. The man has gone as white as the A4 paper I am holding. 'Seb?'

'Yes?' he says, very quietly taking in the scene.

'Are you ready to talk Mike and the stars through what you want?' I ask.

'What?' he mumbles.

'Talk them through things? Like we'd planned?' He says nothing. 'Like in the script?'

'Um,' he says, just standing there.

'I won't do DP,' says Helga, stretching on the sofa.

'I know. You told us earlier.'

'Good,' she smiles. 'You listen.'

'Yes,' I smile back. 'Let me just run through the story so you know what you are doing.'

'You 'ave a story?' says Freddie, who pauses from masturbating for just one second to look and sound surprised.

'Yes,' I say.

'Oh,' he says and carries on wanking.

As I go through my student's interview and professor story, I can't help but think that this should be Seb's job. But he seems to have lost the power of speech for the moment and we have to get the show on the road.

'Oh, that sounds quite a lot more complicated than I'm used to,' says Mike. 'But I'm sure we'll get through it all.'

'Good,' I say, tapping my hands together. 'So I think we can do the professor/secretary scene, if that is OK? Helga? Freddie?'

'Sure,' says Freddie, looking down at his own genitals, checking the firmness of his cock.

'Fine,' says Helga, getting off the sofa.

'You're going to need some clothes,' I suggest.

'And some professor glasses?' Freddie suggests.

'Great idea.' I smile.

Helga walks over and brings her suitcase in from the hall. Small, black and on wheels, it looks like something an air hostess might trail through an airport. She opens it up and pulls out three packs of wet wipes, two white surgical-looking boxes and a whole load of red nylon underwear that you might buy a lap dancer for Christmas. She also has a pair of red, plastic, heavy heels that look like they fell off the back of a lorry in Albania.

'I have this skirt,' she says, holding up something short and turquoise and covered in chains. 'And this shirt,' she adds, waving a short pink T-shirt.

'Thank you, Helga,' I say, rattling around in my bag. Amazingly I had planned for this possibility. Quite frankly, red nylon panties and a pink T-shirt are not really the look I am after. 'Um, I was thinking more along the lines of this.' I hold out a pair of white cotton pants and a short black skirt with a white shirt – a little bit more upmarket for my upmarket porn film.

'What?' she says, looking down her pretty nose at the knickers. 'But those are not sexy.'

'They are,' mumbles Seb from the corner.

'Really?' she says, turning to smile at him. 'These are sexy?'

'Yeah,' he nods.

'You're sad,' she says, plucking the knickers out of my hand. 'I wear the panties, the skirt, but I keep my shoes.'

'OK,' I say quickly. Anything to get this shoot started.

'Right,' she says, bending over to put on the underwear, slipping into the skirt and shirt. 'What do you want me to do?'

Mike Hunt's got his camera out ready to roll. It's not quite what I expected. Small and grey and very much of the handy variety, it looks like the sort of thing you would use to shoot a day out in Margate, rather than a high-quality porn film.

'Is that your camera?' I ask

'Yup,' he says, holding it up to his eye.

'It looks very small.'

'It's served me well through the years,' he sniffs. 'Lets me get into all those nooks and crannies.' He lunges forward to prove his probing abilities.

'Righto,' I say. 'What's the quality like?'

'Oh, great,' he insists. 'Definitely porn standard.'

'Excellent,' I say, thinking anything but. 'Shall we start?'

Everyone in the room looks at Seb. Seb looks back at everyone else. There's a pause. My heart starts to race again. The fucker has frozen on me.

'Mike,' I say quickly. 'What are your ideas?'

'Well,' he says. 'She comes into the room. And then, you know, the usual sort of thing. She goes down on him. He goes down on her. They fuck. They do anal over the desk and then I get the cum shot up the arse.'

'That sounds excellent.'

'OK then,' he says.

'One thing? Could he go down on her first? You know, just to mix it up a bit,' I suggest.

'What?' says Mike. 'Don't be stupid.'

'Why not?'

'Because that's not how it happens.'

'Why not?'

''Cos in porn,' sighs Mike, 'the girl always goes down on the bloke first. Shows she's gagging for it.'

'Right.'

'They expect a girl to go down on the bloke – if you

change it, it won't work. Trust me,' he winks, 'I'm a porn director.'

'Actually Seb's the director,' I say.

'Course he is, mate,' he says, slapping me on the back. 'I'm only here to help.'

'Thank you,' I smile tightly. 'Shall we get going?'

'Absolutely,' says Mike. 'OK, team!' he shouts, with a small game-show whoop. 'Let's get fucking!'

'Yeah!' says Freddie, wearing clothes for the first time today.

'OK, Helga?' asks Mike.

'Fine,' she says, putting on her lipstick.

'So,' says Mike, picking up his camera, 'do you want me to shoot hard and soft at the same time?'

'Sorry?' I say.

'Hard and soft? At the same time?' repeats Mike.

What the hell is he talking about? I can feel my heart racing again. Hard and soft? Hardcore and soft porn, I get that much. At the same time? What does that mean?

'Um,' I hesitate.

'You know, so you can double-bubble at the same time?' A small frown flickers across Mike's tangerine-coloured face as he tries to read my blank expression. 'TV? Satellite? As well as yer video market?'

'Of course!' I exclaim. 'Hard-soft, absolutely! At the same time! Exactly! Exactly what I was thinking! Good idea.'

'Great,' says Mike, turning around like I am some weirdo. 'Oh!' he says, twisting quickly back. 'Who's doing your web-site stills?'

'Um,' I say.

'I am!' says Seb, moving suddenly.

'He is,' I agree, rather too quickly. 'As well as directing . . . a bit.'

I turn around to see Seb pull a Boot's disposable camera out of his jacket pocket. My heart sinks. 'Only a couple of skiing snaps in here,' he whispers in my ear. 'Should be able to get you a few.'

'Thanks,' I say patting him on the back as he walks past. I knew he would be useful in the end.

The shoot finally gets under way. The lights are turned up bright. The crew are quiet. Mike squats down. Freddie takes up position behind Ian's desk and Helga walks into the room, dressed in her skirt, shirt and cheap red shoes. She mutters something along the lines of, 'Good morning, professor, here is your morning coffee.' The opening line, naturally, leads to her going down on him. Freddie, dressed in jeans and a T-shirt, couldn't look less like a professor. Even Pete's glasses do nothing for his intellectual status. He takes them off as he goes down on Helga – a touch that he seems inordinately proud of. All seems to be going OK. Mike is filming away, occasionally pulling back for Seb to point the snappy snap. However, no sooner does Freddie move between Helga's thighs, than she starts to make the most extraordinary noises. She moans, squeals, shrieks and squirms like a whimpering, wounded wild animal.

'Um, hang on there a second,' I say, interrupting her apparent ecstasy.

'What?' she says lifting her head off the desk.

'Very good so far,' I say swiftly. Freddie sits bare-buttocked on the floor. 'It's just that, er, we don't need all those noises.'

'What noises?' asks Helga.

'You know, those sort of moaning noises.'

'Moaning noises?'

'You know, those noises you were just making.'

'How else do you know I'm enjoying myself?' she asks.

'The expression on your face?' I suggest.

'But we always make noises,' she says.

'Well, perhaps not so loud?'

'Oh,' she says.

'Quiet noises,' I smile.

'Whatever,' she replies, lying back down on the table and opening her legs.

Freddie gets back up on all fours and puts his head straight back between Helga's thighs. She starts to shout and scream like I'd never interrupted her. They move on to full sex. They bang away like a couple of rabid terriers and then go on to anal.

I'd always thought that I might be slightly turned on by the process of making porn, or at least have my fancy tickled in some way. But once over the initial embarrassment of watching people have full-blown sex in front of me, all I can think about is: Is Mike getting the shots? And I wish Helga would stop making that noise. She is yelping like a dog now, shouting: 'Fuck me! Fuck me harder!' It's just not the sort of thing I'm after in my movie. It's so goddamn cheesy. I know she is lying. You know she's lying. It's obvious she's not really feeling it. My only hope is that all her fake enthusiasm doesn't come across as plastic on film.

Another person clearly not enjoying all the histrionics is Ian. Standing against his sitting-room door, his face is contorting with every yell, wail and exclamation. His knuckles shine bright white as his hands grip the doorknob. The doorbell goes. His face looks horrified.

'Can't you please try and keep it down,' he says, as he opens the sitting-room door.

We all stand stock still, listening to him mumble away in the hall.

'Helga,' I whisper.

'What?'

'Can you try to keep it down a bit?'

She shrugs and looks away, which I take to be Eastern European for 'yes'. Ian comes back into the room.

'My neighbour,' he stutters. 'Asking if I was OK. She says it sounds like someone is being murdered in here. She says the noise is so loud she can't watch Phil and Fern on *This Morning*. I told her I was watching a movie and she's asked me if I could turn it down a bit. I said I'd try.'

'Helga?' I say.

'All right,' she sighs.

'Shall we go for another take?' I ask.

'Do you know when you'll be needing me?' asks Big Stiff, fully pumped, from the sofa.

'Um. Has your fax arrived yet?'

'Yeah,' he says, pointing to a curl of paper on the desk.

'Oh,' I say. 'Well, I suppose we could bring you in somehow. What do you think, Seb?' Seb shrugs. 'Mike?'

'Ideally we'd shoot some DP at this point. Two boys, one girl, it would be the most natural thing to do.'

'Yes, well,' I say. 'But other than that?'

'Well,' says Mike, appearing genuinely stumped. He scratches his head and adjusts his crotch. 'Um, other than double penetration?' He whistles through the back of his teeth, deep in thought.

'I'll do it,' Helga announces suddenly from astride the table.

'You will?' both Mike and I say at the same time.

'Yeah,' she shrugs. 'I feel turned on now.'

'You do?' we both say again.

'Yeah, why not?' she says.

'Are you sure?' I add. 'I don't want you to do anything you're not comfortable with.'

'No, it's fine,' she says. 'I want to. I like double penetration. Just so long as you guys don't bang around too much.'

'What?' says Freddie, looking surprised. 'Are you accusing moi of not knowing my job?'

'No,' says Helga. 'But you know what I mean.'

'I'll be professional,' smiles Big Stiff, walking towards her, finally living up to his name. 'Where do you want to go, man?' he asks Freddie. 'Front or back?' Freddie shrugs. 'I'll take the back, then,' says Big Stiff. 'I'm a back type of guy,' he smiles and then adds quickly, 'not that I'm gay at all.'

'Let's get on with it,' says Mike. 'Big Stiff, you get some clothes on and come into the room like you are some sort of client for the professor. They are fucking on the table and you come and join in. OK? Do you think that you can do that?'

'Yeah, sure,' he says. 'Give me a minute.'

Big Stiff gets dressed into some jeans and a blue jumper. It's not quite the sort of outfit normally associated with professors and their clients, but I am almost past caring. My morning orgy has disappeared before my very eyes. My star has yet to arrive. I'm in a shitty location. I have some irate granny next-door complaining. Never has the world of porn been less glamorous, or, indeed, so incredibly un-erotic. I am just very glad that Ana is not here to see this rather expensive disaster.

Big Stiff ambles into the room as comfortably as his erection under his tight trousers will let him. He hands over his own Aids certificate and says something plot-defining like: 'Professor, here are the papers you asked for.' Meanwhile the professor is taking his secretary Helga over his desk. Big Stiff removes his trousers and pulls his blue jumper off. 'Do you mind if I join you?' he asks. 'Non,

non,' says Freddie, sounding really quite French again. 'Be my guest.' Somehow Helga contorts herself into a position where she manages to take both men up each orifice while keeping her legs out of the way to allow Mike to get the 'in and out' close-ups. Both boys move slowly back and forth, Helga yelps like a puppy and the front doorbell goes again.

'You deal with that,' says Mike, leaning right in close between Helga's thighs. 'I've got to get this on film.'

Ian goes back out into the hall and returns almost immediately with a slim, curly-haired brunette who I presume to be Shell.

'Oh 'ello,' she says, taking in the lights, Mike, me, Pete, Seb and the double penetration taking place on the sitting-room table. 'Sorry I'm late,' she says. 'That's a shit of a train journey. Took me ages. Do you have any idea how far away Birmingham is? Shaggin' miles.'

'Glad you're here,' I say, glancing back and forth between her and the double penetration.

'Ri-ight,' she says, looking around the room. 'Where's the toilet? Let me just give myself a quick douche and an enema and I'll be right with you.'

'Oh, great?' says Helga from the table. 'Is it dinnertime yet?'

'Yeah,' agrees Big Stiff, still pumping away. 'I could murder a tuna sandwich.'

So while the rest of the stars sit around eating the Somerfield sandwiches that Pete goes out to buy, Shell spends half an hour in the loo 'flushing out her pipes'. I have to say it never occurred to me that porn stars travelled around with enema and douche kits, but I suppose it makes sense. If you are taking it up the backside, the last thing you need is anything unpleasant going on. Still, I'm slightly taken aback by the matter of fact nature of it all. None of the others seems to bat an eyelid as she disappears into the bathroom. Although I can't actually look Ian in the eye any more. Poor bastard. I think I better double his beer order. He can't have been expecting all this. I've spent my life watching porn and even I didn't realise it was going to be so visceral. I can't blame him for standing around outside his bathroom looking increasingly twitchy. Fortunately Mike gives him a distraction.

'Oi, Ian,' he says.

'Yes?' he replies.

'What's the letter in the alphabet that comes after "s"?'

'T,' says Ian.

'Oh, don't mind if I do,' says Mike. 'Milk and four sugars.'

With Ian making tea for the entire room, Shell emerges from the bathroom wearing red panties, a matching bra and plastered in make-up. She looks nothing like the head-shot photo she uses on the internet. She's older and a good deal more ropy, and this girl is supposed to be my star. I wish I'd employed hair and make-up on the shoot. My years in the music business had made me wary of employing them. In my experience hair and make-up are the ones who usually make trouble on the set, either through incompetence or bitching, so I had decided to try and do without. But looking at the heavy line-painting around Shell's pale lips, I am beginning to see the error of my ways.

A Fanta and some solids seem to have perked Seb up a bit: he takes me aside and says that he's ready to direct. I approach Mike, who is sitting on the sofa picking lettuce out of his BLT. I suggest that he might like a break from directing so he can concentrate on filming and he appears to take it remarkably well.

I decide to kick off the afternoon session with the G-G lesbian scene that is to start the film. I am planning to do the links outside later on, where the girls meet, but for the moment I am keen to get the half-hour girl session in the can. And I am relying on Seb to make it happen.

'Right, let's go,' says Seb, clapping his hands together and trying to sound motivational. 'So, um, Shell?'

'Yeah,' she says, her head down; she is fiddling with the front of her pants.

'I would like you to, um, come into the room, take your clothes off, if that is OK with you,' says Seb.

'You what?' She looks up. 'I'm a porn star it's my job to take my clothes off.'

'Quite,' says Seb. 'So you do that. And then, Helga?'

'Yes,' she says.

'You embrace Shell and then you have sex,' mumbles Seb.

'What do you want us to do?' she asks, standing stark naked in the middle of the room.

'The usual sort of thing,' says Seb.

Right! That's it, I think. I have a director who is too posh for porn and who is practically tripping over the word naked. There is only room for one amateur on this shoot and that's me.

'Seb, mate,' I say. 'Maybe you should stick to stills and we should let Mike get on with the shoot?'

'Of course, of course, whatever you want.'

I can see the relief all over his face.

Mike swings into action.

'OK,' he sniffs. 'Shell, you come in. See Helga. You say something like: "What is a young girl like you doing in London?" You take your clothes off and take hers off immediately afterwards. You snog. Lick each other's tits. You go down on Helga. Then she goes down on you. You turn her over and put the red dildo up her arse and then we'll cut.'

'OK then,' says Shell.

'Um,' I say. 'In the script—'

'You're not still harping on about the script, mate?' asks Mike.

'Well, I would like some sort of story.'

'What then?' sighs Mike.

'Could Shell say: "Oh, I am sorry to bother you. Is the professor in?" And Helga says: "Oh, no. He is in a meeting. You might just have to wait".'

'And then they fuck?' suggests Mike.

'Absolutely.'

The afternoon shoot starts in a similar way to the morning. Helga shouts her head off. The next-door neighbour rings the doorbell to complain about the noise. She says that we'd better keep quiet for *Countdown* otherwise she'll be calling the police. I poke my head out of the door after she goes to see if there's any possibility of filming a few link shots outside. Depressive sixties socialist architecture is not the look I want for the film but perhaps there's a park nearby. I look up the corridor and with a jolt realise that our bright lights and screams have attracted a small crowd.

'What are you doing in there?' asks a fat woman with a leathery face, a fag in her mouth and a tight perm.

'Oh, we're making a film,' I smile, taking in the sea of some fifteen faces.

'Porn?' she asks.

'No,' I say.

'Are you Ben Dover?' she asks.

'No,' I reply.

'Told you,' elbows her friend.

'Keep it down,' adds the crone. 'We've got kiddies coming home from school in an hour.'

I go back into the flat to find Helga over the desk with a red dildo up her bum and Shell's face between her legs.

'And cut,' says Mike. 'Good work, you two. Do you want to wipe yourselves down?'

'Cheers,' says Shell as she goes into her suitcase and cracks open a packet of baby wipes. She swabs down her breasts and armpits and starts to walk towards me, wiping her fanny as she does so. 'How much more have we got to do today?' she asks. 'Because I'm shagged out.'

'But you've only just got here,' I say.

'I'm exhausted. Honestly. I can hardly move.'

'Well, you've got one scene with Freddie and then one more after that.'

'Freddie?' she says. 'I don't like French blokes. Can't I work with Big Stiff?'

'I'm sorry. I'd much prefer you to shoot with Freddie,' I say, thinking I am paying this woman five hundred quid and all she has done is ten minutes of cunnilingus and shoved a dildo up Helga's arse.

'This is the last time I am doing a job this shit,' she sighs and throws her wet wipe across the room. It misses the bin. 'Fucking hell,' she yawns. 'Can someone pick that up?'

The next ten minutes are a nightmare. Shell huffs and puffs and strops around the place, creating an uncomfortable atmosphere. Freddie wanks so vigorously in the corner to get hard, he practically gives himself blisters. The poor bloke's been pumping all day. He's come twice and been blown once, and the tension in the room is getting to him. Finally he is able to shoot. Pete turns the lights on. Mike turns over. Freddie walks into the room pretending to be the professor, takes Shell's clothes off and bends her over the sofa. He puts his cock in for the anal shot, Shell shouts, 'OUCH', at the top of her voice and we wrap the film. There is no point in carrying on. My star is not behaving. My boys are exhausted and my director still can't ask porn stars to take their clothes off. I stand at the door thanking them all, shaking their hands and peeling twenty-pound notes off a roll. At the end of the day I am around five grand down. I just hope against hope that I have something to show for it.

The next couple of days go a little bit better. In a bit of good fortune a mate of a mate agrees to lend me a sunny flat overlooking the King's Road. We shoot with the windows open. We are joined by the two other girls I booked from the agency, Olga and Camilla. Olga is a surly Slav with a pretty nose and thick lips. Over from Poland on a student visa, she is lap dancing and shooting porn to supplement her studies. Camilla on the other hand is altogether different. She has a fantastic body, pneumatic tits and an accent that can cut glass. She is a Home Counties girl with a private education and is saving up for her own stables. She will only do G-G and spanking and has the bruises on her backside to prove it.

'Bloody hell,' she says, bending over in her thong, pushing her buttocks in my face. 'Can you believe this?' Her perfectly shaped cheeks are pink, black and blue. 'I can hardly sit down. Some bitch whacked me with a hairbrush!'

None of this seems to hold her back – her moans stop the passers-by in the street. They crane their necks to see what is happening in the first-floor window, much to the amusement of Mike and Pete. By the end of three days I am sure that I have something that I can edit. We shoot Helga and Shell meeting in Battersea Park; Camilla puts on a room service uniform as she gives the girls breakfast in bed and then, after she leaves, Professor Freddie comes in to finish the whole thing off.

Come the end of the week I may be ten grand poorer but at least I have something in the can. Something that I can show investors, something that will help me raise money. Something that means I actually work in the porn industry. I am not just a bloke with plans in the pub. Seb and I go out for a small drink to celebrate. He apologises for being pathetic. He says that the situation got the better of him. I forgive him. He promises to be tougher. And we toast the future of Spring Meadow and Touch Wood Films. It is good to have a real friend on board.

One week later and we are each in an orange chair, sitting in the edit suite with Dave. Since Mike left with his camera neither of us has been able to see the rushes. I am excited, Seb is very excited and Dave can hardly contain himself.

'I never thought you two blokes would do it,' he says, putting the first tape in the machine. 'Far too nice and posh, I thought.' He turns on the tape. 'I am looking forward to this,' he announces as he scrolls forward. 'No need for any of the chat. Let's cut straight to the action.'

Ian's flat comes up on the screen. It doesn't look quite so small on film. I breathe a sigh of relief. The lighting's not bad. And the sound is OK. The first scene is Freddie and Helga over the desk.

'Oh dear,' says Dave. He leans in all concerned. 'Oh dear,' he says again. 'That's not quite what we're after now, is it?'

I stare at the screen. A wave of depression engulfs me. I can't believe what Mike has done. There are legs in the way. His feet in the shot. His reflection in the mirror. And no close-ups of the action at all.

'You need to see it going in and out,' says Dave, looking at me. 'Didn't someone tell you that?' He turns back to the screen. 'Oh no!' He points to the footage of Freddie coming just a bit off-screen. 'Look at that. That's terrible. He's only gone and missed the money shot!'

Three

It turns out that he may be Mike Hunt by name, but he is a total cunt by nature. Seb and I spend three days with Dave in his edit suite in Reigate trying to salvage something of the film. Dave does his best but all we end up with are nine scenes of people rolling around in a poorly lit room. There are some grunts and moans but no clear action at all. It's a pile of crap. My dreams of taking the industry by storm are in embarrassing tatters. Mike appears to have stitched us up good and proper.

Seb thinks he shot it badly on purpose. He pulls out when he is supposed to come in. The focus is blurred. There are legs and buttocks in the way. Seb says it smacks of dirty tricks. That Mike was making sure our project never takes off. Why would you want to help out the new guys? Give a helping hand to the new porners on the block? He wants to keep as many slices of the porn pie to himself.

And part of me thinks he may have a point. After all Mike is supposed to be a professional. He has hundreds of films to his name, half of them with him in them, pumping away with his flaccid old backside on show. How could he fuck up so spectacularly on my project? But then again I can't believe that anyone could be so malicious. I paid him nearly three grand of my savings. I told him that it was supposed to be my wedding money. I even bought him a few pints with whisky chasers in the pub. Perhaps the camera wasn't working? Maybe he wasn't used to working in those conditions? Or the flat was too small? All I know is I shall never find out because every time I phone Mike he drops my call. I return home defeated, with nothing to show for my cash at all.

I sit around the house for a week licking my wounds. Ana keeps asking me what is going on and I think I might have to tell her. Every time we go to the pub or see Seb and Antonia, or any one of our mutual friends, someone drops some sort of unsubtle hint and then everyone sniggers and exchanges looks. It looks like none of my friends is capable of keeping their mouth shut. Everyone's got a cum-shot joke up their sleeve and news of my film failure is doing the rounds. Even though English is Ana's second language, she is more fluent and articulate than most of my friends and she is bound to work it out soon. It's far better that it comes from me rather than Chris after a bottle of red, or Antonia when she's had a few at lunch.

So I book a table and I take Ana to a restaurant around the corner. I always think it is better to break bad news in public, as there is less of an opportunity for a scene. I order a bottle of top-notch white wine and a couple of portions of expensive grilled fish and try to work out what to say. Ana's done her hair for the occasion, it's blow-dried poker-straight down to her shoulders and she is wearing a low-cut black top I haven't seen before. She looks stunning and keeps smiling at me. She clearly thinks that I am about to tell her some good news. Oh shit, here goes.

'I've got some really interesting news,' I say, smiling as hard as I can.

'Great,' she says, taking a sip of her wine.

'I am going to do this most amazing, interesting project.'

'Cool,' she smiles and leans forward enthusiastically. Her tits touch the table.

'It is so exciting and so interesting.'

'Good,' she says.

'It's going to give me so many opportunities. We are going to make a lot of money.'

'Excellent.'

'A lot of money. And I am going to be a real player. There is a chance that I could be one of the best people in the industry within a year.'

'What!' she laughs. 'Tell me!'

'We're going to make a lot of money,' I repeat. 'And I am going to be my own boss.'

'It sounds very exciting,' she grins.

'The only downside is that I'm going to be a hardcore porn director.'

She puts her glass down very slowly and looks at me. 'And I thought you were taking me out to ask me to marry you.' She raises her eyebrows.

'Oh,' I say.

'Yes, oh,' she says back. 'Silly me.'

'I won't be in them myself,' I say, hoping to swing it.

'Of course you won't,' she replies. 'No one would pay to watch you fuck.'

At that moment a waiter arrives with our food. He clears his throat with embarrassment. Ana fixes me with one of her special cold stares. God. If only I knew what she was thinking.

'Um, who's having the sea bass?' ventures the waiter.

'She is,' I reply.

'Cod?' he says.

'Him,' she says.

He puts the plates down on the table and makes the sharpest of exits.

'But you're Scandinavian,' I protest. 'You're supposed to be very level-headed about these things.' She doesn't say anything. 'You're liberated. You're always in and out of those saunas.'

'That's the Swedes,' says Ana. 'I'm Norwegian. It's a little different.'

'I know you're Norwegian, darling!' I lean across the table and take her hand. Amazingly she doesn't snatch it away. 'We're going to have our own company. I am going to be a boss.'

'It's just a shame it's a boss of hardcore pornography. It's not really an ambition, is it? It's not something I dreamed of.'

'We're going to make lots of money.'

'In porn?'

'I'm going to become a serious player in a very short space of time.'

'What makes you think you know anything about the subject?' she asks. 'Actually, of course you know about the subject. You're a bloody super-fan.'

'I know I can be good at it.' I am practically pleading now. I give her my special cute smile. I stroke the back of her hand. 'I promise you. I love you. My heart. My soul. I need you on-board. What more can I say?'

'My parents will never find out?' she asks.

'Never,' I say, zipping my lips.

'Yours?'

'Never.'

'Not even your dad?'

'Most especially my dad,' I say. 'I've got just as much to lose as you.'

'OK then,' she says.

'OK then?'

'OK then,' she smiles. 'Are you really going to make lots of money?'

Well, that was so much easier than I had thought. I'd expected tears, tantrums, tearing of hair, a lecture about morals and a hundred and one questions about whether I was going to mix business with pleasure. But she took it all in her stride. Amazing. That's one of the very many reasons why I love her.

We carry on with our dinner and I omit to tell her that I have already lost about ten grand of our savings and made the worst porn film ever. Instead I fill the conversation with my plans and tell Ana about my ideas for expansion and porn domination. She is sweet and kind and supportive. I just hope she stays that way.

The first time I test Ana's patience is when I tell her Toby is moving in. Toby is an old fuckwit friend of mine who drinks too much and takes too many drugs to be employable in the real world. However, he is brilliant with computers and very cheap, so he is perfect for mine. He's just spent two weeks drying out in hospital when I pick him up outside St Mary's in Paddington. I am hoping he might be capable of concentrating for a couple of weeks on my website.

'Thanks for this, mate,' he says, as he gets into the car and throws a suspiciously large suitcase on to the back seat. 'I had nowhere else to go.'

I tell him not to tell Ana what he's just shared with me. I tell him he is staying with me to help me set up the website, to get Spring Meadow's show on the road, and the business up and running.

Ana is not best pleased when Toby walks through the door. He is unshaven and his hair is matted and unwashed.

He looks more like an eco-protester than the primary asset of an up and coming porn business. Fortunately he is incredibly charming, with the impeccable manners of an expensive education, and soon has Ana wrapped around his little finger.

I practically lock him in the spare room. I delete his coke dealer's number from his mobile and give him strict instructions that he is not allowed out until he's set up the site.

Meanwhile, on Toby's advice, I set about getting some content. I spend a couple of days scrolling through footage of my film – *Sex and the City of London* – trying to work out if I can salvage some clips that punters might want to download. There are a couple of shots of Helga being taken from behind by the big red dildo that someone might pay something for. But the best footage is of Camilla and Olga in the flat in Chelsea. It is good, fun stuff and Camilla actually looks like she is enjoying it. I get out my folder and go through all the paperwork, the ID and the STD certificates, before rootling out her number. She gave it to me as she left, saying if ever I wanted to use her again there was no point in going through the agency. It's a wonder that any of those places make any money because she wasn't the only one to offer direct bookings. Anyway, I give her a call. I have an idea she might be interested in.

Four days later we're in Hyde Park hiding behind a bush. Camilla has tears running down her face as she is laughing so much. She has just been busted with her fanny out in the grass by an off-roading jogger. And I was being so careful. We'd arrived in the park at 11 a.m., which we had hoped would be early enough to miss the nannies and too late for joggers. But apparently not. I was just leaning in for a close-up of her open legs in the long grass when this symphony of yellow and black Lycra tripped over us both. He was so shocked, he couldn't say anything. He looked from me to Camilla and back again. I'm not sure what he thought. All I know is that he got out of there like a rat up a drain.

'That was so fucking funny,' hoots Camilla, picking her pants up off the grass. 'I wish we'd got it on film!'

It strikes me that Camilla is probably the sort of girl who finds almost everything amusing and most things unshocking. When I collected her this morning from Victoria train station, she wouldn't stop talking about the fetish shoots she'd been doing that week.

'Honestly, you wouldn't believe it,' she said. 'I've been dressed up in stockings, I've been smoking. I've been in stockings AND smoking. I've been spanked. Worn a policewoman's outfit and fireman's outfit for some site that specialises in uniforms. And someone's filmed me pissing. Water sports are massive, you know.' She turned to look at me and smiled. 'You should have peeing in all your films.'

Naturally, my idea of having her dress up like a naughty schoolgirl and show her bits in the long grass in Hyde Park was something she took very much in her stride. Even when I made her pose totally naked behind the police station she remained unruffled.

'Christ!' she laughed, as she pushed her parted buttocks towards the lens. 'We used to do this stuff all the time at boarding school.'

The results of the shoot are fantastic. Camilla looks gorgeous and naughty and provocative, and the close-ups are in focus. I'm pleased and Toby is delighted. Something to put on the website at last.

In fact the website seems to be coming on great guns. My house stinks of fags and there are red wine stains all over the spare room's carpet but Toby has really put in the hours. He has set up a domain name called SexyPornFlics.com and a

PayPal account so that punters can pay for vibrators on the site.

'But what you're really after is members,' he explains, taking a drag of his fag and flicking the ash on my cream carpet.

'OK,' I nod, looking at the screen.

'Yes, well, you see, most people come in from the pub, they're pissed, they feel horny; they find a website, become a member for twenty-four dollars a month, fall asleep and forget they have joined. And they continue to pay for months and months before they realise the error of their ways. Smart people join when they are pissed, download what they want and then cancel it when they are still pissed.' He smiles.

'Right,' I say. 'Rather like becoming a member of the gym?'

'Yeah, except once people join the gym they very rarely cancel it because they are always kidding themselves they will use it one day. If they cancel, they have really given up.'

'I see.'

'So with this system you have a few months' grace.'

'That sounds great,' I say. 'But we are ripping them off a bit, aren't we?'

'Not really,' he shrugs. 'If they're too pissed to remember what they've joined, it is hardly your fault. And anyway it is much better than the bad old days of porn when you'd join a site, it would go bust and you'd find yourself still paying out to Red Hot Orgies on the monthly basis. You'd try to cancel. There was no one to cancel with and the credit card companies would refuse to stop your direct debit because they couldn't get in touch with the supplier. In the end the only way out was to cut up and cancel your credit card. So at least with PayPal acting as an intermediary for you, taking the money and billing the customer, both you and your punters are relatively protected.'

'That's true,' I nod.

'Yeah,' he says. 'But also you have to remember that the bastards who complain the most about security on porn sites are also the same bastards who leave their cards behind bars, shove them in any hole in the wall and drive off without them altogether from a petrol station.'

The more I hang out with Toby and the more red wine we drink, the more I realise he knows what he is talking about. During one night session he tells me that to get members on to a website is all about 'traffic'. We have to get as many people as we can to log on as often as we can and then I might have some sort of viable business. We need hundreds of thousands of hits in order to generate money. He says the statistics are not in my favour. A hundred thousand hits, he explains, will get me between ten and fifteen members. And at twenty-four dollars a pop that sort of cash is hardly going to make it into the bank, let alone sort out my dwindling balance. The big sites like Private, he says, have an extraordinary amount of traffic and are taking half a million members a month, at thirty dollars each.

'But you need to update every day,' he says. 'Updating is key.'

I find myself nodding along in agreement, wondering what on earth all this updating will entail and if this is possibly a simple ruse for him to move into my flat permanently. I spare Ana my worries about Toby's increasingly less temporary status in our lives and set about thinking up ways to get traffic going through SexyPornFlics. I think about making the trips to Hyde Park with Camilla more of a regular event. People would log on all the time to see her posh pussy in variously dangerous outdoor venues. Then again I think Ana might be less than liberal about me seeing so much of one porn star. And at £250 a session, there is the expense of booking her week after week. It could become quite a profligate way of getting six more people to part with twenty-four dollars a month. But then Toby tells me something quite interesting. Mind you, I did have to wait until 3.15 a.m. to hear it. Text sells, apparently. Titillate the punter with text and you might have people logging on week after week.

'A bit like Dickens,' he slurs. 'Except with tits and knobs.'

With Toby's advice ringing in my wine-soaked ears, I set about trying to turn the sex surfer on. I think about the adventures of a porn star, then realise it is probably a little too weird an idea. I moot the idea of a man who always gets lucky. But then who wants to read about a man who is more successful at shagging than they are? So I come up with the premise of the horny secretary who is gagging for it all the time. She shags in lifts, under desks, in the back of cabs, with anyone and anything. She is called Bridget Bones and works in the City. I have not worked out exactly what firm she works for yet, but I am pretty sure that's not the sort of detail the punters are after. Toby thinks it is a great idea. He even suggests that we get an advertising firm on-board to start an email campaign where one of her supposed conquests emails his mate about the horny secretary who is always up for it. We'll include some stills or possibly some footage and see if it gets passed around the City.

'It is a very cheap, easy way of getting word of mouth going,' says Toby. 'And that's half the battle.'

I spend the next week or so trying to write like a sexed-up secretary and I can safely say it is a lot harder than I thought it was going to be. By the time Ana comes home at night I am so exhausted by my imaginary sex life I can't get it up at all. Writing about sex is more difficult than having the stuff and writing like a well-fucked woman doesn't come easily to me at all. The only thing that keeps me going and amused is that anyone who pisses me off during the week goes in the column as some hard-nosed pervert. Mike Hunt is in there. He now has a fetish for putting office equipment up Bridget's fanny. I can't wait until the whole site actually goes live.

I am busy writing about putting bottles of correction fluid up my arse over my boss's desk when Andrew calls from the bank.

'Good morning,' he says, sounding breezy and efficient. 'Andrew here, I was just giving you a three-month call to check to see how the business is going?'

'Three months?' I say.

'Yes,' he replies. 'That's when you set up Spring Meadow.'

'Oh,' I say.

'I know,' he laughs. 'Doesn't time fly when you are having fun?'

'Doesn't it just.'

'So,' he inhales. I can hear the metaphorical rubbing of his hands. 'What have you been up to?'

'Oh, right. Hang on there a second.' I save the stationery sex on my screen and try to concentrate. 'You know, this and that. I have made a film.'

'Good!' enthuses Andrew. 'I'd like to see it.'

'You would?' Maybe he is more than a one-porn-tape bloke after all.

'Yes,' he says. 'And so would a couple of my colleagues.'

'Oh, right, good, the porn's in the post then,' I joke weakly.

'Better not,' he replies quickly. 'That's illegal.'

'Of course it is.'

'You should come down to the office,' he suggests. 'Bring it with you.'

'Good idea!' I say, thinking anything but.

'Excellent,' says Andrew. 'I shall look forward to that. In the meantime your account . . .'

'Yes?'

'There doesn't seem to be much movement?'

'Ah, yes.'

'Well, there is movement,' he corrects. 'Just all of it is in one direction. Out.'

'Oh, yes,' I say. 'It is mainly outgoings at the moment.'

'Yes. I have noticed. Quite a lot of outgoings.'

'Yes.'

'Yes,' he repeats. 'Do you have any plans?'

'Well, the website is about to launch.' I try and sound optimistic. He says nothing. 'It's full of interesting things.'

'Money-making things?'

'Absolutely. And I am making a new film,' I announce to myself as well as Andrew.

'That's sounds great,' says Andrew. 'When?'

'Soon?'

'How soon?'

'Next month.'

'I shall look forward to that,' he says. 'Do come into the office and have a chat. And bring a few films with you.'

'Will do,' I reply. 'In the next few days.'

I hang up and stare at the computer. Shit. That's it. I am as good as fucked. There is nothing for it. We have one more shot at getting into this industry and we'd better make it good. There has got to be nothing amateur about the next film. It has to work and it has to work well. It has to be hard-core porn with nothing polite or stammering or middle class about it at all. I have to throw everything at it. I can't keep chucking money away. I've already wasted £10k. I think I've got enough money for one more go. And that's it. Or I return to my dwindling career as a session musician and the long and dull road of increasingly miserable venues with decreasingly attractive returns.

I am sitting racking my brains working out what to do next when it dawns on me. Seb told me some gossip last week in the pub about a very old, very distant friend who might be able to help. And unlike Seb he has proper form. A news cameraman who cut his teeth on 'Local MP Opens Fête' news stories, Kent has since graduated to shift-work on a rolling news channel and has been shooting porn on the side for while. I met him about fifteen years ago when we were both young and hard-drinking and used to stay up late in clubs. I haven't seen him in about a decade. But there's no need to stand on ceremony – from what I remember Kent is a wild kind of bloke who'll either embrace an idea by the balls or tell you to fuck off. So Seb gives me his number and I make the call.

He is neither shocked nor surprised by my telephoning. In fact it is quite hard to work out his reaction at all. He is so monosyllabic and hungover I am surprised he remembers the conversation at all, let alone turns up in the pub on time. Yet he does. Two days later he wanders into the Winged Spur in Clapham dressed like some overgrown schoolboy, in a pair of socks, sandals and shorts. He is six foot four, weighs about twenty stone and is covered in hair. His beard and chest seem to merge into one hirsute mess, and he looks like a yeti.

'All right there,' he sniffs, his long arm extending towards me as he looks over my shoulder. 'Long time no see.'

'Great to see you again,' I say. 'Let me buy you a drink.'

He orders a double vodka shot, no ice, and a packet of pork scratchings, before perching on a stool near the bar. His huge hairy legs unfurl in front of him.

'Sorry I couldn't meet you earlier,' he says, tearing open the packet of pork skin. 'I have been knee-deep in pussy all week.'

'So you're busy?' I say.

'It's more than I can handle, mate,' he says. 'I am shooting and editing back to back. I have the boys from Relish trying to book, Private, everyone always on the blower. Back to back. Shoot. Shoot.' He spins around on his chair, an imaginary camera on his shoulder, taking close-ups of the seven or so other people in the pub. 'I am fucking knackered,' he adds, popping a large piece of crackling into his mouth.

'Right,' I say. 'That's a shame, because I was rather hoping you might come and work for me.'

'Oh,' says Kent, sitting up a bit straighter and wiping his hands down the front of his khaki shorts. 'Well, there's always room for one more.'

'Really? But you're not too busy.'

'Yeah, well, when I say busy, I have a few windows.'

'That's great news.'

'It depends how long you take to shoot and edit,' he says. 'I mean, it takes me a few days to turn things around in the suite.'

'You have an edit suite?'

'Yeah.' He knocks back his vodka in one. 'D'you want another drink?'

Kent and I prop up the bar in his local boozer for the rest of the afternoon. In between the drinks and the pork scratchings and the anecdotes about his last shoot where he worked with some German porn star called Klaus who had 'fucked forty-seven women in a month', I try to persuade Kent to join Touch Wood Films.

'So you're a professional outfit?' he asks, shifting on his chair.

'That's right.'

'How many films have you made?'

'A few,' I say.

'Cool,' he says. 'Any of them any good?'

'Yeah.' My voice squeaks suddenly.

'Good,' he says, taking another swig of his warm vodka. 'There's nothing worse than a poorly shot film.'

'I agree.'

'Well, what's your plan?'

By the time Kent and I stagger out of the pub three hours later we have agreed some sort of business plan. I am to phone as soon as I have booked the girls and the venue and he will film and edit the project on the proviso that I deal with the British Board of Film Classification. Otherwise known as the censor, they view and categorise any film made or shown in the UK, rating it from U to PG, through to 18 or, in the case of hardcore porn, 'Restricted', or R18.

'I just can't bear all the chatting and the toing and froing,' he says, weaving up the street towards his basement flat. 'It does my head in. I am a creative. I can't be doing with fucking detail and I don't understand the rules. I mean, who cares if you wank while pissing when you've just filmed a cock going up someone's arse? How can it be more offensive to fiddle and piss at the same time?'

I have to say that since *Sex and the City of London* was such a total failure I have only had the briefest of dealings with the BBFC. I called them up to ask about whether it was OK to have some spanking in the G-G scene and I found them to be perfectly helpful and polite. It turns out that spanking is fine just so long as it does not verge on abusive and it was consensual in the first place. If the woman doesn't shout out in pain and looks like she is enjoying it and she is not constrained, so that she can withdraw her consent at any time, then the girls can whack away as hard as they like, hairbrushes included. I suppose it is because the BBFC is a government-funded organisation that they are so user-friendly. They have targets, guidelines and systems just like every other institution. How else are they to differentiate efficiently between an 18, an R18 and a banned film?

Back at the flat and Ana is in a filthy mood. Toby's gone out to buy more cigarettes, or at least that's what he told her, and he hasn't returned in over an hour. So Ana went to give his room an air and has found three empty wine bottles under the bed and a large burn in the carpet.

'And there is porn everywhere!' she screams, her blonde hair flying and her face going red.

'Well, what do you expect?' I say. 'That's the business we're in.'

'The business you're in,' she shouts back. 'I don't want to see the stuff in the house. I want to be able to bring friends home,' she says. 'I want to be able to look under the table, to reach for a magazine without finding some naked woman with her legs apart. This is not fair,' she says. 'This is not what I signed up for when I said that you could go into the business.'

I have to agree she is right. There is quite a lot of porn seepage coming from Toby's room. What was supposed to be the office and the headquarters of the website and Touch Wood Films is now spilling over into the sitting room. My younger brother James came over the other day and saw the photos of Camilla in the park that were lying in a folder on the table in the sitting room. I could tell he was shocked. He stuttered and his cheeks flushed pink. I told him they were Toby's and that he wasn't staying long. James didn't think that improved things much.

'How can you have this sort of stuff in the house?' he asked. 'It's degrading to women.'

I told him a cunt is a cunt is a cunt, whatever way it is photographed or filmed, and I didn't see anything too shocking in that. He didn't seem convinced. He shifted about in his suit and didn't stay long. His flying visit was cut even shorter. We don't see each other much. He is quite a lot younger than me. Ten years makes a big difference when growing up. We have always been cut from entirely different cloth. He works in insurance at the moment. I wouldn't be too surprised if, like Dad, he decided to join the Church.

I manage to calm Ana down and promise to tidy the place up at bit. I have to keep her onside. She has been such a star about the whole venture so far. I don't mind getting the Hoover out and spraying some Pledge around if it keeps her happy. The last thing I need is for her to go all crazy and unsupportive just when my plans are beginning to come back together.

After a while Toby falls through the front door, a bottle of champagne in his hand.

'Where have you been?' demands Ana, more jaded than annoyed. Not even she can remain cross for more than a couple of hours.

'We're going live tonight,' announces Toby. 'So I thought I'd stock up to celebrate.' He waves the half-drunk bottle of champagne at both of us and raises up a heavy-looking carrier from Oddbins. 'Go on,' he grins. 'Because you're worth it!'

'What do you mean we are going live tonight?' asks Ana.

'Launching the website,' says Toby.

'Shouldn't we be doing press and things?' she asks.

'Press?' Toby looks extremely confused.

'Yes, you know, telling people we are out there,' says Ana.

'We?' I ask.

'I mean you,' she says.

'It's porn,' says Toby. 'It doesn't need advertising. People will find you, us.'

'Oh,' says Ana, sounding rather disappointed.

'We will start advertising,' adds Toby, trying to keep her interested. 'But we don't have the cash at the moment. Later, when the vibrator sales go through the roof and we have money to burn, we can advertise on the Hun.'

The Hun is one of the largest porn search engines around. Even someone as computer illiterate as me has used it in the pursuit of internet porn. Covered in thousands of small thumbnail photos of various different types of porn, the idea is that you click through to the website advertised and join it. The Hun gets half the money and the porn site itself gets the rest. It is a good shop window in a crowded high street. An even better, but more expensive, way of alerting punters of our existence is to advertise directly on the site, rather than simply post up a thumbnail. However, when Toby enquired the other day, it cost a thousand dollars a month for something that flashes up on the site every couple of seconds. For the moment we don't have the cash flow or indeed the product at the other end of it to justify that sort of expense. When we have more films to sell and more clips to download on SexyPornFlics.com, then it is just the sort of marketing I shall be interested in. In the meantime the fact that we have a website at all and that we are about to launch it on the internet is exciting enough. Even if Ana doesn't quite buy it.

'So,' says Toby, grinning and stumbling towards his bedroom. 'We have about half an hour to go before we launch. Drink?'

'Great idea,' I say, following him into his room. 'Ana?' I turn around. 'Are you going to join us?'

I can tell this is not the sort of glamorous evening that she had in mind, sitting at the end of the bed in the spare room, a warm glass of Lanson in her hand, staring at a screen. But she shrugs and goes into the kitchen to get some glasses.

Half an hour later the three of us are sitting in a darkened room staring at the computer, waiting for something to happen. SexyPornflics.com is up and running. The bright pink logo is flashing away. There are a couple of clips from *Sex and the City of London* for you to download. There are photos of Camilla in suspenders and nothing else posing in the grass. She is also totally nude behind a bush, up against a tree and if you look carefully there is a police sign visible in the background. I have some vibrators for sale. They are pink and made of a soft jelly rubber and are sitting in a box underneath the table in the hall. Toby managed to find a wholesale supplier of these new 'Just Perfect' dildos from California Exotics, so we bought a hundred of them for five hundred quid and we are flogging them for £34.99 a pop. We are hoping to make a killing. My 'Bridget Bones's Diary' looks good, laid out with a few racy secretary poses that I asked Camilla to do as a favour. In fact, as I sit here sipping my champagne, I have to say I am feeling a little proud of myself and Toby. I may have messed up the movie but the website looks great. All we need now is for someone to join.

Ana shifts on the end of the bed. 'How long do you think?' she asks Toby.

'How long is a piece of string,' he replies helpfully.

'But normally?' she asks.

'This is the first porn site I have done,' he says. Now he tells me, I think, squeezing the stem of my champagne glass. 'But it shouldn't be long,' he says. 'The domain name alone will get traffic.'

'Really?' I ask, trying not to sound too desperate.

'Trust me,' he winks. 'SexyPornFlics is a brilliant name. I surf for porn all the time.'

'Let's hope so,' I say, draining my glass, our life savings disappearing before my eyes.

'There!' screams Toby, pointing at the screen. 'You have a hit!'

'A hit? Where?' I lean in.

'There! Look! The figure one at the bottom of the screen!'

'Where?' asks Ana, squinting in the dark.

'There!' Toby leaps off the bed and jabs away at the bottom of the screen. 'One, one! Can you see it?'

'Who is it?' I ask. 'Can you tell?'

'Actually I can,' says Toby, slipping in behind the keyboard. 'I can back-trace it. As it is just one person.' He fiddles and types away on the keyboard for a minute. 'There you go,' he says, sitting back. 'He's called Hard Dick,' he announces. 'From Alabama.'

'Hard Dick from Alabama,' I repeat.

'Well,' says Ana, getting off the bed. 'He sounds nice.'

Ana leaves in a cloud of repulsed annoyance. Her goodwill towards me is wearing thin. This site has to make money and quickly if our relationship is going to last through to the end of the summer. I think about following her out of the room and having some sort of consolatory conversation with her. Something along the lines of the worst being over, that Toby is leaving soon and that we shall start seeing dividends very shortly. But as I get off the bed Toby shouts, 'There's another', at the top of his voice. So I sit back down again and join him.

We sit there most of the night like a couple of schoolgirls at a boy band concert, squealing with delight at every hit we see. They come thick and fast between 11 p.m. and 2 a.m. and after that they trail off a bit. It develops into some sort of drinking game where every time the site takes a hit we have to take a swig of champagne. Then we move on to vodka and finally at four in the morning some Lithuanian spirits that I brought back from a stag weekend. I end up sleeping next to Toby fully clothed, in my shoes. We don't wake up until lunchtime the next day.

By the time Toby and I surface, I find a short note from Ana demanding that I clear up. She has already gone to work. I am worried that I might have pushed it too far, although unfortunately I am not really capable of dealing with it. But I try my best. I grovel and grunt a few apologies down the line to her answerphone. She is dropping my calls, of course. And then I concentrate on eating as many bacon sandwiches as I can in order to soak up the acid and alcohol in my stomach. Toby can't even be bothered to do that. Like a true alcoholic he proposes to smoke through his hangover and contemplates a hair of the dog can of lager at around two in the afternoon.

While Toby's head is in the fridge, slowly making the decision between a can of Stella and San Miguel, I check up on the website. I try and call it up on the computer and it refuses to appear. I try again and the thing crashes.

'Toby!' I shout, my heart beating faster, my hangover hurting, my hands sweating. I can't cope with this venture failing as well. 'Toby! Toby! Get your arse in here.' He must have heard the panic in my voice because he arrives in the room at a trot.

'What?' he asks, cracking open his can of Stella.

'It's crashed. The site is down,' I say. 'Look! I can't get it up on the screen.'

'Don't panic,' he says, taking a sip

'But it's fucked. The site has crashed. Something's wrong.'

'What time is it?' he asks. Toby is not the sort of man to wear a watch.

'Um, two,' I say looking at mine.

'Don't worry,' he shrugs. 'It's all the Yanks coming online.'

'I don't understand?' I say.

'You don't have enough bandwidth,' he says. 'They've slowed it right down.'

Toby goes on to explain that American porn habits are a little different from ours. In the UK most punters download porn after they have come home from the pub. So the busiest amount of traffic on the internet in the UK is between 11 p.m. and about 2 a.m., when they usually pass out. The weekends are quiet because that is when punters are playing with their kids, however there is a surge on Saturday nights. In the US, they download porn as soon as they come in to work. They hang up their coats, get themselves a latte, check their emails and then log on to TeenVirginSluts.com.

'It's quite interesting,' opines Toby, taking another sip from his beer. 'With a bandwidth as narrow as yours, you'll be able to see what happens when each state comes in to work. You'll get an East Coast and then West Coast surge. Then it will quieten down until the Brits get home from work. The entire plant is looking at dirty pictures the whole time,' he smiles. 'Welcome to the world of twenty-four-hour porn.'

And as the day progresses Toby is proved right. The early surge at 2 p.m. makes way for a greater one between 4 p.m. and 5 p.m. when the Angelinos get into work. Then the system frees itself up for a few hours until the drunk Brits start to come on-board. It is fascinating to watch. However, it is not particularly lucrative. Toby and I watch the website for a whole weekend. We watch the peaks and troughs and the traffic going through it. And by Sunday night we have had just fewer than half a million visitors and no members at all. We have not shifted one dildo. Not one membership.

'It's early days,' says Toby, sucking a fag and flicking the ash on the floor. 'What you need is content. I mean, why would I join when all you are offering so far are a few fanny shots and some ropy old anal?'

There is nothing for it. I have to empty the bank account, call in some really big favours and make another film as soon as I can, otherwise I am going under and I am taking Ana and the flat with me.

So I pour myself a shot of vodka, pull out my old address book and ring up my very old mate Simon. He owns a gin palace of a house in Oxfordshire. It's big. It's swish. It's very upmarket. And amazingly, after ten minutes of begging on the telephone, he actually agrees to let us film there. I call up Kent.

'Get your cameras together,' I say. 'We're on.'

Four

Kent and I are sitting in a traffic jam on the M40 on our way to shoot *The Good Life* in Simon's big fat pad in the country. It's a lovely day. But I have to say I am already exhausted. Who would have thought that organising for six people to meet up for a shag in the countryside could be so goddamn difficult?

On the last shoot it was Seb (we have since parted our porn ways. He is happier and so am I) and the location that let me down; this time it's the bloody porn stars. In an effort to cut corners, build up some sort of porn loyalty and get out of paying the 20 per cent agent's fee, I decided that it was a good move to go with the same boys as before. Big Stiff was only too keen to come on a weekend in the country and Freddie was also enthusiastic. But just as I was congratulating myself on my own efficiency Big Stiff rang up to tell me he'd had a porn accident and that he was in hospital.

'It's the ligament in my cock,' he explained in muffled whispers down his mobile. 'I was banging away at the wrong angle and, pop. The thing went. It was very painful.'

'I can imagine,' I said, crossing my legs. It didn't bear thinking about.

'I'll be out of action for six months or more,' he groaned.

'Oh, God,' I said. A porn star who can't fuck. 'That's terrible. What will you do?'

'Oh, you know, go back to my painting and decorating job, I suppose.'

Poor bloke, it sounded like agony. But I was a little annoyed. Good men are hard to come by and I had rather liked him. With Big Stiff out of action, it was back to the agency drawing board. But at least I had Freddie. Or so I thought. I was just scrolling through the Total Babes site trying to find some girls when he called. He sounded very French and rather sheepish.

'I am afraid I won't be available,' he said.

'Why not?' I asked. 'I booked you a week ago. It seems a little unfair to let me down at such short notice.'

'Well.' He paused. I heard him trying to decide whether to go with the truth or not. 'I've got Chlamydia.'

'Ah.' The truth, then.

'Ah, oui,' he said. 'I have given it to four women and they are very angry.'

'Where did you get it?' I asked.

'I'm not sure,' he replied. 'But I have been having some sex outside work.'

'That might be it,' I suggested.

'That, or some girl from Poland,' he said. 'You know, the ones who come over for two weeks and lap dance, escort and shoot as many movies as they can back to back?'

'Oh, no, I didn't know about that,' I said.

'Well, they are always quite high risk,' he declared. 'Anyway I can't work for a couple of weeks. Until the infection has disparu.'

We were back to square one. Fortunately Kent remembered a couple of blokes who he'd met and worked with before. The first is a bloke called Ray from Yorkshire who has his own website, fan club and, from what I can tell from his photos, appears to be permanently a shiny, bright orange. It says on his CV that he used to strip for a living, so I look forward to seeing that display after a few beers. The other bloke looks rather serious and very professional. He calls himself Tony and says he's from Essex; he has a great body and has appeared on TV a few times, so he should be OK.

Amazingly, with this being a big shoot, the girls this time have been a lot less problematic. I have managed to secure myself a star. She calls herself Trisha Bigtits, even though her real name is Debbie and her tits aren't actually that big at all. She is one of the new stars on the block and everyone seems to know her name. Kent sounded pleased when I told him on the phone that she was coming to Oxfordshire.

'She is just the sort of star we need,' he said.

However, if booking the four other girls and Trisha Bigtits was easy, getting them to Simon's pad has been a total nightmare. I have had to send them all train timetables from various market towns all over the country that include changing in London, in order to get them to arrive anywhere near Oxford. I have booked three hundred quid's worth of cabs to cart them across country, to get us all to Simon's house. Although if the traffic stays as bad as it is at the moment, with Kent and I sitting here on the M40, it looks like they are all going to get to Simon's before we do.

'This is a fucking nightmare,' says Kent, as he raises himself on to one buttock in the car and breaks wind. 'Ah,' he sighs. 'They're going to get there before us.'

'Jesus!' I say, rolling down the windows. 'That smells disgusting. What the fuck have you been eating?'

'Pork pie,' he says.

'Well, don't,' I reply.

'Nothing wrong with a bit of bum gas,' he says. 'Anyway

you'd better get used to that sort of thing if you're shooting porn.'

I sit in the car in silence, feeling a little sick. This is going to be a very long weekend.

Finally Kent, the equipment and I turn left along a country lane and then right into a thick gravel drive. As I park up my Range Rover next to Simon and Claire' matching 4×4s, I see Simon come rushing out of the front door. Tall and well-fed with brown hair, in a jazz shirt with navy-blue shorts, he looks very white and pale for such a hot, sunny day.

'There you are,' he says, poking his head through my open window. 'Hurry up and come inside.' He sounds panicked. His face is tense. 'Claire is fucking furious.'

I leave Kent to unpack the car and follow Simon down the hall and into his rich cream drawing room, where I find a small gathering of my stars. Now when I was booking the girls, and indeed the boys, I did specifically tell them that we were shooting in the country and that they should dress appropriately. This suggestion has fallen on deaf ears. Granted, it is a hot day in the middle of July, but none of them appears to be wearing anything. Trisha Bigtits is sporting a candy pink mini-skirt that just scrapes over her arse and a tight white T-shirt that, just in case anyone was in any doubt about what she does for a living, says 'Porn Star' in bright-pink letters across her chest. Ray is wearing a white vest and what appears to be a pair of pants and chaps. A couple of the other girls are in cropped tops with Playboy bunnies on their tits. Only Tony appears to be normally dressed. But even then if you look a little more closely his jeans are just that bit too tight.

'A word,' hisses Claire, from the other side of the room. 'Now!'

She bundles me out and frogmarches me into the kitchen, shoving me right up against her bright red Aga, which despite the hot weather appears to be switched on to maximum heat. I stand gently singeing my buttocks against the oven door.

'You can't stay here,' she says.

'But—'

'You can't. I won't have it.' She is wringing her hands. 'I just can't deal with it.'

'But, Claire, you can't . . .' I am in such a panic I might actually start to shake. I have got ten grand in cash in my back pocket, I have porn stars here from all over the country and now she might be about to close the whole operation down. 'You can't do this to me.'

'You can shoot here,' she says, curling her expensive blonde bob behind her ears. 'But you are not staying.'

'Oh . . . right.' The relief.

'I have booked you all into the motel down the road,' she declares. 'I just don't think I can cope with all that fake tan on my sheets.'

'But we are supposed to be pitching tents in the garden.'

'I just can't,' she says, her bottom lip trembling.

'Oh, OK,' I say, smiling, patting her on the shoulder. 'That's fine. Of course.'

'It was a very witty idea of Simon's,' she continues. 'Until I see it in the flesh. And now . . .'

'Don't worry.' I squeeze her arm. 'We can still shoot here, though?'

'Of course,' she smiles. 'I'm not that much of a bitch.'

I don't think it is wise to say anything else just in case she calls the shoot off altogether. So I go straight back into the drawing room and pull all the porn stars out, telling them to wait in the sunshine while I go and sort out our accommodation. Luckily the local motel is not busy and I confirm the bookings for a party of eight without too much bother.

By the time I make it back to the house I am sweating my balls off in the heat but thankfully Claire seems to have calmed down. I pull up in the drive to see her in the garden with Ray, his orange arm wrapped around her shoulder. She is talking him through the flowers in the herbaceous border. Thank God for northern charm.

Inside the house Trisha Bigtits seems to be having the same effect on Simon. He is laughing and pink-cheeked and making tea with five sugars when I find them both in the kitchen.

'So are you ready then, Trisha?' I ask.

'Whenever you want,' she says, straightening her Porn Star T-shirt.

'Is it OK if the others stay here?' I ask Simon. 'While Trisha and Tony and Kent and I go and film?'

'Sure,' says Simon. 'They all seem like very nice girls.'

As well as the porn stars and Kent, I have also booked a make-up artist and an assistant for the shoot. I have learned my lesson from the last time around and while I don't want the girls to look like they have just arrived fresh off the train from Bucharest, I also don't want them to look too natural, either. Kent shoots on high-quality video and widescreen and what we don't want are widescreen spots on buttocks or bruises on legs. Kelly has come along to cover up more than enhance and she has a load of skin-coloured creams in her bag to prove it. She also has tattoos on her arms and very bleached white hair, and is a veteran of many *FHM*, *Loaded* and porn shoots.

'I've got gloss, hairspray, nails and here,' she says, picking up what looks like a squeezy bottle that you'd use for tomato ketchup, 'I've got cum.' She shakes the transparent bottle of milky-coloured liquid in my face. 'You know, splodge,' she says, squeezing the thing. 'For yer cream pie, should you want one.'

'Cream pie?' I ask.

'Yeah, you know,' she says, snapping her chewing gum between her finger and thumb. 'When the sperm comes back out between the labia.' She puts her finger and thumb together to make some sort of sandwich. 'It comes out? Like a cream pie?'

'Oh, that!' I say.

'Everyone's doing it these days,' she says. 'Only sometimes it takes so long for the sperm to come out, you know, it's much easier just to shove this in.'

'Of course!' I laugh.

'My own recipe,' she smiles, flashing a couple of gold fillings at the back of her teeth. 'Milk and lube,' she says. 'It looks just like spunk on film and doesn't do yer bits any harm. It's taken me a while to perfect.'

'I bet.' I nod.

'It's all organic,' she adds.

'That's good to know.'

I pack Trisha Bigtits and Tony into the back of the car along with an Australian mate of Kent's called Connor. He is assisting on the shoot but also works behind the bar at the Winged Spur in Clapham. It appears that Kent only recruits from within a five-minute radius of his flat.

I have been a guest of Simon and Claire's many times over the years and was brought up not far away so I know this area well. We set off in the direction of Lower Bridge, a small village near Simon's house where I remember there's a nice Norman church and a stream.

'The plot of this film is quite simple,' I explain as I drive along.

'Thank God for that,' says Trisha. 'I really hate it when they make things difficult.'

'You're the star, Trisha, and it is basically about you being a naughty girl who lives in the English countryside and it is sort of what you get up to on your average day.'

'OK,' she nods.

'So, Tony?'

'Yeah?' he says.

'What I want is for you to walk along down the lane, past the church, which you can see over there.' I stop the car and pull over.

'Yeah.' Tony is evidently a man of few words.

'You find Trisha coming out of the church, you go up to her and you ask her if she knows of anywhere you and your mates can camp? And she says, "I am only an innocent country girl but my uncle does have a farm around the corner and he has a field you can use." Then you ask where it is and we cut to Trisha giving you head near the stream.'

'You're opening with a blowjob?' asks Kent, itching his balls in the front seat.

'Yes?'

'You can't do that,' he says. 'You have to open with anal or double penetration.'

'You don't have to,' I say.

'Yes, you do,' he says. 'That's what we always do.'

'Exactly,' I say. 'That's why I'm not.'

'On all the other jobs I've done—'

'Please, Kent!' I say. 'Just go with me on this.'

'If you want,' he sniffs. 'It won't work.'

'Everyone OK with what they are doing?' I ask, ignoring him. Jesus, he is a grumpy bastard.

'Er, not quite,' says Connor. 'What d'you want me to do?'

'You're on lookout, Connor. You're there to make sure that we don't get caught.'

'Oh! OK there, mate.' He winks. 'I'll keep my eyes and ears on red alert.'

Trisha slips behind the car to change into the white shirt and denim mini-skirt I bought along with me, while Kent marches up and down the lane looking determinedly through a square he has made out of his thumbs and fore-fingers. I direct Tony to walk around the corner further up the lane and once Trisha is dressed she teeters over towards the church. Connor is dispatched further up the road and told to whistle if he sees any walkers or approaching locals. Kent picks up his camera and checks the sound is working. He mounts it on his right shoulder.

'Rolling,' he says.

'And action!' I shout.

Tony walks around the corner and comes towards the church. Meanwhile Trisha positions herself by the church gate and appears to frot it slightly between her thighs.

'Well, hello there,' says Tony as he comes towards her.

'Hiya,' she replies.

'I am new around here.'

'I can see that,' she says, biting her lip as she looks him up and down.

'I was wondering if you knew of somewhere where me and my mates could camp?' he asks, perching his elbow on the church gate.

'Oh,' she says. 'I am a very naive country girl but I know my uncle has a field around the corner where you could stay.'

'Why thank you,' says Tony.

'Follow me,' says Trisha.

'Cut!' I yell. 'That's a wrap!'

'What?' says Kent. 'Don't you think we need to do it again?'

'Why? I ask.

'Because,' he says, 'you always need to do it a few times.'

'Why?'

'Because that's what professionals always do.'

'Listen, Kent, I have spent enough time on video shoots to know if you have it, you have it, there is no point in doing it again. It is not going to get better.'

'You're the boss,' he shrugs. 'It's your call.'

'Good,' I say. 'Let's go to the stream. Connor!'

'Yeah?' comes a voice from around the corner.

'We're moving!'

'OK!'

We decamp to the towpath under the bridge. I suggest that Tony and Trisha walk towards the camera, talking about something and then they stop. She drops down on to her knees. Tony gets his cock out and she blows him by the stream.

'I want you to be able to see the water and the towpath first before you go close in for the action,' I explain to Kent.

'I don't know why you're bothering with the story,' he mutters under his breath. 'If you are playing with yourself in Albuquerque, the last thing you need is backchat. The other people I have worked for would never do this. I thought you were a professional outfit.'

If I had a pair of tits, Kent would be getting on them by now. He won't stop muttering and undermining me. For a bloke who has just joined the team, he is throwing his substantial weight around. I think he thinks he knows it all. He may well have a lot more experience than me but there is no need to keep pointing it out. I am going to have to have a word before the end of the day. Meanwhile everyone else seems to be doing their job well and not complaining, which I'm beginning to suspect is unusual for a porn shoot.

'So action!' I say again.

Trisha and Tony walk towards me hand in hand. Her plastic shoes look a little incongruous on the Cotswold towpath but the white shirt sets off her orange tan very nicely.

'I think you are very sexy,' says Tony.

'Oh, really,' says Trisha. 'But I am just a naive country girl.'

'But you are very sexy,' he says.

'Thank you. You are quite sexy, too,' purrs Trisha, running a nail extension down his chest.

'You naughty girl,' says Tony.

'You naughty man,' says Trisha.

They stop in the middle of the towpath. Tony pulls out his extremely large, hard cock and Trisha falls to her knees.

'You naughty, naughty man,' she says as she wraps her heavily glossed lips around the end of his knob and sets to work on the shaft with her hands. Tony leans back against a handy oak tree and closes his eyes. He looks like he is enjoying himself. Trisha clearly knows exactly what she is doing. Kent moves in for the close-up. I hold my breath, hoping he is getting it all on film.

'Baby, baby,' moans Tony. 'You naughty girl.'

'Um, excuse me?' comes a clipped cut-glass voice from behind me.

I spin around. 'Good morning!' I say in my poshest, smartest voice. Standing in front of me are an elderly couple with two fat black Labradors. She has a neat brown bob and is in a sensible skirt and walking shoes. He is completely bald with huge milk-bottle glasses.

'Shit!' says Kent behind me. I move close to him, hoping to block the view.

'Fucking 'ell,' says Trisha, as she scrabbles to her feet. I hear Tony zip up his fly.

'What are you doing?' asks the elderly woman, trying to look over my shoulder.

'Filming,' I say.

'I can see that,' she replies.

'What sort of film?' asks the husband.

'A student film,' I reply.

'Students?' she queries. 'Students?' She frowns, looking both Kent and me up and down. We are both dressed in shorts but we are obviously kidding no one. 'Aren't you a little old?'

'It's special interest,' says Kent very quickly.

'Oh,' says the elderly man. 'What sort?'

'Got to keep moving,' I say. 'I'm terribly sorry. We are working to a schedule.' I tap the back of my hand, where a watch would be.

'Yes, of course,' says the man, stepping to one side. 'Don't mean to keep you.'

'OK, everyone?' I say. 'Off we go!'

We all march off in the opposite direction looking busy and motivated. As soon as we turn the corner, Trisha and Tony start to laugh.

'I was just playing for time so you could get your skirt down and Tony his trousers up,' I explain.

'Well, thank God for you!' says Trisha. 'That was right close.'

Connor comes out of the undergrowth and ambles towards us.

'All right there?' he says, sounding surprised. 'You finished already?'

'Where the fuck have you been?' barks Kent.

'What, mate? Don't look at me,' replies Connor. 'I just went into the bushes for a piss.'

'Well, don't,' says Kent. 'You very nearly got us all arrested.'

'Sorry,' huffs Connor. 'Keep your hair on.'

'No,' says Kent. 'This is serious. We could have been prosecuted under the Lewd Behaviour Act or whatever it is called. You need two witnesses for that and there were two right there.'

Kent is so furious at his near arrest at the hand of his assistant that he sulks all the way to Burford High Street, which suits me just fine. I could do without any more earache from him about how other people shoot. And if I hear him question my professionalism again I am going to kick him out of the car.

It's mid-morning in Burford and the traffic is heavy. The place is packed with tourists and there is nowhere to park.

'OK,' I say to Trisha. 'What I want is for you to go into the sweet shop over there and we will film you come out with a bag of sweets. You don't have to do anything. It is just a pick-up shot to link up later in the film so that we see you going around your country business.'

'OK,' she nods.

'Do you need me?' asks Tony.

'No,' I say.

'So I don't need to pump myself up?' he says, looking down at his crotch.

'No,' I smile. 'You can give your cock a break.'

I double-park the car outside the Ye Olde Sweet Shop, thinking it might speed up the process. Kent gets his camera out of the back and we are immediately surrounded by a group of some eight or nine elderly American woman who all look identical with white curled hair and pistachio pant suits.

'What are you filming?'

'Can we be in your film?'

'How great is this?'

Kent is swatting them away like flies.

'It's special interest,' I can hear him say. 'Very special . . . No . . . I can't really say.'

Meanwhile Trisha Bigtits gets out of the car and shimmies into the sweet shop in her plastic heels, mini-skirt and bleached-blonde bouffant. Half the street comes to a standstill. I can't really cope with the chaos we are creating. There is a queue of traffic building up behind the car. Drivers are beginning to sound their horns. I walk around the back of the car and open the boot. I am thinking, maybe if I get the red triangle out and place it behind the car, people might think that we have broken down and cut us a little slack. I search through the stuff right in the back and as I do so I knock open a cardboard box at the front. Out pop all the fucking sex toys. I can't believe it as I see six red vibrators and two pink rabbits tumble from the boot and bounce down the middle of Burford High Street.

'Connor!' I shout. He turns towards me. There is terror in my voice. 'The toys!' Connor looks at me and then the road, and sprints off down the street. He picks up the first three quite easily but two pink rabbits are really breaking for the border. I look the other way and pretend it has nothing to do with me. It's not often that I pull rank but surely chasing sex toys down the street is a job for staff?

Kent is still surrounded by his coach party of US nearly-deads and Trisha is nowhere to be seen. Where the hell is she? She was supposed to be in and out of that sweet shop in a two-minute take. I walk into the shop and find her at the pick-n-mix, biting the end of her nail.

'Oh, hiya,' she says.

'What the fuck are you doing?' I hiss.

'Buying sweets,' she says, like I just asked the stupidest question in the world.

'I can see that.'

'I just can't make up my mind if I want lemon bonbons or a sherbet dip dab,' she says.

'When I said go into the shop and buy some sweets I didn't mean for you to spend hours trying to work out which ones you want.'

'Oh,' she says. 'You should've said. So it was pretend-buying sweets?'

'That's right,' I smile. 'Just pretend.'

'Oh, I'll have the pear drops then, if we're not going to eat them.'

Having created chaos in Burford, I gather everyone back together again, along with as many sex toys as we can muster, and head off back to Simon's. We have one more scene to do before this afternoon's orgy and need to hurry up if we are going to make it to the gastropub before the kitchen closes for lunch. At the house the other three porn stars all pile into the back of the car and I put my foot down in order to get to the pub.

Frequented by weekending Londoners and the odd Liz Hurley or Kate Moss type of local international celebrity, the pub is packed when we arrive. Luckily I got Simon to book a large table outside. As we all pour out of the car in front of the pub, I can see people muttering to each other, wondering who we are. Maybe it is the mix of accents, or the neon colour of most of their tans, or the fact that they are not wearing much, but we certainly don't look like a group of chums going out to lunch. I have to say I am too tense and exhausted to care. I just want to get this shot in the can and then I can relax. We need to get our food order in as soon as possible. Then I will try to work out how to shoot in a very busy pub without anyone suspecting that we might be filming porn. The waitress comes out with her notepad and suddenly a new hell is unleashed. I find out that porn people don't eat in the same way that other people do. I suggest we all have sandwiches to keep things simple. Silly me.

'Oh, no,' says Ray, holding his orange stomach with his orange hand. His flat northern vowels cut through the Sloaney trilling. 'I can't do tomatoes. I'm allergic.'

'Really?' I say. 'You're allergic to tomatoes?'

'Yeah,' he nods. 'I don't like them.'

'Oh, right,' I say, feeling the temperature rising on an already hot day.

'So just chicken in mine.'

'No lettuce in mine,' says Trisha. 'I don't eat anything green.'

'What's tuna?' asks one of the Polish girls, called Krista, who as far as I can work out from the headshot I have on file, I didn't actually order.

'Can I not have any gherkins?' asks Kent joining in.

My head falls into my hands. This was supposed to be a simple scene in which Trisha comes out of the pub where she 'works' and hands around the orders to her mates, before we all go back to Simon's for an orgy. Instead I've got to cater for the hypo-allergenic needs of a bunch of porn stars who would have been much happier with a plate of chips each. At last we get the order in and the waitress disappears. I can see the owner of the pub sitting on the other side of the garden from us. He is smoking a cigar, nursing a pint. He looks across at our table, checking out the camera equipment. His eyes narrow. He looks like he is about to come over and ask some difficult questions but he gets distracted by a drinker. Our food arrives. It comes devoid of anything green. Not even cress. And while the owner is looking the other way, I get Trisha to take the plates off the waitress and walk out of the pub holding them. She greets the table like a long lost friend and hands round the food. Kent films away as surreptitiously as he can and I knock back a double vodka and think of the money this is costing me. Just a quick orgy to do this afternoon and then we can relax.

We head back to Simon's house all squashed into the back of the car. The sun is so hot everyone is beginning to get a little tetchy. Fortunately by the time we pull up in their drive both Simon and Claire are out shopping. So we pitch our tents in the back of the garden for Tony and his mates to 'camp' in and get going on the G-G scene that I have planned. Trisha is supposed to come back home and find her cousin, Krista, swimming naked in the pool. She threatens to call the police unless her cousin shags her. She is then interrupted by Ray, Tony and Ingrid, who are looking for a place to camp, and then we have the orgy with the sex toys, etc.

Krista gets into the swimming pool while Trisha sets about drinking three cans of lager. It is a hot day and I want her to piss all over Krista, so she needs the liquid. The words of Camilla are ringing in my ears. I wasn't going to include a water sports section in the film, because it isn't really my bag, but if we want to appeal to as many people as we can with this film a peeing scene is vital to the equation. So Krista swims; Trisha comes into shot; they have an argument that ends up with them having sex on the grass by the pool; and then Krista lies down in the grass and Trisha straddles her and pees all over her. The lager clearly did the trick because I haven't seen that much piss since I walked past a police horse outside Stamford Bridge last year. Kent is furious because it splashes all over his sandals and dribbles in-between his toes. He stamps and swears and throws his shoes across the lawn. But I have to say it's Krista who I feel sorry for as she stands there, stark naked and absolutely drenched. The girl looks horrified. I don't think this was in her game plan when she flew over from Poland last week. She dives straight back into the pool to wash it all off. Luckily Simon and Claire are still at the supermarket. They must be doing a very large shop.

Only the orgy scene to go. Ray and Tony disappear off to get themselves hard while Kent and I discuss our plan of action.

'Right,' says Kent, rubbing his hands. He has a glint in his eye and is clearly excited. 'We've got three girls and two boys and loads of toys so we'd better make the most of it.'

'Absolutely,' I agree. Having never choreographed an orgy myself, I am actually rather interested in what he has to say. I am not sure I know exactly what to put where and how to keep everyone occupied.

'Your main problem is you don't have enough pricks,' he says.

'I'd prefer it like that,' I say.

'Much more difficult to shoot,' he says, scratching his crotch.

'We should start with Trisha and Krista and then get the others to join in one by one, as they arrive at the campsite.'

The conversation goes back and forth and eventually we end up deciding that we start with a G-G and then Ray joins them, and then Ingrid and Tony come in with the sex toys in the end.

'So for the cum shot,' explains Kent, 'you two are taking Trisha and Krista up the arse, and, Ingrid?'

'Yes?' she says, pulling apart her long brown hair.

'You end up with two vibrators, one up the front and one up the back,' says Kent.

'Oh, OK,' she replies.

While Kelly gets her cover-up out, Kent picks up his cameras to get the show on the road. He disappears off in the direction of the pool to work out where and how he will shoot. I am talking to Ray when I hear a tirade of shouting and swearing and histrionics. Kent is yelling down a mobile phone. I watch as he kicks his camera and throws his mobile across the lawn. He looks like a very large, very rotund schoolboy having a hissy fit.

'Jesus fucking Christ,' he says, walking towards me, all hair and temper and shorts. 'The camera's fucked.'

'What?' I say.

'The camera's fucked and I have just phoned the cunts I rented it from and they say that it's the fourth camera to be fucked today and they don't have a replacement.'

'Sorry?' I say. He is talking and spitting so quickly and loudly that I don't understand. 'What's happened?'

'The camera's blown up in the heat,' he says slowly. 'And I can't get another one sent down here.'

'Shit,' I say. This is all we bloody need.

'You can use my handicam, if you want,' says Ray. 'I've always got it with me.'

We end up filming my expensive orgy scene in one of the most stunning locations in rural England with the sort of equipment your nan would use at her grandson's party. It's worse than the piece of shit that Mike Hunt used. Kent assures me that we won't notice in the edit, which makes me doubt both the quality of the stuff we were shooting earlier and indeed his word. We also have to wait about twenty minutes for Ray to come. He blames the heat and the fact that he has been sitting in the car all day. I think my bad luck has got to run out soon.

Simon and Claire come back just as we wrap and

announce they are throwing a party and that we are all invited. It sounds like they have told some of their friends they are shooting porn in the house. They all want to come and have a gawp.

'It's just a few of us,' smiles Simon. 'You know, booze and bangers on the barbie.'

'Sounds great,' I say. I could do with a drink. 'I'm sure Connor will help. He's Australian – they are born with a pair of tongs in their hand.'

Five hours later and everyone is naked, hurling themselves in and out of the swimming pool. Given a bucket of Pimm's and a few vodka shots, it is hard to tell the difference between the porn stars and the toffs. In fact I think the toffs are more badly behaved. They are so overexcited at being able to press the porn star flesh, as it were, that they get quite giddy and out of control. Trisha and Krista are a bit overawed at first. They have not spent any time in a big house in the country before. But the boys take it all in their stride. In fact they are in their element. Perhaps it is because women are used to discussing things like sex, but within about ten or fifteen minutes of the party starting the boys are surrounded by posh birds asking questions, flicking their hair and laughing loudly at their jokes. It is two in the morning by the time I manage to gather the porn gang together and squeeze them all in the car and get them back to the motel.

The next morning we are all looking rather shabby and hungover. We shuffle down to the buffet breakfast hardly capable of conversation. I am sitting in the corner with two boiled eggs and three rounds of toast on a plate with a bird-bath sized cup of coffee. I am hoping to eat my way better; it is the only way forward. With my mouth full of buttered toast, I look up and suddenly see someone I know. It's fucking Nik

Kershaw. Shit. I toured with him in the eighties. We didn't like each other at all. Try not to move. I keep as still as I can. I don't want to attract his attention. Try and blend in with the blue and yellow wallpaper behind you, I think.

'Oh, look!' declares Ray at the top of his northern voice. 'Bloody 'ell. There's Nik bloody Kershaw! He's a celebrity. Hello there, mate!' He waves his orange arm. 'Nik! Nik Kershaw. Over 'ere. I loved your stuff.'

Nik Kershaw looks over and sees me, sitting in the corner, surrounded by a sea of orange. I am well aware that I have put on a few pounds since we worked together and that sitting hungover surrounded by porn stars in a motel in Oxfordshire is perhaps not the best of looks, but I decide to brazen it out. They could be my mates. He doesn't know what I am doing here. And anyway he is staying in the same place.

'Hello there,' I smile.

'All right?' he says.

'Good,' I say. 'You?'

'Touring,' he says. 'You?'

'This and that,' I nod.

'We're making a porn film,' beams Ray.

'As I said,' I smile, 'this and that.'

'Good . . . good for you,' he says. He gives me the most piteous look I have ever seen and then walks straight out of the dining room. I look down at my eggs and toast. No amount of food is going to make me feel any better.

Back at Claire and Simon's house we are welcomed back with open arms. In fact Claire seems to be so overexcited by her porn experience that she asks to be allowed to come on the shoot. I try to persuade her that perhaps it is not the best idea, but she insists.

'Don't be ridiculous,' she says. 'I mean, how much of a lightweight do you think I am?'

Twenty-five minutes later she has her answer. The shoot has hardly got started before she retches into her hands and walks off the set. Trisha is giving Ray a blowjob but Claire finds even that too difficult to watch.

'I am off,' she says, her face the palest of greens. 'And when I get back I would appreciate it if you weren't here.'

As Claire speeds off to seek sanctuary with a friend, Simon takes me aside to explain that he's also out for the day but that they have two handymen from the village coming to mend the gates at the front of the house.

'Now whatever happens,' he warns, 'they must not know what you are doing here. It's fine that our close friends know that we're shooting porn in the house but they can't know in the village. If they knew what was going on in the big house we'd never hear the end of it.'

'Of course,' I nod. 'They won't see us at all. Ships in the night. That sort of thing.'

'Thanks,' he says, patting me on the back. 'I know I can rely on you.'

An hour later Mr Jones and Mr Jones – a father and son outfit – arrive to mend the gate. Mr Jones, Snr is so old he looks incapable of lifting the powerful drill he is carrying, let alone using it. Junior is evidently not the brightest of sparks. I make them tea and direct them to the gates, while trying to keep my stars well hidden in the back garden. Ray and Tony are both naked and wanking and getting themselves ready for a spanking scene, so it is perhaps best that the four of them don't meet.

We start to film. Both of the boys are spanking the girls and the noise is rather more than I had banked on. The smacking noise that hands make against naked buttocks carries much further in the countryside, as does the yelping of the girls. And Kent is encouraging them.

'Harder! Louder!' he shouts.

I don't know what to do with myself. Should I stand near the gate and gauge Messrs Jones's reactions or keep an eye on Kent and the filming? In the end I send Connor to make sure the Joneses don't get too curious. He is instructed to keep them the other side of the house, whatever it takes. Still, even this simple task of chaperoning a pensioner and his son is beyond Connor because half an hour into the shoot, just as Ray is slipping a second dildo up Ingrid's backside and Tony is spanking Trisha and Krista, I look up to see their faces pressed against the kitchen window. Jones, Snr is sipping his tea like he is enjoying some sort of floor show, while his son is just standing open-mouthed. There is nothing to do except smile and wave and carry on. The father raises his mug of tea and they turn, walk out of the kitchen and get back to work.

Neither of us really disturbs the other for the rest of the afternoon, save for the occasional trip around the house to ask them to stop drilling during a few of the more intense scenes. Otherwise we just carry on working.

The only other interruption of the day is at about three in the afternoon when a young girl arrives at the front door in a pair of jodhpurs. We are between takes at this point so she only witnesses a collection of strangely coloured folk wondering around in short skirts and T-shirts. The Joneses direct her to the riding school at the farm next door.

Before long it's five in the evening and we start to pack up. I have got three runs to the station to do before taking Kent and the equipment back to London. The gates are fixed and the tents are packed away, when Simon comes roaring up the drive in his 4×4. He stares at me through the windscreen. He looks hot and bothered and very pissed off indeed.

'You little shit,' he says, getting out of the car, slamming the door.

'What?' I say. 'What have I done?'

'I asked you to do one thing,' he says.

'What?' I say, holding my hands up, my heart beating faster. The last thing I want to do is upset him.

'One thing,' he repeats. 'And you can't even do that.'

'I don't understand?'

'I've just stopped to fill the car up in the village. It seems the Joneses have been talking.'

'What?' I say. Oh, God, I think.

'It seems everyone in the village knows we've been shooting a porn film.'

'But they only left half an hour ago,' I say. Shit.

'It's a very small village.'

'I am so sorry, mate,' I say. 'I really am.'

'You'd better fuck off quickly,' he says, quietly. 'Because if Claire catches you still here, she's going to fucking kill you.'

Five

Claire still isn't speaking to me. Simon has returned one of my many calls but Claire is still steadfastly sending me to Coventry. I have heard through the grapevine that the fallout from the shoot has been quite substantial. So I can hardly blame her. Apparently they fall silent in the post office and the petrol station whenever she arrives, and she heard someone refer to their house as the 'porn palace' when she was in her local shop. I suppose I wouldn't be very pleased with me if I were her. And I feel terrible about it. They were so very kind and generous. I wish Connor had done what he was told. I am not hiring him again. I hope that one day they will forgive me.

Thankfully, I have been too busy editing the film with Kent at his flat in Clapham to be able to dwell on things too much. And I think he's done a great job. The film looks good and Simon and Claire's house is fantastic. The church looks stunning, as does Burford High Street. You can see all the ins and outs. The girls aren't overly shouting. They are pretty. The boys are all hard and come at the right time. The only thing that is a bit worrying is the blowjob scene by the stream, which cuts rather abruptly; but I think we have got away with it.

However, the British Board of Film Classification has

other ideas. No sooner have Kent and I sent *The Good Life* in for certification than it comes straight back. This is the first time that I have dealt properly with the BBFC. We talked briefly about *Sex and the City of London* but it was such a load of old rubbish I never bothered to get the whole thing certified because I knew I wouldn't be releasing it. So I console myself. There are bound to be a few teething problems. There is a sliding scale of payment for each film, ranging from £900 for under two hours to £1200 for over two and a half hours. And they check everything. Firstly the films are checked for technical glitches. You are not allowed blank frames, or gaps in sound or pictures. Kent tells me it is to stop you slipping in other dodgy frames at a later date. Your work has to be whole and complete. Secondly they check the content. Frame by frame. And they are so much more regulated and meticulous than I had thought. I can understand why Kent was insistent he didn't want to deal with them right from the start. Fortunately they run a helpline, so when they send back *The Good Life* with a jargon-filled letter explaining their reasons for doing so, it is my first port of call.

'Hello BBFC helpline, Madeline speaking, how can I help you?'

'Oh, sorry?' She sounds more like a doctor's receptionist than a porn adviser and I am a little wrong-footed. 'Is that the porn line?'

'Yes, that's right,' she says. 'You'll have to excuse me, I'm terribly sorry if I sound odd. I'm eating my lunch.'

'Oh, right, what are you having?'

'A prawn sandwich.'

'Good.'

'Well, it isn't actually,' shares Madeline. 'There's a little too much bread.'

'Right,' I continue. 'I was just calling about my film *The Good Life*. It has been sent back pending an R18 certificate.'

'OK,' she chomps.

'There's this, um, p . . . urinating scene that seems to be causing a problem.'

'Mmm?'

'And I am not sure . . .'

'Well,' she clears her throat, 'you can urinate but not auto-eroticise at the same time.'

'She isn't.'

'Is she urinating on someone?'

'Yes.'

'Ah, well, that's it.'

'You can't pee on someone?'

'No.'

'Oh, I thought that was the whole point.'

'I know,' she laughs. 'But sadly no.'

'I also have a fisting scene.'

'Oh, OK,' she says. She sounds so breezy. I suppose she must have these conversations every day.

'I thought that was OK?'

'Fisting is OK,' she agrees. 'But just so long as you can see all the knuckles.'

'Oh, right!'

'I know, it's a common problem. Just going in that little bit too far.'

'Really?'

'Oh, you would be surprised. If I had a pound for every fisting scene we've had to send back . . .'

'You'd be a millionaire!' I laugh.

'Not quite,' says Madeline.

'No, of course not,' I say quickly.

'That all?' she asks.

'Yes,' I say. 'And thanks for your help.'

'Pleasure,' she replies.

'Enjoy your lunch,' I say.

'Actually, I've finished,' she replies.

I hang up. Kent stares at me.

'What?'

'There's no need to fraternise with the enemy,' he says.

'What on earth are you talking about?'

'That's the censor,' he says, his small eyes narrowing. 'It's us against them.'

'Who do you think you are?' I ask, suddenly rather nervous that I am spending so much time with this man. 'Some sort of porn terrorist?'

'I was just saying,' he shrugs.

'We are all in this together,' I say. 'It's a business, not some sort of anti-establishment lifestyle.'

'So we need to cut the fisting,' says Kent, turning to look back at his computer.

'Yup,' I nod. 'We need knuckles to pass.'

'OK,' he sniffs.

'And the pissing scene,' I say.

'What about it?'

'We need to lose Krista.'

'What?' he looks at me. 'You mean I ruined a good pair of Birkenstocks for nothing?'

'Well . . .'

'I'll charge you for those,' he says, looking at the scene. 'They were expensive.'

Kent and I spend another fractious day together re-editing. I talk to Madeline three or four more times, much to Kent's annoyance, and then we send the film back to the BBFC. A week later it comes back.

'What now?' bellows Kent down the telephone when I tell him.

'Um, apparently Trisha Bigtits is gagging in the last orgy scene and it looks like she is not enjoying it, or something like that.'

'She's a porn star, of course she is enjoying it!'

'Can I trust you to take it out and send it off?' I ask.

'Who do you think I am?' he shouts, before hanging up the phone.

The film gets sent back for the third time with a technical error: we have a few frames missing. Kent forgot to shuffle everything forward once he'd taken Trisha's choking out of the film. What should have been a relatively simple job has now taken over three weeks. But now we have a completed film of high quality that has been passed by the BBFC and is ready to go into production. I am stupidly pleased.

I bring the first copy home desperate to show it to Ana.

'Here it is!' I say, waving the DVD in her face as I come through the door. 'My first proper film!'

'Great,' she smiles, standing in the hall, dressed in her pyjamas.

'Shall we watch it?' I enthuse.

'No,' she says. 'You know I don't like porn.'

'But it's not just any porn,' I say. 'It's my porn.'

'Your porn, my porn, anyone else's porn, I don't want to watch it,' she shrugs. 'Sorry. I'm going to bed.'

I stand there, deflating like an old party balloon. I know she doesn't like porn, but she could at least sit and watch a few frames with me, just to be supportive. Perhaps things will change when the money starts to come in? If it ever does. Happily Toby is keen. He has been sitting in his room all day trying to write 'Bridget Bones's Diary' and he welcomes the distraction. It could also provide just the inspiration he is after. We settle down on the bed and turn on the computer. I wonder if it is such a good idea to watch porn with another bloke in the room, especially if you are both stone-cold sober. But I remind myself that this is work and I am interested in his reaction. The film starts. We open with Trisha Bigtits at the church gate.

'You don't have any music?' says Toby.

'No,' I say. 'I think it's much better with real sound. You can get all the real grunts and groans. It's much more natural. Much more of a turn-on.'

'Oh, OK,' he says. 'If you say so.'

We settle back.

'That blowjob was a little brief,' he complains again.

'I know,' I say. 'And the BBFC have just asked me to write a letter confirming that it was done on private land so that no member of the public was offended.'

'Have you?'

'Yes.'

'Was it?'

'No.'

'Oh, by the way,' says Toby, letting off an enormous yawn, 'the Paul Raymond Organisation called and wondered if you would be up for shooting a movie.'

'Really?' I sit up straight. The Paul Raymond Organisation is one of the biggest players in the country. The company behind *Mayfair*, *Men Only* and *Razzle* magazines, as well as its famous Raymond's Revue Bar, they are people to take very seriously indeed. 'God, word gets out quickly.'

'I know,' says Toby. 'Porn's a small world.'

'It might bring in some money,' I say.

'I know,' he says, staring at the screen. 'The website's not exactly rocking, is it?'

He is right about that. We have something like fifty members who have shelled out the $24.99 to join and a few hundred downloads of the *Sex and the City of London* clips. We haven't sold a single vibrator. So much for them flying off the shelves. I am now giving them away. Quite literally. Every time Ana has a girlfriend's birthday, they get given a Just Perfect vibrator. This embarrasses her and costs me money so I am in a lose-lose situation. Still, there is not very much that I can do about that. I've got to get rid of them somehow. A big box of the bastards has been cluttering up the hall for months now. Even worse, PayPal called up the other day and withdrew their services. They said that we were a porn outfit and that they didn't deal in porn. I told them we were only selling toys and they said that that wasn't entirely true. So now I am back to square one. I am practically accepting cheques. But now we have some real product to download from the website things should start looking up a bit. All I have to sort out now is the manufacture and distribution of the DVDs.

Kent, I have to say, has been no help at all. For a man who professes to know all there is to know about porn and who has been constantly undermining me for being unprofessional, he seems to have shag all clue about how the industry works. He has no idea where to get DVDs manufactured and it seems neither does anyone else. The porn industry is like some secret club run by Mike Hunt, where I don't know the password, my name is not on the list and I am definitely not coming in.

I call around DVD manufacturers for about a week. None of them seem to have any qualms about doing porn alongside their *Friends* episodes or *Little Britain* box sets; the problem is that they are all so bloody expensive. I only want five thousand copies for my initial run. I have yet to sort out any distribution and have no idea what sort of sales we might get, so I am playing my cards a little bit closer to my chest than I did with the dildos. As a result my numbers are too small to interest these large companies. They make something like half a penny on each DVD, but when they are dealing in ten thousand to a hundred thousand copies at a time that sort of makes sense. Numbers like mine are hardly worth turning the machinery on for. The lowest offer I have so far is £1.40 a copy, which is just far too much.

I pick Wedding Video Dave's brains. He is quite matey on the phone. He tells me he is having an affair with a Polish porn star. 'Talk about mixing business with pleasure,' he sniggers. Needless to say, his wife doesn't know. Anyway, he proves as clueless as Kent. Eventually it is a mate of Seb's down the Water Rat who comes up with a lead. Surely there must be a better way of doing business than scribbling numbers down on the back of beer mats? But apparently not.

Film Stuff turns out to be a bit of a find. I talk to this girl called Susie-Anne on the phone who seems to be able to cut me some sort of deal, if only I could get a word in sideways. She is the sort of person who barely draws breath and even then she can speak and inhale at the same time. She tells me her dad has a Jag within the first ten minutes of talking to her, but she comes in at eighty pence a copy, so I am not complaining. All I have to do now is send her the master copy and wait.

'Well, I think it's great,' says Toby, stretching out on the bed. 'And take it from me, I have seen a lot of porn.'

'Yeah, you have,' I nod.

'I like the sound, or lack of it,' he says. 'And the locations are great.'

'Thanks. So you think we have a future?'

'Oh yeah,' he coughs. 'Definitely.'

Copies of *The Good Life* won't be ready for three weeks and we have a bit of a cash-flow problem – a lot of it is flowing out and nothing is coming back in. For this reason I decide to take the offer of a job from the Paul Raymond team. I am a little reluctant to do so. The whole point of Spring Meadow and Touch Wood Films is that I am my own boss, creating my own films to my standards. I have spent a lifetime working for other people. Independence was one of the main reasons for getting into the porn business. But Ana is becoming increasingly worried about our lack of cash. She keeps reminding me that I have been in this business now for nearly five months and I don't appear to have got anywhere. Thank God she doesn't know about the amount of money I've steamed through and the failure of *Sex and the City of London*.

I send the Paul Raymond Organisation one of the few copies of *The Good Life* and they appear to love it. They call me in for a meeting at their offices in Soho, next door to the Windmill Theatre, and tell me they want more of the same. In fact exactly the same. A romp in a big country house. And can I organise it? We agree a flat fee of £25k and they ask me to sort it all for next week.

As I have burnt my bridges with Simon and Claire, I am now a little short of country houses to shoot in. Word has got out about the Joneses and how I can't be trusted, so every estate that I know north of Watford has closed its gates to the adventures of Touch Wood Films. We are therefore reduced to renting. I find a company called Country House Cottages and rent a beautiful-looking house on an earl's estate on the south coast. I admit, I tell a few white lies when I make the booking.

'So you know that we don't take corporate bookings?' asks the woman from the estate office when I call.

'Oh, yes,' I reply.

'You are a family unit then?' she asks.

'Absolutely,' I say. 'One big happy family.'

Our big happy family turns up at the estate in a convoy of incongruous cars. Jenny Saint, a well-known porn star famous for being able to put four fingers up her backside, arrives in a pink Mazda. Ray makes it down from Yorkshire in his souped-up BMW. Tony's in his Porsche. I'm in my Range Rover. Adam and Sean from Paul Raymond are supposed to be coming down together but Sean's wife hits the roof at the last minute about him spending a long weekend with a load of porn stars. He's no longer allowed to stay the night and has to commute back and forth from London. Which, considering what he does for a living, is kind of an odd situation. Anyway, in the end, including Kiki Hard, Alexa and Pippa, plus Kelly in make-up, we have something like ten cars cluttering up the driveway to the estate.

My voice is hoarse and my ears have turned purple for shouting directions down my mobile. It seems that they all have sat-nav in their car but not one of them knows how to use it. I only just manage to stop Jenny Saint from driving all the way up to Northamptonshire because she'd found a village with the same name. The other problem is that the house we have rented – a gorgeous bit of Georgian real estate with eight bedrooms and a huge kitchen and a swimming pool – is right next-door to the estate office. They can see everyone coming and going from the house. Every extraordinarily pimped car. And of course every tight pink T-shirt, short skirt and virulent orange tan.

In order to pre-empt any passing snooping or any overly curious visit from any of the Earl's employees, I pop into the office as soon as I arrive to introduce myself. The first person I meet on walking in is the Earl himself, holding an air rifle. He must be in his late eighties but looks remarkably sprightly.

'I am renting your house for the weekend,' I say, after introducing myself.

'Jolly good,' he says, cupping his left ear towards me.

'There are quite a few of us,' I say.

'Good,' he nods.

'A bit of a gang.'

'Righty-ho.'

'My cousins,' I say.

'Cousins,' he nods.

'We're making a film. So there will be lots of bright lights and things. I have written a script. I'm taking it to Hollywood . . .'

'What?' says the Earl, bending closer.

'Hollywood, sir,' I say, raising my voice.

'You're from Hollywood?' he repeats, looking increasingly confused.

'No, sir,' corrects a rather tweedy member of the estate staff. 'He's making a film for Hollywood.'

'Oh, really?' says the Earl, raising a distinctly bushy eyebrow. 'Bravo!'

'Thank you,' I smile. He is rather a sweet old chap and I am now feeling a little guilty. 'So we will be doing a sort of run-through,' I explain slowly and a little too loudly.

'Well, off you go,' he replies. 'Don't let me delay you.'

'Thank you, sir,' I say, and then I bow. I'm not sure why. Anything to get out of there with a bit of dignity intact.

Inside the house, chaos has already broken out. The girls are complaining about having to share a room and the boys are offering to bunk up with them. Jenny Saint is saying that she is a star and deserves a room of her own and Kent is

offering to sleep with everyone. It takes a while to sort
things out. Eventually the girls are persuaded to share and
the boys have a room each. Kent and I are also sharing,
which seems to annoy him enough to go and have a small
strop in the garden. I'm afraid I ignore him. I have six porn
stars to tame who could wander out of the house at any
moment and give the game away.

If there is one thing I have noticed in the short period
that I have been hanging out in the porn industry it is that
all porn people talk about is sex. They just can't shut up
about it. Even when you've asked them to keep quiet and
incognito, they can't seem to help themselves. And Ray is
the worst of the lot. Within five minutes of arriving at the
house, he's chatting away in his loud northern voice in the
drive. He's discussing the fact that some girl on some shoot
he did last week wouldn't do anal.

'I mean, anal is one of yer basic porn shots, don't you
think?' he asks Kiki Hard as he unloads the car. 'What's the
point of turning up on a shoot if you don't do anal. I mean,
you do anal, right?'

'Yeah,' she agrees.

'I know Jenny does anal, she can fit almost anything up
her arse. I mean, I don't see what the problem is.'

And so he goes on and on.

I call a meeting as soon as the great room debate is sorted
and hand out some very specific instructions. The curtains
are to be kept closed at all times. There is to be no nudity in
the garden. No wandering around in underwear and no
standing in doorways and pumping cocks. These people
think we are a family unit, I explain, and we are rehearsing
a Hollywood film. It is imperative that this illusion is not
shattered and they have no idea that we are shooting porn.

'Maybe the girls should get out of their "Adult Channel"

T-shirts,' suggests Adam, pointing at their chests with his cigarette.

'Mmm,' I agree, my voice shooting up an octave. I can't believe I didn't notice those. 'That would be an excellent idea.'

'You got an Adult Channel contract?' Pippa asks Kiki Hard as Kiki peels off her T-shirt.

'Yeah,' says Kiki. 'Haven't you?'

'No,' says Pippa.

'Shame,' says Kiki. 'They pay a fortune.'

Another thing I've noticed about porn people, apart from the constant chatting about sex, is that not only do they kiss instead of shaking hands but they're usually extremely nice to each other. They aren't bitchy in the slightest. They are very sweet and helpful. Then I suppose if you are about to have sex with someone inside fifteen minutes of meeting them, it is probably better to start off as friends. However, where money is concerned they lie like children caught stealing sweets. They lie about what they were paid on the last shoot. They lie to each other about how much they are getting. And they always tell each other they have a contract with one of the adult channels.

These channels are one of the more glamorous ends of the porn industry. For a fee of around £200 an hour, all the girls are required to do is sit in a studio in Great Titchfield Street, Canary Wharf or Milton Keynes, wearing a whole load of satin and marabou, and answer the phones. They usually work in pairs and play around with whips, chains and dildos, teasing punters from Gerrards Cross, and occasionally snogging each other. They say things like 'Do you like my underwear?' or 'Would you like me to kiss my mate Julia?' It is all fairly tame and everyone makes money on the premium phone lines that the punters use to call in.

Kent taught me to recognise the girls with the contracts in one of our many conversations stuck in traffic. The girls with adult TV contracts have the best nails, the longest hair extensions and the most expensive suitcases. They usually have two of the most up-to-date phones – one for business and the other for mates. And they are covered in designer labels. They were once the prettiest girl in Leatherhead and they want everyone to see how far they've gone. They do also always take you to one side at the beginning of every shoot and tell you that, as they are under contract to the Playboy Channel, they can only shoot hardcore porn. Their soft porn image is exclusive to Playboy.

Judging by her nails and long red hair extensions, Kiki does bear all the hallmarks of an Adult Channel girl, even if she does have a bright-pink wheelie suitcase. In fact all four of the girls have got the same virulent pink suitcase. They were on offer at Asda, so Kiki tells me.

'OK, everyone,' I say, clapping my hands together and trying to get some sort of order and attention. 'Let me just run through the story of *Sex Lives and the Countryside.*'

I explain the plot, such as it is. Two couples and a lesbian couple book the same house for the weekend. There is a bit of friction but they decide to move in together and then the lesbians decide that they are not lesbians any more. It ends with a large orgy in the grass. Everyone is nodding their approval.

'Sounds good,' says Ray. 'I like your films, they are always nice and complicated.'

'Good,' I smile. 'Now I need photocopies of your certificates and your IDs please.'

'Photocopies?' asks Jenny.

'Yes,' I say.

'Oh,' says Ray. 'I've only got the originals.'

'Me too,' says Kiki.

'I've forgotten mine,' shrugs Pippa, like they're the most unnecessary things in the world.

'What?' I say. I am incredulous. What is it with some porn people? It is not as if they need to remember very much. A thong, some heels and the address, as well as a couple of bits of paper. It is not bloody rocket science. 'Jesus Christ,' I say, my head in my hands.

'Well, we could always get them faxed through to the estate office?' suggests Kent, playing with his balls through the pocket in his shorts.

'Yeah,' nods Adam and points at Kent with his cigarette. 'Good idea.'

'No, it's not.' I shake my head. 'We can't photocopy HIV certificates in the estate office. We're supposed to be a family unit rehearsing a film; why would we want to know each other's HIV status?'

'Good point,' Adam points and nods again.

'You need to find a place that does secretarial services,' suggests Sean.

Thank God, I think, someone with a plan.

Half an hour later Pippa and I are trailing through the back-streets of Folkestone looking for Red Rose Secretarial Services. Glancing at our reflection in the window of the local chemist, I can't help thinking we make an odd-looking couple. I am stocky, with dark hair and a middle-aged spread and I certainly look a fair few days over forty. She, on the other hand, is blonde, tiny, with large breasts, a pair of hot pants, more or less no top and is all of nineteen. The look on Mrs Aston's face as we walk into Red Rose Secretarial says it all. Are we husband and wife? Father and daughter? Hooker and pimp? Her slack rose-pink mouth indicates that she can't decide.

'Good morning.' She manages a smile. 'How can I help you, sir?'

Looking around the musty, fusty shop, it is easy to work out that Red Rose is one of the more salubrious secretarial outfits. Run by Mrs Aston and Miss Welsh, who both sport smart short-sleeved shirts and handy name badges, you can tell they are more used to legal documents and CVs than porn stars' driving licences and HIV certificates. I explain that we need some photocopying and a fax number and that we are in something of a hurry. Mrs Aston smiles but her nostril curls as if someone has farted. And Pippa isn't helping. On her mobile to her boyfriend relaying the fax number and the whereabouts of her certificates, she can't stop talking about where she is and what she is doing.

'Can you believe it?' she squeals. 'I'm working with Jenny Saint . . . Yeah . . . That's the one. Four fingers up her . . . I know . . . Isn't it great?'

All I can do is stand and smile at Mrs Aston as she licks her plump fingers and counts how many STD certificates we want photocopying. Before long Pippa's HIV status curls through on the fax and Mrs Aston hands over all my photocopying in a large buff envelope. By the looks of it she has read what she is photocopying because she chooses the buff envelope rather than the transparent plastic folders that all the other photocopying is presented in. But she is too polite to say anything. Instead she takes my cash and I'm sure heaves a sigh of relief as I walk and Pippa teeters out of the door.

We return to the house to find it deserted. All the cars have gone, the windows are wide open, the door is ajar and there are a couple of escaped sex toys lying on the kitchen floor.

'Hello? Hello?' I am shouting. 'Hello? Anyone here?' My

mind is racing. The suitcases are still here. What's happened? Where is everyone? I'm thinking all sorts of scenarios. We've been discovered. The Earl has thrown a shit fit and they are all in the estate office, explaining themselves. I go into the garden and, sitting on a lounger with his shirt off, I find Sean. He's on his mobile phone.

'No . . . of course not. I'm not going to sleep with them. No . . . no . . .' He smiles at me as I approach and rolls his eyes. 'Wife,' he mouths. I nod. 'Listen,' he says, 'I've got to go. The director's turned up. Yes? Yes, bye . . . Me too.' He hangs up. 'Sorry about that,' he says.

'Where is everyone?' I ask.

'Oh,' he replies. 'They've gone to the shops.'

'What, all of them?'

'Yup.'

'Each in their own car?'

'Yup.' He nods. 'Some wanted cigarettes, others wanted food. It was a big expedition.'

'You can say that again.'

It is about three in the afternoon by the time I manage to guide the last lost car back to the estate. Adam is beginning to get twitchy about the lack of filming. We've all been here since about eleven and so far we have nothing on film, so I can hardly blame him. But it does make me think twice about what I am doing. I didn't really come into this business to dance to somebody else's tune. I wanted to be my own boss and I am compromising already. However, I am not stupid enough to kick up a fuss. I've got about £25k of business riding on this project, so I have got to make it work.

I have heard that one of the big cheeses at Paul Raymond likes a bit of car action, so our first port of call, while the sun is still warm and the light good, is on the back seat of my Range Rover on the North Downs Way. I leave Tony, Kiki,

Pippa and Alexa behind, with specific instructions not to leave the house or to walk naked around the garden, and I take Jenny and Ray off in the car. It is not going to be a difficult scene, just a quick wham bam to keep the corporate guys happy – a little gentle B-G to kick off the film. Kent has the cameras set up. Kelly is covering a bruise on Jenny's inner thigh while Adam and Sean are chain-smoking by the car. Ray comes up to me.

'Listen,' he sighs. 'I'm wondering if someone else could do this scene?'

'What?' I reply, squinting through my sunglasses.

'Well, I've shot with Jenny six times over the past three weeks. I've fucked her so many times. She's like my sister.'

'Oh,' I say. 'Your sister?'

'Yeah,' he nods. 'I'd much prefer to fuck someone new.'

It takes me ten minutes to persuade Ray to fuck Jenny. He walks around in circles by the side of the car, complaining that she just doesn't do it for him any more. I don't like doing it but eventually I call into question his credentials as a porn star. It's his job to get hard at the drop of a hat, otherwise any old fool could spray themselves orange and shag for a living.

That seems to do the trick. Another four minutes later and he's as hard as a rock, going at it like a train on the back seat of my car. Kent's in the front balancing on the dashboard and the whole thing is rocking up and down. Adam and Sean are standing about trying to look important, and Kelly and I are keeping a lookout on the bridlepath. Two blokes are walking towards us. I nudge Kelly and she goes and knocks on the door of the car. They don't take any notice. If anything, Jenny's screams get louder and Ray's groans increase.

'Hide!' I hiss loudly and all of us clear off into the bushes.

'Don't worry,' whispers Kelly in my ear as the two blokes close in. 'They look gay to me.'

Quite why that makes a difference I have no idea. But it calms me for a second. Maybe they won't notice the car is bouncing around like a bunny on heat. Or that there is a very bright film light on in the interior. Maybe they are liberal. I smile as they walk past. Perhaps they are not gay at all. They turn back and walk very slowly towards the car. They're going in for a second look.

'Fuck me, fuck me, fuck!' shouts Jenny. Poor Ray, I think, I can understand why the bloke's had enough. My sympathy is short-lived though, as I watch one of the men reach into his pocket and pull out his mobile phone. I have visions of the police. Sirens. Arrests. Lawyers. Expense. Of explaining it all to my father. Ana. And the Earl. But instead of dialling 999, the bloke sticks his phone out in front of him and presses record. He films for all of twenty seconds and then he and his mate start to laugh as they walk away. We all let out a huge sigh of relief. I reach into my pocket and pull out a fag.

That evening back at the estate house Kent cooks up a storm. For a bloke who lives on his own, he can really handle himself in the kitchen. I always thought that his large girth was indicative of a fast food addiction, but he's just a bloke who's very keen on his grub. While all the porn stars were buying fags and telling anyone in the local pub what they were doing at the estate, Kent was in the supermarket stocking up. He cooks roast lamb with new potatoes and piles of roasted veg. Needless to say, the porners eat only the meat and the spuds but Adam, Kent and I really tuck in. We drink bottles of red wine while Ray, Tony and the girls knock back the sambuca.

'God, did I tell you what happened to me the other day?' says Alexa to the table. A pretty girl from Stroud, I booked her because she has the most amazing pair of natural tits I have seen on the website. I smile at her down the table. I have some filthy plans for her tomorrow. Although the poor girl doesn't know it yet.

'No?' I say. 'What happened?'

She tells us that she was booked to do a day's shoot in Holland, which is not unheard of. She says she arrived at the airport and was met by some bloke who explained that they weren't shooting until later and did she mind sitting in the car while he did some errands. Why should she care? she says, she was being paid. She was driven around for a while, and then she ends up in the suburbs of Amsterdam. Two guys come in and say they are ready for sex. She asked them for certificates. They don't have any. They say they don't need any as they're not porn stars, they're two blokes who are out for a good time. She says that she eventually persuaded them to wear condoms and had sex with them to get out of the flat. After two hours of being locked up, she managed to make a run for it and find a cab in the street.

'I mean, can you believe it,' she says, sipping her drink. 'My agency didn't bother to check them out. They let me go all the way to Amsterdam, just because two blokes fancied having sex with a porn star.'

'Jesus Christ,' I say. 'I can't believe they don't look after you better. It must have been terrifying.'

'Happens all the time,' confirms Jenny. 'I have a mate who ended up in a flat in Tooting with a bloke on his own and a handicam on Christmas Eve.'

'I'd have told him to fuck off,' says Ray.

'I know,' says Jenny. 'She's just way too nice.'

Kent opens more bottles of wine and sambuca and every-one starts to get quite drunk. Ray regales us with stories of his striptease past and offers to give us all a turn. He backs down at the last minute when he realises that he hasn't packed his Velcro trousers.

'They're fitted down the leg and come off with one tug,' he shares with the group. 'My mum made them for me last year.'

By midnight I am beginning to get a little worried. The last thing I want is a full-blown party on my hands and a whole load of bedroom hopping. I have shelled out a lot of money on this shoot and I really need it to work. The more they drink and mess around the more my profits disappear. I don't really want them up fucking each other all night and then being too hungover to perform tomorrow. The sexual tension is mounting. It's probably just as well Sean's on his way home; otherwise there is no telling what temptation might have come his way. I turn the music down and start to clear up. After a few minutes I suggest we all turn in. Luckily Adam agrees. Kent shoots me a look like I have just pissed on his parade, but quite frankly, despite his delicious dinner, I don't mind if I hurt his feelings.

The next morning I am woken at 6 a.m. by the sound of smashing and crashing downstairs. I go down into the kitchen and find Kent attempting to clear up.

'What the hell is going on?' I ask, holding my head.

'Fuck off,' he says, turning to look at me. Jesus, he looks rough in the morning. 'I'm not talking to you.'

'Why?' I ask.

'You were so fucking rude to me last night I can't forgive you.'

'What?' I am stunned. I was pissed last night, but not that pissed. I did end the party, but I can't think of anything that I said to Kent to upset him this much. 'What did I say?'

'I don't know,' he shouts, all hairy and sweaty and full of halitosis. 'I can't fucking remember. All I know is that you were so fucking rude that I had to go to bed.'

'It was so rude you can't remember?' I ask.

'Yes! That fucking rude!' he yells.

'What?' I stare at him.

'Fuck off,' he says. 'I'm not talking to you any more.'

'Fine,' I say, walking out of the room. I make a mental note to myself. When dealing with Kent I should always hire and always talk through an assistant.

Over the next three days we manage to get the film done but not before I nearly give myself a coronary. Trying to keep porn stars locked up in a house without any of them strolling off half-naked around the Earl's grounds and bumping into one of the gamekeepers or gardeners is enough of a full-time job without Kent sulking and Jenny throwing a hissy fit because Ray isn't paying her enough attention. I lose count of the amount of times I have to tell Tony or Ray to stop wanking in the window or walking in the garden with just their pants on. The problem is, they can't see why anyone would think it strange to go for a walk in your Y-fronts and I am too exhausted to explain why.

We do quite a bit of al fresco shooting. I have to admit that open-air sex is one of my things. I went to a rather conservative boys' boarding school so didn't have sex in a room until I was nineteen. I think I might be forever trying to recapture my youth.

Anyway on the Sunday we spend the day near the greenhouses shooting a few foursomes, breaking off from filming every time a plane flies overhead. There is an RAF base close by so these flights are quite frequent and a little annoying. Come lunchtime Kent reckons they are getting more and more frequent – he says they can see what is going and are buzzing the estate to investigate. By tea I'm afraid I agree with him. Some of them are coming in so low I can actually see the pilot's face.

Apart from Jenny's arguments with Ray, morale on the shoot remains good. There is a hiccup when Alexa gets her period. I had somehow never imagined that porn stars ovulated, let alone had periods. This, however, doesn't seem to stop them from working. Alexa says she can't use a tampon otherwise it will get in the way of her DP, so she dispatches Kent and me to buy her a sponge in the local chemist. After a frantic dash up the aisles, we come back with a bright green one in the shape of Thomas the Tank Engine. Well, the stock was limited and we were in a hurry, and we didn't quite understand that it was the contraceptive sponge that she was after. Alexa doesn't bat an eyelid when we give it to her. Instead she cuts it down to size with her nail scissors, pops it up and tells us to keep an eye open just in case the thing falls out.

Thomas does us proud. Alexa completes all her scenes and we wrap the film more or less on time. I would like to think that the Earl and his estate are none the wiser as we leave. But there is something in the eyes of one of the gardeners as he wishes us good luck with the film that makes me think otherwise. Perhaps they were in on it from the start? Perhaps they didn't mind at all? Maybe we could have been upfront from the start and saved ourselves a lot of hassle.

I hand over the tapes to the Paul Raymond boys and they seem pleased. Sean even shot some extra stuff on my handicam during the weekend to add a little something to the DVD.

A week later I am sitting next to Toby in the spare room discussing 'Bridget Bones's Diary' when I get a call from Adam.

'Hi there,' he says. 'I just want to ask you something?'

'Yes?' I say.

'Um, you know the extra stuff that we shot on your camera? Well I have the footage in the office and we have been scrolling through . . .'

'Right?'

'And all we can see so far is two old ladies on a coach trip in Scotland?'

'Two old ladies on a coach trip?' I repeat. Toby looks at me.

'Yeah,' says Adam. 'Does anything else happen?'

'What d'you mean?'

'Like in the old days, when naughty boys used to hide hardcore in-between footage of children's birthday parties?' he asks.

'Um', I'm confused. Then Toby taps me on the knee.

'Sorry,' Toby says. 'I lent your camera to my mum for her holiday. She and a mate went on a coach holiday around Scotland.'

'Adam?' I say.

'Yeah?'

'I think you're looking at the wrong tape.'

Six

Shit. Would you believe it? I still haven't made any money. What with paying the rent on the estate house and entertaining all the Paul Raymond guys and the dinners and the petrol and the extra bits here and there, I didn't even cover my outgoings. I've actually made a loss. It is only £1253, but it is still a loss. How am I going to explain to Ana that I am not raking it in, like I expected? This industry is a lot harder to crack than I thought.

I think I'm spending too much time on each film. We have got to speed up the process, cut down on editing time and get the product out in the shops. When I first started thinking about breaking into the industry I had some sort of a plan. I'd churn out a film a month, get a kind of production line going, a bit like a woman called Cathy Barry, just outside Bristol. She has a huge warehouse where they shoot any number of porn films all day every day and she's coining it. My idea was to emulate her, only to take it all a little bit more upmarket. But so far so fucking bankrupt, so don't tell the girlfriend.

As far as Ana is concerned things are going well. I have to say that to her. Otherwise the shit would hit the fan and I might be out on my ear. I'm not lying exactly. Things are going well. Just not financially. It does feel weird though. I always used to tell her everything, now I have to be selective. Things have to get better soon. She's begun to get telephone calls from her girlfriends. I suppose it is naive to expect gossip this good not to get around town quickly. But they're all calling now. Mostly to offer a shoulder to cry on. I mean, how ghastly to be living with a pornographer? I suspect what they're really after, though, are details. They always want to know how the shoots went and what sort of things I'm up to. But, you know, if you live in Fulham and your husband's a banker, anything to brighten up your day.

After my shooting for the Paul Raymond Organisation I get a call from Playboy. Initially I am excited. I am honoured. They're Playboy, for chrissake, and they want to talk to me. But in the end I travel back and forth to their offices three times and I suddenly realise that this is a major jerk off and a bit of a distraction. They want me to come to see how they work. But I've done two films now and I know what I am doing. Why would I need to spend time learning the ropes from them? Also I can't spend my life being employed by someone else. I have spent the last fifteen years playing other people's tunes. It is about time I played my own. I have to make a success of Touch Wood and Spring Meadow; otherwise, quite frankly, my life won't be worth living. I have already been a failed musician, I can't add failed porn director to the list as well.

Just to make matters worse my father calls to check up on how things are going.

'Your mother and I were wondering how you are,' he says in the special voice he usually reserves for parishioners. 'We haven't seen you for a while.'

'I know,' I say, sounding defensive. I always sound defensive when talking to my father. I become defensive. And positively teenage. How come my father always makes me feel fourteen even though I'm bloody forty-three? 'I have been very busy.'

'Good, good,' he says. 'Music going well?'

'Yes.'

'Just so long as you're busy, the devil makes work, as you know.'

'Yes, Dad.'

'So are we going to see you before Christmas?' he asks. He tries to make it sound exciting. But we both know that it is simply a duty call.

'Um . . .' What excuse can I think of this time?

'You're coming up for Emma's wedding, aren't you?'

'Oh shit . . .'

'Don't swear.'

'Sorry.'

'She is expecting you. You've been friends since playschool.'

'I know, Dad, I know.'

'So we'll see you then?'

'Absolutely.'

'Send our love to Ana. Such a lovely girl.'

'Of course.'

'See you in three weeks.'

My heart sinks. I don't want to see him because I'll only have to lie to him. And I hate doing that. This career better be worth it. I have got to start making money and it's got to happen soon.

Two days after the phone call with my dad the first consignment of DVDs arrives at the flat. I can't tell you the sense of achievement I feel as I look at the three cardboard boxes stacked up in the hall. I open one up and take out a copy of *The Good Life*. They even smell fantastic – all new and shrinkwrapped in plastic. The cover is great. It is racing green with a photo of Simon and Claire's very expensive electric gates. They are much more minimalist than the usual gang-bang shots that grace the cover of porn videos. Toby's impressed.

'Now this is classy,' he says with a sniff. He turns the thing over. 'I'm glad you have a few blowjobs on the back,' he adds. 'Otherwise my mum might put it on thinking she's going to catch up with Tom and Barbara from the olden days.'

He laughs uproariously. Looking at him I can't help thinking that Toby's gone downhill of late. His face has taken on the white, waxy hue of someone who has recently been exhumed and his eyes are becoming increasingly bloodshot. I know we have just slid miserably from autumn into winter and that Christmas is only a couple of months off, but he is looking more rough than ready to hibernate. I am worried that he might well be back on the drugs. If he is, he's keeping it quiet.

Now that I have finally got some product, it's time we set about shifting it. The only problem is, I am not quite sure how to do it. Yet again calling around my increasingly long list of contacts, no one seems to know how to sell stock. Apart from downloading off the internet, the only other place to sell hardcore porn is in a licensed sex shop but there appears to be no distributor to call or company to do the groundwork for you.

The licensed sex shop business is one of those retail oddities that I can't really understand. There are something like eighteen of them in Westminster alone, which is the highest collection of porn outlets in the country, and at £29,102 a licence per annum they bring in over half a million a year to the council. What must be classed as rather a nice little earner. How they make their money and afford to pay for their licence and their rent I have no idea. They must be shifting shitloads of videos and DVDs. Selling at something between twenty pounds and twenty-five pounds a pop, they are not exactly expensive fast-moving consumer goods. I have been told by Kent that I should try and sell them to the shops at between six pounds and ten pounds but I have to say, having phoned up three of them so far this morning, I can't fucking give them away.

'Oh, no,' says some bloke in Soho. 'Our customers don't do sophisticated.'

'Really,' I say. 'Have you tried giving them anything a little upmarket?'

'Oh, no,' he repeats. 'There's no call for that around here.'

'How do you know if you don't try?'

It is like banging my head against a brick wall. I can't help thinking I must be missing a trick. I bet the big companies don't cold-call and hand-deliver product. They probably have reps doing this stuff. Or something? There must be a distribution company somewhere?

In the meantime it's me and my motor in the backstreets of Soho, selling to fat, bald white blokes and sharp, smooth Indians round the back of their shops. I manage to charm a few into taking between ten and fifteen copies, but mostly they take five or six at a time. Half of them pay me around five quid for each one, and the rest I hand over on a sale or return basis. It is relentless, exhausting and downright disheartening. Wouldn't it be nice if something in this life were easy?

Sitting at home, I count the cash from my DVD sales. I've got something like £650, which I suppose is not a total washout for an afternoon at the coalface of porn. Just as I am wondering what to do with the spoils, the phone goes. It

is an American porn company called Digital Sun who want
to buy *The Good Life*. My heart jumps. They tell me they've
seen it on our website and they want to put it on theirs to
download. Christ. They also want to sell it in the US, they
say. They make their offer. The figures they are talking are
risible. They say they'll give me twenty thousand dollars for
the rights to everything, and for a second I am tempted. We
have only enough money left to make one, or possibly, with
the help of credit cards, two porn films and the cash would
come in very handy. But I have realised through my research
that the only way to make big money on porn is to get yourself a back catalogue or a body of work so good and
irresistible that people will pay top dollar for all of it. You
need about ten films to make it work. And some sort of bar-
gaining tool to sell in bulk, to get a good price. US
distributors want quantity as well as quality and that's the
only way you are going to make any cash. Toby looks at me
like I am some sort of nutter as I turn them down.

'Don't tell Ana,' I say as I hang up.

'Sealed, mate,' he says, zipping his lips.

Not that he and Ana talk much these days. Toby is
becoming increasingly nocturnal and Ana, now the main
wage earner in our relationship, is really putting in those
fashion hours. Bless her. Thank God someone is making
some money. Anyway they didn't have that much to say to
each other at the best of times, but their different lifestyles
now make things a little easier. There isn't so much tension
in the house. More a resigned stalemate.

I suppose my relationship with Kent could be described in
similar terms, except with a little bit more aggravation and
jaded annoyance. I mean, he always sighs when I call him
up, like I am disturbing him from some higher purpose and

not from wanking in front of *Richard & Judy*. Which I know he's doing. The trouble is, he's good. He's also always available and he has his own edit suite, of course. So while I book him for another shoot, I have to ignore the fact that he is a fat, hirsute, moody pain in the arse.

It is the night before we shoot our next film, *The Painter*, and in an effort to economise on hotel bills, I've got Ray staying in the flat. Ana originally said that she didn't mind because she was going out to dinner with a mate but she cancelled at the last minute, so now we are all sitting watching *The Bill* with bowls of spaghetti bolognaise on our laps.

Ana was a bit uncomfortable when Ray arrived, mainly, I think, because he is so tall and beefy and bright orange; but he bought her a bottle of wine and some carnations, so she softened slightly. Then again I would still say the atmosphere in the sitting room is a little tense. All I can say is thank God Toby's gone out.

'This is one of my favourite shows,' announces Ray, his mouth full of spaghetti. 'But they do things wrong, don't they?'

'Really?' says Ana.

'Oh, yeah,' he nods. 'Last week they had some bloke going mad on steroids and we all know they're fine.'

'Are they?' asks Ana.

'Yeah,' he says. 'All the boys are taking them.'

'You do?' I ask.

'Yeah,' he replies. 'I wouldn't look like this if I didn't take them.'

'Oh,' says Ana.

'I'd be half the size.'

'I didn't know that,' I say.

'So would most of the guys,' he says.

'But aren't they illegal?' asks Ana.

'Are they?' asks Ray.

'Maybe it's just sport,' I say.

'I think that's it,' says Ray. 'I've got this very friendly chemist. Gets me everything.'

'Oh, right,' I say, searching for my liberal face.

'He's dead useful,' says Ray. 'He gets me these super-strong antibiotics. I take them once a month. Just in case. Keeps the system cleaned out.' He smiles at Ana. 'Great spaghetti, by the way.'

'Thanks,' she says, a small tight smile on her face.

Having been let down again by my so-called mates in the location department, I have decided to splash out and book a hotel room to shoot *The Painter*. As a result the next day I am standing outside a very upmarket establishment in Kensington, with Ray, Kent, an assistant, a hair stylist, a make-up girl, Jenny Saint, Freddie, who's recovered from his dose of the clap, and two girls I haven't ordered. I was expecting Alexa and another girl Louise; instead I've got Maddie, a lap dancer from Birmingham, and Dorota, a lawyer from Warsaw.

'What happened to Alexa?' I ask Maddie.

'Oh, you know,' she shrugs. 'She's got flu.'

'You mean, she is working?' I ask.

'I dunno, you'd better phone the agency.'

I call the agency to complain that instead of Alexa and Louise, I have a Brummie and a Pole, neither of whom I ordered.

'Well, unless you want to shoot tomorrow, that's yer lot,' says the agent down the phone.

'Why can't you just be honest when I call in the first place?' I suggest. 'Then at least we would all know what to expect.'

I am already in a bad mood, and mentally rewriting the

script as I start to deliver my lecture. The hotel doesn't know we are shooting a porn film, so could we please all try to be discreet? Although, judging by the fact that no one is wearing any clothes and it is mid-winter, we don't exactly look like a group of doctors on a conference. I explain that we should go through the lobby and up to the room one at a time and try to draw as little attention to ourselves as possible. I tell them that the hotel thinks I am interviewing and screen-testing for a film so we have to keep the porn talk to a minimum.

Twenty minutes later we are all safely in the room, which the hotel has very kindly upgraded to a suite. Kent is setting up the cameras and the lights, with a new assistant called Geoff, and I breathe a sigh of relief. So far, so good, so incident free. There's a knock at the door. I answer.

'Your douche, sir,' says the bellboy, standing there with a white paper bag in his hand.

'I'm sorry, my what?'

'Your douche,' he repeats, his cheeks turning red.

'Ta, thanks,' says Maddie, barging past me with a ten-pound note in her hand. 'Very kind of you, I'm sure.'

'Thank you,' I say, tipping the bellboy another tenner.

He now knows exactly what we are doing, and money is the only way to keep him sweet. I heave a huge sigh. I don't know why I waste my breath explaining things to these girls when they don't take a blind bit of notice. I walk back into the room to find Jenny is pissed off. She is refusing to have sex with Freddie because his STD certificate is six weeks old.

'I don't mind,' says Maddie, standing by the bathroom door holding her douche, 'I'll shoot over six weeks.'

'Well, I won't,' says Jenny. 'It's dangerous.'

'Who do you think you are?' asks Maddie.

'I'm just looking after myself,' shrugs Jenny.

'Are you suggesting I don't?'

'Well . . .' Jenny looks Maddie up and down.

'Right, that's it!' shouts Maddie, chucking her douche in the air. 'I'll only fuck him with a condom.'

The row carries on for another ten minutes, with Maddie accusing Jenny of being up herself. And Jenny telling Maddie that she's the star so she calls the shots. Meanwhile I sit on the bed with my pen and paper trying to working out how to shag my way around a bloke who no one will sleep with. They have both said they'll use a condom but I'm not going to shoot with one of those. No one gets off on a condom. Quite a few of the US porn films use condoms and nearly all gay movies are shot with condoms, as they have to promote a safe sex message. But they don't float my boat. Nor indeed do they float the gay boat much either, which is one of the reasons why some gay men watch straight porn. That and the fact that straight stories are better, apparently.

I ask Geoff to order up room service to see if some club sandwiches without lettuce or tomatoes can calm the situation down a bit. And while everyone tucks into their food, I take Freddie to one side and bollock him for wasting our time. I send him home and tell him that I don't want him to come to the shoot tomorrow. He has really pissed me off. He has a reputation for giving the girls an itch and the very least he could do is turn up with pieces of paper telling everyone he is as clean as a whistle. As I watch him pack up his wheelie suitcase, I am quietly fuming. I've spent two grand already this morning and I have yet to get anything on film.

We rework the scene I had planned with Ray instead of Freddie. But I am not sure what to do with Dorota so ask her to sit the first scene out. She gives me a look, asks if she will still get paid and gives me a petulant shrug when I reply that of course she will.

'OK, then,' I say, desperately hoping that Ray and Jenny have got over their brother-sister thing and haven't had to shag together for a few weeks. I inhale and go for it. 'This is the plan. Jenny and Ray are going out. And while Jenny is asleep he sneaks out and meets up with Maddie. He brings Maddie back to the room. You shag.' They nod at me. 'Then you, Jenny, wake up and say something along the lines of, what are you doing with my boyfriend?'

'OK,' she says.

'And then you fuck Maddie.'

'Maddie?' She looks at her and then sighs. 'OK. I am a professional.'

'Good,' I say. 'That's the spirit. And then you piss and while Ray is shagging her and taking her up the arse, you roll back, put your legs behind your ears and do your signature pose.'

'You want all four fingers up my arse?' she enquires.

'That's right.'

'OK then,' she says. 'And where do you want to shoot the water sports?'

'Kent?' I ask.

'The bath?' he says. 'So much easier than having to clear up here.' He indicates towards the bed. 'We've only got this room, right?'

'Yes,' I nod.

'Then water sports in the bathroom and back here for the fingers.'

'Excellent. Oh, then,' I add. 'Dorota?' She looks up from her book.

'Yes?'

'Then you can come in as the maid and have sex with

both girls and blow Ray at the end.' She looks at me like I have offended her in some way. 'Is that OK?'

'Yes,' she sighs. 'But why am I always the bloody maid?'

We are just about to start filming. Kent has lit the bed and Ray is walking around naked pumping his cock. Maddie is choosing her thong. There is a knock on the door to the suite.

'OK,' I say. 'I'm getting this. You keep quiet please. I want you all to stay out of sight.' I answer the door.

'Hi!' says an immaculately dressed man holding a huge fruit basket. 'I am the duty manager on today and I thought seeing as you were in the suite all day, um, interviewing, you might like one of these.'

'The duty manager?' I cough.

'Yes, that's right,' he smiles. 'I hope everything is to your satisfaction?'

'Absolutely,' I smile. 'Perfect.'

'Good,' he says, looking through the cellophane of his fruit basket and over my shoulder. I follow his gaze. Ray's bright orange buttocks walk past. He turns around, looks at us and nods, all the while vigorously pumping his cock. 'Just so long as you have everything that you need.'

'Yes,' I say, pulling out my wallet and searching for a fifty-pound note. 'Thank you very much.' I hand over the note. He hands it back.

'Don't worry,' he smiles. 'Have a good day.'

The whole hotel is in on it now. There is nothing much I can do except try to keep the noise down and not blow the electrical circuits with the lights. Oh, and keep tipping heavily.

We start to shoot and it is immediately apparent that my first resolution has gone straight out the window. Maddie is a screamer and as soon as Ray starts shagging her, she begins to yelp. It becomes progressively louder until by the time he takes her up the arse over the bed she is screaming so loudly I think the whole floor of the hotel must be able to hear. Sure enough, just as Ray is ready for the cum shot, the phone goes beside the bed.

'Hello?' comes this man's rather deep voice.

'Hello,' I reply.

'I am an airline pilot,' says the voice.

'I am so sorry,' I say.

'And I am trying to sleep down the corridor from you and you've woken me up.'

'I'll try and keep it down, I'm sorry,' I say. 'I really am.'

'Well, the thing is,' the pilot clears this throat, 'I was wondering if I could join in.'

'Sorry?' I take the phone away from my ear and look at it in shock. What the hell . . .? I put it back to my ear.

'Yeah,' he continues, 'I was just, you know, wondering if you would mind . . .'

'Um, I'm sorry, this is a private orgy.'

'Oh, OK,' he says. 'You can't blame a bloke for trying.'

It seems it's not just the pilot who is keen to get his rocks off. Throughout the afternoon our various G-G, B-G and orgy scenes are interrupted continually by calls from various airline staff all over the hotel asking if they can come up and join in. These guys must be the horniest airline in the world. From the pilots to the stewards to the flight attendants, they are all partial to an afternoon shag with a stranger.

Come six o'clock we have done almost everything. There's just the final scene where Ray shags Maddie and Jenny, and Dorota comes in and joins them. The light is fading outside so the film lights are on full blast. Despite the cold, the room is boiling hot. Ray is walking around pumping himself up and the girls, all naked, are choosing which sex toys they fancy and are applying lube. Kent is being his usual irritating self so I walk out on the balcony. It's a cold winter evening and it feels good to clear my head and my lungs. I stretch out and yawn and turn back to look inside the room. All the curtains are open and with all the lights on full beam you can see absolutely everything that is going on. My heart lurches suddenly. I look back in front of the hotel. There is a small patch of raised ground directly opposite the room and on it are sat some fifteen to twenty people all staring at me. I look from the people to the porn stars and back again. Barring Kent and me, it is clear they have the best view in the house. I wave weakly from the balcony. They spontaneously burst into applause. I throw my cigarette over the side. I am going to need some serious money to tip myself out of this one.

In the end I left the hotel about £250 lighter, handing over fifties to the guy on reception, the bellboy, the concierge who bought the douche and any other random soul I came across. In fact I was so bloody generous they practically gave us a royal send-off. But I tell you something, I shan't be using a hotel suite again. I don't think my nerves could deal with it.

The next day's shoot is fortunately at a German mate of mine's place in Wandsworth. It is a sexy, swanky sort of a pad with a mezzanine and huge pieces of modern art on the walls. Florien is an old architect friend from the days when I had cash and celebrity mates. I was surprised he agreed, but he's said that we can film in the flat if he is allowed to watch. I did think of asking my stars if they minded him peeking from the top of the mezzanine, but then again they are all exhibitionists so I can't really see the problem.

I am already in the flat, moving chairs and sofas around,

when Kent lumbers through the door with another skinny-looking bloke in spray-on black jeans who I presume to be his new assistant. They never seem to last longer than one shoot. I can't for the life of me think why.

'All right,' says Kent, with a sniff. 'Seen this?' He shoves a well-worn copy of a Sunday newspaper in my face. 'It's from the weekend,' he says. 'Didn't notice this until I had a dump this morning.'

'What?' I say, pushing the paper away.

'Centre pages,' he says. 'Alexa.'

'What about it?' I say, leafing through.

'Claims she is a secretary who slept with her boss,' he says. 'It is some article about girls who have slept with their bosses and she is one of them. Look.' He points to a photo of Alexa all dolled up in a suit with stockings and a suspender belt. 'It says that she is from Harpenden, and we know she is from Stroud. And that she works in an office. There's no mention of her being a porn star.'

'It also says that she is twenty-five,' I say. 'I know she's twenty-one. I've got a copy of her birth certificate.'

'Can you believe this stuff?' says Kent, looking a little incredulous.

'I know,' I nod. 'Shocking, isn't it?'

'Are you taking the piss?' he asks.

'Yes,' I smile. 'I wonder how much she got paid?'

'I've no idea,' he huffs. 'I was just a little shocked to see her there.'

Kent stomps around the flat sorting out his light and his assistant, whom he sends out for bottles of water. The man must have a hangover, because he is very grumpy. I didn't wait around after the Kensington hotel experience last night as I had no cash left and I didn't really want to have to shell out more on buying the drinks. It looks like Kent must have found someone else to booze with because, as well as the bottle of water, he is on his second bacon sandwich of the morning.

With Freddie off down some Harley Street clinic seeing if he can get his tests done in a day, I have had to find myself another leading man. And almost as soon as John walks in the door, I know I have made a mistake. Within minutes of arriving he is walking around in his white jockey pants, demanding to know where the girls are.

'I'm hot and raring to go,' he grins. 'Bring 'em on.'

I mean, he is practically roaring. He starts strutting around the sitting room like a ram in rut rubbing everyone up the wrong way. He manages to piss off Kelly, Kent and me within the space of a few minutes. It turns out that John is a student and this is his second film. He is financing his way through college by shagging and he's loving it. Over the months that I have been doing this, I have come to realise that there is a very strange and subtle male dynamic on a porn shoot. What could be a big baboon chest-beating exercise is kept very much in check by the porn stars themselves. The successful guys are not the swanky alpha-male types who wang their wazzer in your face at every opportunity. They are quiet and soft and nice and know who is paying their wages. Although they may well walk around pumping their cocks, they never show off or get excited about their prowess. They don't puff themselves up and don't show you just how bloody big they are. And most of them are huge. That's why they are porn stars. Cocks like forearms, always hard and ready to go. Whereas this bloke is all pants and no brain. I feel like saying to him, you may be here to get your rocks off, mate, but, the thing is, I'm paying for you to do it. Thank God Ray turns up to diffuse the situation. Well, he is so big and orange and pumped. It would be hard to out-cock him.

I have also booked Camilla who, according to her

updated website, is now doing B-G, as well as G-G and spanking. She breezes in with another girl, Katie, whom the agency promised would be a cracker. The agency lied. Still, Camilla looks fabulous.

'Darling,' she says, kissing me on both cheeks. 'Great to see you again. Such fun. I must be so much more useful to you now that I'm doing the old B-G.'

'What made you change your mind?' I ask.

'God,' she sighs. 'It was so goddamn boring just doing girls and hairbrushes. I thought B-G might be a laugh. And it is!' she giggles. 'However, I do draw the line at DP. A girl's got her limits.'

'I haven't,' grins Katie. 'It's my birthday today and I've given myself this as a treat.' She rubs her hands together. 'I'm so excited. I can't wait. When do we start having sex?'

'Have you done this before,' I ask.

'No,' she grins. 'Can you tell?'

Well, honestly, looking her up and down, I can. Her mousy hair is hanging lankly to her shoulders. She is too thin and as she takes her shoes off to remove her jeans, I can tell she needs a pedicure. Ray takes me aside immediately.

'Jesus Christ,' he whispers in my ear. 'I can't shag her.'

'Why not?' I ask.

'Have you seen her feet?' he asks.

'They look like they need a bit of TLC,' I admit.

'I can't fuck girls with bad feet,' he says. 'It's my thing. When I need to come, I think of feet.'

'You do?'

'Yeah, quite a lot of us do,' he says.

'Really?' I say. How odd is that, I think. Maybe it's because they've had so many tits and arses that the feet are the last things left to fetishise.

'Yeah,' he nods. 'Tony's the same. He can't look at a girl with shit feet, he finds it such a turn off.'

'OK, don't worry,' I say. 'You can shag Camilla and John can have Katie.'

'Thanks, mate,' he says, looking Camilla up and down. 'She's gorgeous. I love a new girl.'

We get down to shooting and Katie goes off like a rocket. She is all over John, blocking camera angles and trying to take over. The chemistry is non-existent and she is screaming like a stuffed pig, too. I stop the cameras rolling and take her to one side.

'Katie,' I say.

'Yeah?' she replies, wiping her mouth on the back of her hand. She has just been blowing John.

'You've got to calm down a bit.'

'You what?' she says.

'Just calm down,' I say. 'You're frantic.'

'Oh, right,' she nods. 'I am just a bit excited. You know with it being my birthday and all that. I've been looking forward to it. If you see what I mean.'

'Right,' I nod. 'What d'you do normally?'

'Oh,' she says, putting her thin hair behind her ears. 'I work for a housing department. So this is a bit of a treat from me, you know.'

'Yes,' I say. 'Just don't let everyone see it.'

The afternoon goes from bad to worse. Katie carries on screaming and blocking the shots, so we introduce a foursome scene in the hope of hiding her in an orgy. I tell Ray to shag Camilla on the sofa and I say to John to sit next to Ray and take Katie up the arse, and then while he does that we will home in on him for the money shot.

It all starts off OK. Ray gets going with Camilla. She has such a lovely pair of tits that I make her bounce up and down on his cock facing towards the camera. Meanwhile John has Katie bent over the back of the sofa so all we see is her arse. Her screams and overexcited facial expressions are made in the opposite direction of the camera. I glance up to see Florien looking over the top of the mezzanine; he has a bird's-eye view of proceedings. Everyone bangs away. Camilla is playing with herself on Ray's cock; she's enjoying herself that much. But John seems to be struggling. He is slapping around Katie's backside, his eyes closed, straining to come. Kent's got his camera right in there, so the pressure is mounting. There's a tension in the room. Katie's screams are waning. The poor girl's getting tired. I can see beads of sweat gleaming on John's bare shoulders. Katie's gone quiet. Camilla moans. She's clearly had an orgasm. But John's is nowhere to be seen.

'Um, how much longer there, mate,' says Kent, tight and focused on Katie's arse.

'One minute,' squeaks John. 'Nearly there.'

Then suddenly he lets out the most enormous roar, pulls his cock out of Katie's backside as he comes and spreads her buttocks apart. Kent leans in for the money shot but as he does so Katie lets off the most enormous fart and all of John's sperm and the contents of her colon shoot out and land on Kent's shoulder. He screams, Florien retches and the whole shoot grinds to a halt.

I've grown used to bum farts and fanny farts and endless discussions about bodily functions and fluids, but this is the first time someone has shat on set. Kent is so freaked out that he takes his jumper off and throws it out of a window, saying he never wants to see the thing again. Katie is so mortified that she bursts into tears. I have to say I feel for her. It is not really her fault, poor love. John was taking so long, banging around up there, something was bound to happen. But the most horrified person is Florien, who leaves the shoot altogether, asking us to tidy up and post the keys through the letterbox as we leave.

I send Kent's assistant out for a bottle of vodka to try to calm things down a bit. There is one more scene to do before the end of the day and I am determined to get it in the bag otherwise we may as well bin the whole shoot. I give everyone an hour to have a drink and mop themselves down with baby wipes before getting going again. On Kelly's advice, Katie goes off and gives herself an enema during the break and returns renewed and invigorated ready for her final scene.

It is supposed to be a DP scene, but as Camilla won't do DP and Ray won't sleep with Katie we come up with an odd scene. Where John takes Katie from behind while she blows Ray. It seems his hatred of her feet draws the line at knob-sucking, which gives us a tiny bit of leeway. The scene is going fine. Katie can't scream with Ray's cock in her mouth, so I might have some sort of usable footage. I step away from the scene to find myself an armchair to sit down in. Just as my back is turned, I hear Ray shout:

'Get your fucking fingers out of my arse!'

'What?' I say, spinning right back around.

'Oh, God, man, you tell her,' says Ray, shaking his head and putting his hand over his erect penis. 'I don't let anyone put their fingers up my arse.'

'Oh, I'm sorry,' says Katie. 'I thought you'd like it. You've had your fingers up Camilla's arse all day.'

'That's different,' he says.

'Why?' asks Katie.

'It just is.'

I look at Ray and Katie and Camilla and John and realise

that this is just not bloody working. None of them like each other; there's no chemistry on set and no amount of editing is going to get us out of this disaster. We have another two days of filming booked. I am just going to have work the backside off Freddie when he finally gets his certificates. We wrap the shoot and I start peeling tenners off the roll in my back pocket. John's straight out of the door without so much as a handshake. Camilla is charming and delightful and I promise to book her again. Ray is steaming slightly over the finger incident but he is too good-humoured to let it ruin his day. He says that he'll see me in the pub over the road and gives me a slap on the back. Meanwhile Katie seems to have cornered Kent. She's had a few more slugs of vodka and having been sexed-up all day, she clearly thinks that she is irresistible. Somewhat uncharacteristically of Kent, he is having none of it. He keeps moving his hairy head from side to side as she, with equal determination, tries to kiss him. In the end he gives in and she kisses him full on the mouth.

'Jesus Christ,' he says, his mouth all screwed up as he pulls away. 'Your breath tastes of cock.'

Four days later I drop all the footage off at Kent's flat and disappear up to Oxfordshire to stay with my parents for Emma's wedding. Ana is under strict instructions to say nothing about my new career and I am more tight-lipped than a Catholic priest. My brother, my parents, Ana and I all sit around a chilly kitchen table for a cold-cuts lunch and we manage to have one of those stiff hour-long conversations where much is talked about but nothing is actually said. The state of the village, my journey and the weather are all discussed with gusto. Luckily my career is given a wide berth. As we tuck into our quiche I can't help thinking my parents have aged a lot since I last saw them. The broken veins have grown across my father's nose and cheeks, and my mother's face hangs more hound dog than before. They have both been working too hard, keeping the community going. If they found out their son had over one thousand copies of hardcore porn in the back of his car they might well choke on their scotch eggs.

The wedding that afternoon is a jolly affair. Packed into a tent at the back of the old vicarage in the next-door village are various mates, conquests and blasts from the past. There are lots of shouts of recognition, whoops of delight and glasses of champagne. We are all much older and fatter than before. The girls look like their mums, squeezed into bright-coloured silk suits with ankles like piano legs. The blokes have all lost their hair and put cushions down the front of their trousers. But it is good to see them all. There is something very relaxing about seeing old friends that you grew up with, especially after a few glasses of fizz. Actually, quite a few glasses. Come the sit-down dinner, I am a little bit pissed.

'So how are you?' asks a buxom blonde called Belle, who I once took from behind in a horsebox when we were both nineteen.

'Very well,' I say. 'You?'

'Oh, you know, married, two children, bored. The usual,' she smiles and shoves a large forkful of rice into her mouth. 'You?'

'Got my porn company,' I say.

I think I say it to shock her more than anything. Or perhaps amuse. Or maybe I am a little bored of my bourgeois surroundings and want to shake things up a bit. Then again I could just be showing off. Whatever the reason, it works. Belle's eyes almost pop out of her head. She thinks it's hilarious. She always was one of those horsey, hearty and jolly sex sort of girls. She asks me for all the details. How large are the blokes? And are they any good?

'God,' she says, knocking back a large glass of red wine. 'It sounds like heaven to me. I haven't had a good seeing-to in years.'

The gossip spreads through the tent in about half an hour. Most of my old mates think it sounds like the best career move they've heard in years. They come to shake my hand and ask me all sorts of questions.

About thirty minutes later Ana comes to find me standing in a field surrounded by fifteen or so friends. The boot of the car is open. The interior light is on and the sound of 'Come on Eileen' filters from the disco through the trees.

'Hi,' she says, picking her way towards me over the damp grass.

'Oh, hi there,' I smile.

She stops and takes in the crowd, the open boxes and the fistful of tenners in my in hand.

'What the fuck are you doing?'

'Nothing, darling,' I smile. 'Just selling some porn.'

Seven

Ana is furious with me for a whole week. She only speaks when it is absolutely necessary and there's a moment when I think that she might actually move out.

The night of my porn car-boot sale we had a blazing row at my parent's house – all done in whispers and hisses so that we could not be overheard, of course. She said I embarrassed her so much she wanted to cry. Stomping back and forth in her nightie, she said she'd stuck up for me all night as one chinless Sloane after another asked how poorly my music career was going. She even lied for me, telling everyone I was doing something terribly exciting on the net. They'd all laughed and winked but she'd insisted I was making money and was about to really make my mark. And then an hour later she catches me selling porn out of the boot of my car like a 'fucking market trader'. And I do have to concede she has a point.

My agreeing with her is apparently not enough. It's symptomatic of my lack of respect. My not listening to anything she has to say. And my not including her in the decisions I am making or the plans I might have. In the end I manage to win her over by asking if she would mind designing the covers for the DVDs.

'They are remarkably classy,' I say. 'And you have an eye for that sort of thing.'

'Do you think?'

'Oh, yeah,' I say. 'I have always respected your opinions on art.' I am not actually aware of Ana passing any opinions on art, but should she ever, I am sure I would appreciate them.

In the end I eat more humble pie than a politician caught with his pants down. Anything to stop her walking out of the door. And after spending an evening with some of the hearty lasses from my past, it has made me realise quite what a gorgeous girlfriend I have.

Two days later, following on from the sort of minimalist feeling we devised for the cover of *The Good Life* – using Simon and Claire's front gates – Ana has come up with a simple paintbrush design for *The Painter*. And this is obviously the best idea I have ever heard.

The other piece of good news is that *The Good Life* is beginning to sell. We have had five or six telephone calls from the Westminster sex shops asking for more stock. We're not talking huge numbers – ten here, twenty there – but they are beginning to add up. So I get on the phone to that chatty girl Susie-Anne from Film Stuff and ask for a few more copies. I also tell her that I'm about to deliver another film – *The Painter* – which I would like to be in the shops in time for Christmas.

'We're slick and cool and with it,' she tells me from her wireless phone somewhere on the North Circular. 'We can sort that for you.'

'That is excellent news,' I say.

I spend the next week sitting in a darkened room with Kent on the phone to Madeline at the BBFC. We are both a little worried about the amount of noise Katie is making in her anal scene.

'Does it sound at all like gagging?' asks Madeline, munching on a biscuit.

'I'm not sure,' I say. 'Can I play you a bit?'

'If you think it will help,' she says.

'Well, I just can't afford to have the film delayed,' I say. 'I am planning to release it for Christmas.'

'OK, then, let's hear it.'

Kent and I sit in silence as I hold the phone next to the speakers in the edit suite. We play Katie's anal scene and it sounds awful. She is moaning and squealing and making the weirdest noises. It looks pretty ropy as well. Needless to say, it is not the most aspirational scene we have shot.

'What d'you think?' I ask, when Katie's finished shouting.

'Well, I have a little motto,' says Madeline.

'Really?'

'Yup,' she says. 'I tend to find it useful – if in doubt cut it out.'

'D'you know, I think you're right,' I say. 'I can't use the cum shot anyway as it went a bit wrong.'

'Really?' says Madeline. 'Then I think you have your answer. Not that I want to persuade you into doing anything you don't want to do.'

'No, no,' I agree. 'But it doesn't look good anyway.'

In fact the whole of that afternoon looks a bit crap. John and Katie are not attractive to watch and Camilla and Ray aren't really doing anything that exciting. In the end Kent and I decide to cut the lot.

'D'you think it matters if the film is a tad short?' I ask him.

'Not really,' he says. 'I always find most porn films too long anyway. That's why I watch them all on fast forward.'

'Right,' I say. Helpful as always.

'That's what I keep saying to you anyway,' he sniffs. 'I don't know why you bother with the story and all that nice background shit, when everyone only scrolls through for the fucks.'

My ability to ignore the drivel that comes out of Kent's mouth is now becoming something of an art form. Our relationship is like some sort of dreadful marriage of convenience. He is constantly critical of everything I do and I constantly fail to react to what he says. If I could find someone else for eight grand a month in cash who is free to shoot on the days that I want, and who has access to an edit suite, believe you me, I would hire him. In the meantime I have to make do with this bad-tempered yeti who is as abusive as he is essential. I just occasionally wish that he would change out of his shorts. Our travelling band of spray-tanned players must look bizarre enough without a giant dressed as a schoolboy coming up the rear.

As luck would have it *The Painter* takes only five days to edit so we get it to the BBFC in good time for Christmas. That's if they don't send it back to us, of course.

While we are waiting for them to rate the film and give us a VFC number (which means we are ripe and ready for distribution), I set about doing a bit of PR for Touch Wood Films.

After all this time and many conversations I have managed to track down a magazine that deals solely with the business side of the porn industry. There are plenty of mags that talk about porn, photograph it and run articles about the stars, but as far as I know *ETO* (*Erotic Trade Only*) is its only trade magazine. Set up four years ago and packed with columns and stories about how the industry works, product reviews and interviews with the players, it seems like the perfect place to advertise *The Painter* and *The Good Life*. A way to announce our arrival to the porn world, as it were. That might get the orders going.

For two and a half grand I take a whole page in the Christmas issue. Ana designs the advert, using the covers of both the DVDs, and we send it off to the magazine. I am incredibly excited and so is Ana; after all this is the sort of thing that she can understand. All we need now is for the BBFC to clear the film and the DVDs to arrive.

There's been a bit of a delay in the delivery of the next lot of DVDs from Film Stuff. I have been calling for a couple of days now, asking where the copies of *The Good Life* are so that I can restock some of the London shops and start on trying to sell some more up north. I have managed to speak to some bloke who stocks a chain called Nice and Naughty and someone else from Pulse and Cocktails, and another from ABS. They are all inclined to give Touch Wood Films a go. We just need some stock to send them.

Susie-Anne is a bit evasive when I call. Either her handset cuts out or she offers to phone me back and never does actually return my call. It is only when I threaten to send *The Painter* elsewhere that some *Good Life* stock finally arrives. And I have to say that I am more than a little pissed off. Half of it is not shrinkwrapped, which means we can't sell it on, and there are DVDs missing from some of the cases. I spend a whole day going through the boxes and then have to send about 60 per cent of the consignment back. They are no use to me if I can't sell them. And anyway Ana won't have them blocking up the hall.

Another thing that Ana is having increasingly less truck with is Toby. And I have to say I am beginning to agree. The website is failing and Toby's behaviour is becoming ever more bizarre. I am sure now that he is back on the drugs but I don't manage to confront him about it because we almost never see him. He has become entirely nocturnal. Ana and

I hear him rattling around the kitchen at about three in the morning, and by the time one of us has summoned the energy to get out of bed to talk to him, he has usually left the house. We leave him notes, which he ignores. He does sometimes leave money for food but he only really cooks himself a fry-up every few days, so it does seem a bit mean to charge him.

The website is going from bad to worse. I have been so busy filming, I left Toby in charge of Bridget Bones and if I'm honest he has not been up to scratch. Her encounters are not terribly erotic. In fact her sex life has become a touch lazy of late. All she ever seems to do is shag her boss over his desk and blow the bloke on reception. If we had any subscribers I'm sure they would complain. But we don't really, so they don't. The only thing is, I am a little lost as to what we should put in her place. The dildos didn't sell. We have only a few clips to download. The whole venture is proving to be a bit of a disaster.

The only good thing Toby seems to have done recently is set us up with a company called CC Bill. After PayPal knocked us back, we needed to find a safe way for punters to hand over their credit card numbers and it doesn't appear to come safer than CC Bill. In fact it is so goddamn safe it has taken Toby more than two months to sort out. They know more about me and my life than my father. Or should I say Ana. Or actually when it comes down to it, Kent.

Based in Phoenix, CC Bill protects the customer and the provider from being ripped off. In the last months I have sent them my birth certificate, my passport details, my VAT number, my address, my company registration number and as many fax and phone numbers as I can muster. In turn they have given me a list of countries not to deal with and have advised against taking any Congolese credit cards. We are protected to the hilt. Our customers are as safe as houses. All we need now is some business.

The BBFC calls up and says that *The Painter* is on its way. There are a few tiny tweaks to make and a glitch to clear up. When taking out Katie's anal scene Kent has again failed to shift all the content along. There's a seven-minute gap in the film. Clear that up and a few shots where Jenny pisses on Maddie and we have ourselves another R18 film.

We clean it all up and get our classification, and send it all off to Film Stuff. We're cutting it fine but Susie-Anne has promised to pull her finger out. Everything is going to be ready in time for Christmas. We have the advert ready to run and some forty sex shops waiting. God, don't you just love it, when a plan comes together?

It's been nearly two weeks since I sent off the master tape of *The Painter* and I am still waiting for Susie-Anne to call. I have spoken to her a couple of times and she assures me that they will all be ready in time. The advert comes out next week so I am counting on her. But just to make sure and give them a friendly boot up the arse, I travel up to north London to see them.

As I park outside the small office on an industrial estate off the North Circular, I am a little bit taken aback. All my dealings with the company have been on the phone and I have always sent my films over to them by bike, so this is the first time I have been to see them. I was expecting to see a small DVD factory. Or at least some sort of a shed full of presses. But there is nothing. Not a single sign of any manu-facturing. Susie-Anne laughs when I ask her where everything is.

'Oh, God,' she says flicking her brown WAG hair and

clicking her nail extensions on the keyboard in front of her. 'No one makes anything in this country any more. It's all done abroad.'

She goes on to explain some laborious process whereby DVD manufacturers from all over the world bid online for the work.

'So the master tape could be made in Taiwan and then pressed in Mexico. We're only the brokers here.'

'Oh, so do you know what has happened to the DVDs?' I ask.

'D'you know where they are, Terry,' she asks her colleague at another desk.

'Um,' he says, tapping away at his keyboard. 'Somewhere between the Philippines and here.'

'The Philippines?' I ask.

'Yeah,' he nods. ' Looks like it's been DHL-ed from one of our factories over there.'

'What? There is only one DVD?'

'Oh, yeah,' confirms Terry. 'They've made the glass master there.'

'Where are the others going to be made?' I ask.

'It's a toss-up between one of our places in China or Mexico,' he says. 'But I think the Mexicans have got it. Although it doesn't say so here.'

'So they're your factories,' I ask, a little puzzled.

'Not quite,' he says, 'We only send them stuff.'

'So they aren't actually your factories, then?'

'Er, no,' he agrees.

'Do you know when I might be getting the DVDs, then?' I ask.

'Well,' says Terry.

'Soon,' interrupts Susie-Anne.

'But when?' I ask.

'Well . . .' says Terry.

'Not long,' trills Susie-Anne.

'The thing is,' admits Terry, 'as you're a small order you will be at the back of the queue. So a couple of weeks? A month maybe?'

'What! But you said . . .' I turn to look at Susie-Anne.

'No . . . right . . . yes,' she says.

'What?' I say.

'Absolutely,' she says.

'What?' I stare at her. She smiles back at me and points to her right ear with a white-tipped nail. It appears that she's not talking to me at all. She is chatting into her earpiece, having picked up a call on her mobile phone.

I am shaking with anger by the time I leave the office. The DVDs are not going to arrive in time. The ad campaign is a total waste of money. And all the pre-Christmas orders we have from the various sex shops around the country are not going to be fulfilled. My company is going to be an industry joke before we have even got off the ground. My grand opening is going to fall flat on its face. And I shall go bust just before Christmas.

I get into the car, turn on the engine and burst into tears. I am not crying out of sadness, although I am pretty down. I am crying out of frustration. All this work and all this planning, only to have it pissed against the wall by some little daddy's girl. It's my own fault, really. I should have realised that things weren't right from the beginning. Should have hung up then and there. I am such a bad judge of character. I am an arsehole and a total twat. I hit the steering wheel in frustration. The horn honks. And now I am a bust arsehole twat. My mobile goes. It's Ana.

'Hi,' she says. She sounds scared. 'Are you far away?'

'No,' I sniff.

'You'd better get home quickly.' The panic rises in her voice. 'It's Toby.'

'Right?'

'I think he is having some sort of attack.'

'Call an ambulance.'

'Are you sure?' she says.

'Absolutely. Dial 999.'

By the time I get back to the flat the street is packed with squad cars, ambulances and flashing blue lights. I arrive to see Toby leaving on a stretcher and Ana in tears, wringing her hands. There are people everywhere asking questions. Does Toby live here? How old is he? Does he have a history of convulsions? I grab hold of someone who looks official in a green jumpsuit and explain he has a history of drug and alcohol abuse.

'Andy!' he shouts to his colleague in the back of the ambulance. 'It could be a coke-induced heart attack.'

'All right, thanks, mate,' says the colleague and carries on with his job.

At the mere mention of drugs, a copper at the scene pricks up his ears.

'Drugs, you say,' he says, taking out his notebook. 'Mind if I take a look around?'

'Be my guest,' I say, knowing he'd go in anyway. 'Take as long as you like.'

It takes him all of three minutes to find the stack of DVDs in the hall. Well, they aren't exactly hidden.

'What's this lot?' he asks, nodding towards the boxes.

'Hardcore pornography,' I say.

'Yeah, right,' he laughs.

'No, it is,' I smile. 'And I am a pornographer.'

'What did you say your name was again?' asks the policeman, licking the end of his pencil.

'I don't think I did.'

An hour later the copper leaves. Turns out he's quite a nice chap. He looks through my DVD collection and pronounces it rather good. He says he spent a while looking at porn once when he worked for the Met and found it boring. They always used to have to watch the films all the way through, he says, just in case someone had slipped something really awful in among the normal hows-yer-father. He likes the look of my stuff, though. I offer him a couple of DVDs for his mates, but he says he'd better not, seeing as he is on duty.

Thankfully Toby's seizure didn't last long and he was put on a ward around 10 p.m. Poor bloke. He had been back on the gear for a while, which is why Ana and I only saw the back of him as he left our place to score. He spends a few days in hospital. Ana and I go in a couple of times to hold his hand and tell him to get better. He is then released into the care of his parents. I think they're planning one more attempt at rehab. They've booked somewhere nice and expensive like the Priory and are crossing their fingers, hoping that this time it'll work.

In the meantime Touch Wood Films has still got no DVDs and now there is no one to run the website. I decide to take a long hard look at things. I realise it is time to cut our losses with the site and cut the thing right back. There is no way that I can compete with the big boys in Holland and the US who are shooting clips every day and employing up to a hundred people to update their sites as soon as new stuff becomes available. The 'Bridget Bones's Diary' has not really worked and I have long since given up trying to flog sex toys. The adverts we did eventually place on the Hun porn search engine worked a bit, but there is no point placing new clips up there. There is so much stuff pouring into that site on a daily basis, ours are pushed right down the bottom of the list within hours of posting. And I just don't have the energy, or the resources, to keep that particular kettle boiling. It is time that we kept things simple and played to our strengths. I am a content provider and that is all. I shall make films and I'll post them on the SexyPorn Flics website for punters to download. They can become members of the site. They can watch lots of little clips but the main thing they can do is buy the films. If I keep the site simple, it will cost something like six hundred quid a month to keep going and we can make more money selling clips to other people and other sites. They go for between one grand and two grand a pop, which is much more lucrative than trying to sell the latest vibrator.

It seems Toby's relapse was a bit of a blessing in disguise. Now that he's gone and I have made the decision to calm down the website, I have to say that I feel relieved.

I am still going bust, though. I am desperate for the Christmas stock but it shows no sign of coming. Then Kent and I get an invitation to attend the Erotica Fair in Kensington, which is somewhat of a welcome distraction.

Taking over the Grand Hall in Olympia for a long weekend at the end of November, the Erotica Fair is where the porn industry lays out its wares and gives them a public pole dance. And it's popular. Very popular. They say that it is the biggest adult lifestyle show in the world and has a larger footfall than the Ideal Home Show. They don't appear to be lying. There are at least a couple of thousand people milling around on the pavement outside when Kent and I arrive. They are mostly men. The majority of them are dressed in denim with short or shaved hair. There are a couple of iffy-looking girls with piercings and leather and then there is the fetish crowd. Both Kent and I are rather excited as we queue up behind a couple clad head to foot in black latex, one taking the other around by a lead.

We are soon inside. The place is packed. There are rows of stalls selling anything from lube to latex nurse outfits and the latest swinging holidays in France. Kent just stands there and inhales.

'Don't you just love it when the porn industry wakes up and tucks into its bacon sandwich?' he says.

Look up and down the aisles I can see what he means. The doors have only just opened but most of the girls are already greasing their poles. Others are powdering down their red latex catsuits. Or laying leaflets out on the stands.

'Shit!' says Kent, picking up a leaflet from a stand selling Solo Sex Machines. 'Isn't that Dorota?'

I flick through the pages and see Dorota straddling what looks like a large metal cock poking up through a wooden chair. There are rubber knee pads in the seat and a sort of lever to hold on to. The idea, or so it seems, is for the woman to ride this metal cock. Called 'Wild Rider', it claims to be a 'fusion of design, innovation and engineering, creating a new experience in self-pleasure for you and/or your partner'. The whole thing looks rather dangerous and uncomfortable to me.

'Shit,' says Kent again. 'Don't you remember?'

'What?' I say.

'That she claimed she had a sore fanny after some sex toy shoot the day before we filmed her?' he says.

'No?'

'Well, she did. You probably weren't listening,' he says.

'Maybe I was worrying about something else.'

'Maybe,' he says, inspecting the photographs more closely. 'It must have been very sore. This looks fucking painful to me.' He shakes his head. 'How about this one?' He reads: '"Solo Rider – this little number is designed for those of us who adore vibrating. The Solo Rider takes it one step further with total control of the level from 0 to 5000 vpm. The beautifully crafted stimulator tops off this roll of love." What the fuck does that mean?' he asks looking at me.

'I have no idea,' I shrug. 'But I know it's an odd type of love they are selling. It's not going to send you flowers.'

'That's true,' he says, putting down the brochure. 'Oh, look,' he says, pointing ahead. 'They're about to put on a show.'

Kent settles himself down at a red plastic table, right near the stage, while I go for a walk among the 250 or so stands. In among the rows of black rubber cocks, there are stands covered in red nylon underwear, stands with penis enlargement kits (to help reduce shrinkage due to age) and stands with gaudy bronze porno art. I am drawn to one selling bespoke bondage and leisure furniture that looks like something out of the Tower of London. There's a flogging bench, a corner cage, a rack and a spanking bench. But the most bizarre of all is the 'discreet bondage bed'. Made of black wrought iron, with places to attach handcuffs or whips or whatever you fancy, it is obviously kinky and not fooling anyone.

The stage show at the far end of the exhibition kicks off. I can see Kent with a pint of lager in a plastic cup in front of him, settling back to enjoy it. Girls in leather bikinis and stratospheric heels come strutting out to the front of the stage, followed by a man in red latex pants, a cape, devil's horns and three-foot-high hoof stilts attached to the end of his feet. His face is painted red and black; he blows fire at the audience and a couple of fat blokes at the front clap. The music is loud. Poles come out of the stage and the girls start to dance. They are joined by more girls in bikinis, some in black lurex bodysuits, a couple of rather chubby blondes in pink and a whole load more guys just in their pants. There is much writhing and moaning and auto-erotic dancing as the devil weaves his way through the crowd of worshippers, flicking them all with his whip. Kent has a bit of a grin on his face and has almost finished his pint. I watch as he is joined by a group of guys, none of whom seem to know each other. They all nod and a couple stiffly shake hands.

The go-go dancing continues. There's a lot of rolling around on the floor. A few girls lie on their backs and split their legs at the audience. Kent's table sits and stares. No one's missing a trick. A police siren sounds on stage. More girls in black bathing suits slashed down the front pour on stage. They are also sporting black metal tit guards, blue police helmets and small round perspex riot shields. Some high kicking and more leg splitting follows, with a bit of G-G action as they pretend to clear the stage. There is some mock booing coming from the audience and a few jeers. It is clear they are all on the side of evil in this show and then eventually everyone troops out, turning cartwheels and with a few high kicks, to rapturous applause.

I leave Kent queuing for another beer downstairs and walk up to the second floor to check out the DVD porn. There are stalls stacked with the stuff all around the R18 Video Village area. Provided mainly by Private and Harmony, the shelves are six rows high and about three films deep. I walk along them checking out the competition. *School of Cock, Grand Theft Anal, Crack Addict,* the titles are usually some sort of pun. I pick up *RearEnders* and turn it over. It promises 'three hours of hardcore action with girls getting their backdoors bashed in'. There are series called *Slam In* and *Slam It In Harder.* A pregnancy selection

called something like *Milking It*. And an OAP section fea-
turing women over sixty-five years old. Every whim,
penchant and diversity is taken care of. No fantasy is too
obscure. However, the really odd thing about these films is
that they all look the same. No one has thought to brand
their stuff. It is difficult to tell who has made what and who
is starring in each film. The Relish guys have shoved their
logo on the top of their *Weapons of Mass Satisfaction* video
but the layout is still a mess and it looks exactly like the one
next door.

I stand and look at them all. Piled high, all shouting for
attention in the same sleazy way. It is almost as if what's in
each film doesn't matter. It's the same girls being shagged by
the same blokes, watched by the same people to the same
end. Perhaps I have been kidding myself all along. There's
no market for sophisticated porn. No one wants an upmarket wank. They want rubbish sex in shit locations in a
crappy, unsubtle cover. I'm in the wrong business. I stare at
some film called *Hot Milky Hooters* and sigh.

'Excuse me,' asks a small bloke in black leather trousers,
sporting a bolt through his bottom lip. 'Can I help you?'

'Um, no, thanks,' I say. 'I'm just looking.'

'Right,' he says, looking at the blowjob on the telly screen
behind me.

'I'm sort of checking out the competition,' I say.

'Right,' he says, still rather distracted.

'I am a porn director.'

'Mmm.' He isn't listening.

'I have made a few films.'

'Right.'

'*The Good Life*?'

He turns and looks at me. '*The Good Life*?' he checks.

'That's right.'

'I bloody love that film,' he says. 'It's dead classy. And the cover's great.'

'You do?' I say. 'Thanks.' I am grinning with delight. 'So you've seen it?'

'Just the other day,' he says. 'Oh, it's great. Are you going to do any more?'

'I have just shot one,' I say.

'Oh, you must speak to Morris over there,' he points. 'Get him to stock your films.'

While Kent is sipping beer and taking in another show, I spend the rest of the afternoon trying to network porn distributors in the far corner of the hall. There is a special bar for trade only and Morris very kindly gets me in. He introduces me to a couple of blokes who do actually distribute porn around the country. It seems there aren't that many big boys in the industry. It is a very interesting and informative afternoon and confirms to me that the industry is behind the times. These blokes are talking about the sex shops being the major porn outlets and are either ignoring or ignorant of the internet, I can't quite work out which. There are about 280 sex shops in the whole of the UK and they are mostly in insalubrious parts of town. Not the sort of streets you would want to walk after dark, let alone shop on during the day. I tell one of them that I think the sex shop market can only really decrease and he laughs, blowing cigar smoke in my face.

'No one under twenty-five is going to go into a sex shop,' I say. 'They are only really for the older generation or the fetish brigade.'

'Yeah, right,' he guffaws. 'Tell that to my bank manager.'

Kent is plastered by the time I manage to peel him off his red plastic seat and get him out of the Great Hall.

'That was a great afternoon,' he slurs as he bumps into

me, walking along the pavement. 'It was very interesting.' For once I have to agree with him.

It is three weeks before Christmas and the stock still hasn't arrived. I call Film Stuff every day for updates and every day Susie-Anne promises that the consignment will arrive tomorrow. Every day she lets us down.

Adam from the Paul Raymond Organisation calls up to congratulate me on the advert in *ETO* magazine and says that if ever I want to film for them, they'd be only too delighted to have me on-board. I like those boys from Paul Raymond; they are nice blokes with a bit of a sense of humour. I tell him all about our Film Stuff hell and he commiserates. He says that it happens all the time and that in future he'll keep an eye on them. He offers to take me out on the piss to take my mind off things.

At 2 a.m. over a pair of buttocks and a silver thong in Spearmint Rhino I confide in him that I am about to go bust. I tell him all about the marketing plan and the launch of the company and how it is all going tits up because of my lack of stock.

'You've got to hang on in there,' he says, taking a sip of his champagne, while watching this Czech girl bump and grind. 'If you can get through the next couple of months you'll be fine.'

'I don't know,' I say.

'Have you ever thought of getting in some shareholders?'

The next morning I wake up with a hangover the size of Bristol and Ana's cold buttocks in my face. She normally gives me the cold buttocks when she is pissed off and this morning as I didn't get home until after 3 a.m. I kind of expected them.

'You awake?' she asks, from the other side of the bed.

'Mmm.'

'The bank manager called,' she says. 'He wants to see you.'

'Ah.'

'Ah?' she repeats, sitting up. 'Is that all you can say?'

'Well, what else do you expect me to say?'

'Thing is,' she says, 'I have been through your bank statements and I know what is going on.'

'Oh.'

'Yes,' she says. 'You're broke. We're broke, the company is broke and we are on the point of being bankrupt.'

'Ah.'

'Is that it?'

She throws back the duvet. We're both naked. It is bloody freezing, but she is so angry she doesn't appear to notice. She gets out of bed and stomps around the room throwing clothes and pillows and anything that comes to hand. I curl up on the mattress. I'm in fear of my manhood. She could reach for the nail scissors and Bobbitt me in a second. She is shouting and screaming now. Telling me I am not to be trusted. That I have stolen the wedding money. I try to get her to calm down. I say that things are not that bad. She rants some more about how I am irresponsible and that I don't know what bad is until it is too fucking late. I tell her to stop shouting. That shouting never got anyone anywhere and that I will sort it.

'How?' she yells.

'I've got some investors,' I say. It's a little white lie. Any port in a storm and all that.

'Oh,' she says, picking a pair of pants up off the floor. 'Why didn't you say?'

'Well, if I could get a word in.'

The first person I call is Chris. He feels guilty about letting me down right at he beginning, and is incredibly enthusiastic down the phone. Raising money and investors should be no problem at all, he insists. I can almost hear the relief in his voice as he realises I'm not asking for the use of his swanky bathroom, just about fifty grand in cash. That, he can do something about.

When setting up Spring Meadow and Touch Wood Films I had always thought I would draw the line at shareholders or investors of any kind. I didn't want to answer to anyone. I didn't want to talk to them on the phone, to listen to them throwing their weight around, asking if a mate of a mate could come on set. But I suppose needs must. If selling 15 per cent of the company is the only way to stop me from going under then I can't see that I have much choice.

I pop in to see Andrew at the bank. He greets me at the door, still sporting his grey suit, grey tie and grey shoes, with his grey hair.

'How are you?' he asks. His handshake is warm and his smile is wide. We are almost like old friends. I suspect it is the fresh £50k in my bank account that is making him this pally.

'Bit of a tough time at the coalface of porn,' I smile, sitting down in the chair opposite his desk.

'But it all seems to be sorted now?' he says.

'It'll all come good next year,' I say.

'The first few months in any business are hard,' he says.

'It has been a bit difficult. It is not the sort of industry where you can ring people up and ask their advice.'

'I can imagine,' he nods.

'Anyway,' I smile. 'I have brought you all some films.'

'Oh, really?' I can see some colour returning to his cheeks. 'Not too dirty, I hope.'

'Absolutely filthy.' I smile. 'And don't worry, I have enough for the whole office.'

It is the week before Christmas and five and a half thousand copies of *The Painter* are delivered in brown cardboard boxes to my door. Unfortunately too late for any of the sex shops. Too late for Christmas. Too late to be any bloody use to anyone. I call up Susie-Anne to give her a customary bollocking and she screens my call and sends me straight to the answer machine. What really makes me laugh is that in among my useless stash of porn DVDs she has included an invoice for £5500. If she thinks that I am paying that with any speed or attention, she has another thing coming. I had to sell part of the company to finance her fuck-up. I'd rather see her in the small claims court than write out Film Stuff a cheque.

I call around a few sex shops in Westminster to see if they might want to shift a few copies in the Christmas rush. They are all perfectly pleasant. But they inform me that it is a no-go. So I pack them all into the back of the car and drive up to my parents' for Christmas. The plan is to push on to Birmingham and Manchester after the festive season and try to shift a few copies for New Year.

Christmas at my parents' is the usual sort of stiff event where we all drink a little too much just to get through it. Ever since I sold a bit of the company Ana has been incredibly sweet and supportive. She is even charming about the third bath hat my parents have given her in almost as many years. I didn't think you could still buy them these days but apparently they are all the rage near Didcot. My father likes his bottle of whisky and puts it to one side to save until after he's given the 6 p.m. Evensong sermon at church. My mother tucks into the box of Just Brazils that Ana bought for

Nelly the dog and my brother James continues to ask difficult questions. He keeps on and on about the internet, like he knows what I'm up to. Three times he asks me exactly what I am doing and I find it difficult to remember what I've said before. He is so curious and determined that I am beginning to wonder if someone has actually told him what is going on. But every time I look into his eyes, he returns my look with his usual guilelessness. I can't tell if he is hiding something.

Christmas dinner is the same as it always is. The meat is dry. The sprouts are overcooked and the pudding is rich and heavy. The meal is accompanied by the faint smell of dog flatulence as Nelly the black Labrador is allowed to sit under the table. My father leaves early, before the Stilton, and my mother and James retire to watch the Bond film on the TV. I slip upstairs for a postprandial fag out of my old bedroom window. There is something quite pathetic about a forty-three-year-old man whose parents don't even know that he smokes, but let's not even go there. As I hide the butt in the guttering, I look down into the drive and notice that my car has gone.

'Mum?' I shout from the top of the stairs.

'Yes, dear?' she shouts back from the sitting room.

'Where's my car?'

'Sorry, dear?' She walks into the hall adjusting her pink paper party hat.

'My car?'

'Oh, your father's borrowed it. He's driven it to church.'

'What? When? Why?' My heart is racing. There are five hundred hardcore porn DVDs on the back seat. Boxes and boxes of them. Some are opened. He's bound to brake. The boxes will go flying. There'll be porn everywhere. Jesus Christ, why is God doing this to me?

'He thought it would be easier to take your car than getting you to move it,' she says, looking up at me. 'You don't
mind, do you?'

'No, not at all.'

'You all right, dear?' she asks. 'You look very pale.'

'I'm fine,' I say. 'Perhaps I've had a little too much brandy
butter.'

I think I'd better go and pray for another kind of
Christmas miracle.

Eight

They say that the Lord moves in mysterious ways and on Christmas night He obviously decided that my father was not meant to find the stash of hardcore porn DVDs in the back of my car. And instead of my life collapsing around me, and my drowning under waves of disapproval from my family, I got away with it. My father drove to church and back in my car and told me the tyres needed some air. My mother finished the box of Just Brazils. James gave up asking me questions. And Ana and I drank a whole bottle of Baileys. I continued my journey on up to Birmingham and Manchester and shifted over a thousand DVDs in the next three days. Had I got the stock in before Christmas, they all told me, I would have sold more. But they liked the two covers, and the ideas behind them, and they all said that they would take more.

With money coming in from the northern sex shops, some reorders in London and the revenue from the shareholder sale, the mood at Touch Wood is a lot more buoyant than it was before the festive period. Ana even has a smile on her pretty face. She admits to me over a glass of wine in the kitchen that she likes sending out invoices. It makes her feel more involved and a little in control without getting her fingers dirty. I immediately put her in charge of paperwork and set about organising the shoot for the next film.

The Surveyor is going to be my biggest, best and slickest film yet and two friends of mine, Mitch and Laura, have offered to lend us their London flat. Well, strictly speaking Mitch has offered to lend us the flat. Laura doesn't know too much about it as she is spending the weekend in France with her mother. But, as Mitch points out, what she doesn't know won't hurt her, and I have assured him that we will take good care of the place.

The day of the shoot I get an early morning wake-up call from Kent. It is 6.15 and I am still half asleep. He has done this before. I am beginning to wonder if it is actually developing into some sort of habit.

'You awake?' he asks.

'I am now.'

'I have been thinking about the shoot . . .'

'Yes?'

'And I don't think it's going to work.'

'Why?'

'We should have checked it out beforehand.'

'I have been to the flat before.'

'I know but if you were a professional outfit we would have seen it before.'

'I am professional.'

'No you're not. Not compared to the people who I've worked with.'

'Well, work with them then.'

'See you later.' He hangs up.

I sigh and lie back in bed. I think Kent might have a screw loose. His behaviour is becoming increasingly bizarre and obsessive. I think I might have to have a word.

Mitch and Laura's apartment is a prestige pad overlooking

the river. Mitch works in finance. He has also invested money in Spring Meadow, which is part of the reason that he has lent us the flat. The other part, I suspect, is to prove to himself that he is not under the thumb. Laura was a beautician and has adapted to her new life as banker's wife with a great deal of gusto. She spends money like water and is so interior-design-obsessed that she records all the makeover shows on Sky Plus. Mitch did once suggest that we film in their flat just before Christmas and Laura kicked up such a fuss in front of his mates that I have a feeling today is some very gentle form of revenge.

I have learned my lesson from the last couple of films and kept the plot of *The Surveyor* very simple. Trisha Bigtits is a property surveyor and she goes from apartment to apartment getting into scrapes with her clients and whomever she chances upon there. Never has checking over houses been so hot and horny. At least that's what the cover will say. Ana is out and about today with her camera photographing houses in and around St John's Wood High Street, with a view to finding something for the DVD cover.

In the meantime Mitch has left the apartment keys with the porter and I have let myself in. This is a very nice place. It has a fantastic open-plan sitting-room area with white sofas and some sort of nondescript modern art on the wall. There's a great long table down one side and a huge balcony with a view overlooking the Thames. Mitch is renting the place at the moment while they do up his house in Kensington. It must be setting him back a few grand a week.

The first person to arrive is Camilla. She is wearing a pair of jodhpurs and is fresh from the stables. She does, however, look different from the last time I saw her.

'Oh,' she says, when I tell her. 'It's probably the make-up.'

'Didn't you wear it before?'

'No, not really,' she shrugs. 'Oh, by the way, I have grown back my hair like you asked.'

'Oh, thanks,' I say. 'I didn't really—'

'It looks like a right old growler.' She smiles.

I did have a conversation with Camilla before Christmas about growing back her pubic hair. I didn't so much as ask her to do it but make the suggestion that it might look a little bit more interesting and different for a future film. The lack of hair in porn is one of the things I find unattractive. Most of the girls have some sort of landing strip or Velcro-like line down there. Some of them have even done away with it altogether, which I always think looks strangely infantile and not at all sexy. I know Kent is a no-bush man as he says that it is easier to shoot. But I quite like a bit of hair and would even go so far as to say that I'm partial to a full seventies triangle. So I am looking forward to seeing what Camilla has grown for the occasion.

Trisha Bigtits, Freddie, Alexa and Tony all arrive more or less at the same time. Freddie has been on holiday in the Caribbean and got himself a natural tan.

'I also have all my documents,' he says, with a large grin. 'So no bloody fucking mistakes this time. I am STD-free and ready to work.'

'Can we all check them?' asks Trisha, taking Freddie's paperwork off him. 'Forgive me,' she says to him, 'but you are a bloke with a bit of a reputation, having given half the industry lice.'

'It was Chlamydia,' he says.

'Whatever,' says Trisha. 'I know my rights.'

Before anything gets too heavy and difficult Kent arrives. He high-fives everyone as he walks around the flat and introduces another new assistant.

'She's called Helen,' he whispers in my ear. 'And she's hot, if you know what I mean.'

Within ten minutes of setting up the shoot it becomes clear the Helen is indeed quite hot. She has a lovely arse and long legs in her tight black jeans. But Kent has been nowhere near her and is obviously desperate to change this. It is a strange idea of foreplay to bring a girl on a hardcore porn shoot. Each to their own, as they say. Unfortunately for Helen, she's only had two hours' sleep, after a lock-in with the landlord at the Winged Spur, Kent's one and only recruiting ground. She is so hungover, poor love, that she needs a bit of a lie-down. So she beds down in Mitch and Laura's bed for the morning, occasionally surfacing for a glass of water or a cup of five-sugared tea.

The first scene we shoot is on the terrace. The idea is that Trisha Bigtits comes into the apartment to show Camilla around. Camilla is her posh client and the first thing she wants to see is the view. They go out on the balcony and Camilla pisses on it. Next they go into the sitting room together, snog and then fuck on the sofa using a double-ended dildo. They are interrupted by Alexa and Freddie who are coming back to their flat and they all join in. I am trying to keep things simple because I want to try and shoot as many scenes in the day as possible. It is a question of speed-ing up the process, if we are to make money on these films.

'So,' I say, rubbing my hands together. It is bloody freezing on the balcony. 'Camilla, you come out here, say you can't hold it in any more, raise your skirt and piss in the corner, while, Trisha, you watch, OK? Do you want another glass of water, Camilla, before you start?'

'No, that's fine,' she says turning around and taking her pants off, before slipping into a short white mini-skirt. Her backside is small, pert and red and purple all over.

'Jesus,' I say.

'Ferkin' 'ell,' says Freddie, from the white sofa. 'What 'appened?'

'Oh, you know,' says Camilla, 'the usual spanking movie.'

'I think you should cut down on those and give your arse a rest,' I say. 'Surely you have enough money for the stables by now?'

'I got that ages ago,' she says pulling up her skirt. 'My boyfriend manages them.'

'What are you still doing working?' I ask.

'Well, you know,' she smiles. 'Fun?'

Kent and I stamp our feet on the balcony, waiting for Kelly to touch up Camilla's legs. Trisha is made up and ready to go.

'Finished,' says Kelly, stepping away.

'OK then, everyone ready?' The girls nod. 'Action!'

Trisha opens the sliding doors and walks to the edge of the balcony. 'So here is your view,' she turns around to see Camilla squatting down to hitch up her skirt.

'I am sorry,' says Camilla. 'I am a naughty little girl from London – I just can't wait.'

She opens her legs to reveal the hairiest black bush I have seen in years. The girl's done herself proud. If that is two weeks' of hair growth, God knows what her pussy looks like after a month.

'Jesus!' says Kent. 'What the fuck is that?'

She then starts to pee. I have no idea how much water she's drunk but she doesn't seem to be able to stop. There's steam rising up from the terrace and it is splashing over Kent's camera. The bloke is furious. And still Camilla carries on. The puddle grows larger and larger, taking over almost a third of the terrace. Eventually she stops.

'Cut!' I yell

'God,' Camilla says, stepping over it all in her white high heels. 'I really needed that.'

Back inside the apartment and we move quickly on to the G-G scene. Trisha and Camilla start fiddling and fondling each other on the white sofas. Kent has to shoot this a little more cleverly than his limited talents usually manage, due to the state of Camilla's arse. The scene concludes with them both banging away together with the dildo up their backsides. Kent gets right in for the action shot.

'Now that,' he says as he lies on his back and shoots them moving back and forth overhead, 'that is very tasteful, indeed.'

Unfortunately it is not so tasteful for Laura's white sofa as some lube mixture dribbles all over it. The make-up has rubbed off Trisha legs and there's a black eyeliner patch in the middle of one cushion. Kelly spends a good ten minutes scrubbing away with some cleaning product, but to no avail.

'Fuck it,' she says to me. 'I think we should just turn the cushions over.'

I agree it is the only real option. So we get Kent to shoot the orgy scene on both of the white sofas just to make sure that we don't ruin anything else in the flat. By the time both Freddie and Tony make their cum shots, there is a skid on one sofa and a whole lot more lube on the other. In fact they are so trashed I think we should replace them. But Kent talks me out of it and Kelly cleans them up a bit, and we all kid ourselves that we have got away with it. However, no matter how hard any of us pretend, all it takes is one close look and they are what is known in the trade as 'fucked'. It looks like I shall have to send the covers off to the dry cleaners after all.

We break for lunch and finally Helen surfaces and she is sent to get some sandwiches. While we are all sitting down tucking into nothing more exotic than cheese and pickle, hold the pickle, my mobile goes. It is Wedding Video Dave and he sounds like he is in a right state.

'The wife's found out,' he says very quietly down the phone.

'The wife's found out what?' I ask, chewing on my sandwich.

'About the affair.'

'Oh, dear,' I say. 'I am sorry.'

'I am such a fool,' he says. 'Falling in love with a porn star.'

'Ah.'

'What was I doing?'

'I don't know.'

'I am such a fool,' he repeats.

'How did she find out?'

'The girlfriend is pregnant,' he says. 'Everyone knows. Even my children.'

'But she's a porn star,' I say, genuinely shocked. 'How can she get pregnant? Isn't she on the pill?'

'No,' he says. 'You'd be amazed. The majority of porn stars aren't.'

'But they don't use condoms,' I say.

'I know,' he agrees. 'You would have thought.'

I commiserate with Dave a little more. I feel for the guy, but the man is right about one thing. It is madness to fall in love with a porn star. They are not the most reliable of people. And fancy getting the girl pregnant. I hang up and pick up a cheese sandwich.

'My mate Dave has just told me that quite a lot of the girls in the porn industry aren't on the pill,' I announce to the group. They all turn and nod at me in agreement. 'What?' I am totally taken aback. 'But you have sex for a living. Surely it is in your interest not to get pregnant?'

'The boys don't come inside you,' says Trisha. 'So what's the point? You need to see the sperm in the shoot. So it's not very likely.'

'But it is still possible,' I say.

'Maybe,' she says with a shrug. 'But, you know, why bother?'

'That is so irresponsible,' I say.

'No, it's not, she says. 'Everyone does it.'

'But that's crazy.'

'I think you're talking to the wrong crowd,' smiles Camilla, shoving in the last of her sandwich.

We move on to our last scene of the day. It is supposed to be a foursome that is interrupted by Alexa, playing the part of the maid, and it finishes with her joining in, getting off with Camilla, while Trisha Bigtits ends up doing DP with Freddie and Tony. Everyone is happy with the plan. However, since we have a fantastic table along one side of the flat, I think the DP should take place on it so we can show the furniture off.

'DP on a table?' says Trisha turning up her nose. 'I don't think so.'

'Really,' I say, 'it is not impossible. Just a little uncomfortable.'

'I don't do uncomfortable,' she says. 'I'm a star. And you don't pay me enough to give me bruises.'

'I'll do it,' says Camilla.

'But I didn't think that DP was your thing,' I say. 'I thought that's where you drew the line?'

'Really?' says Camilla, looking a little surprised. 'That must have been a while back. I've been doing DP for a bit. In fact I quite like it. There's a lot less bashing around.'

Unfortunately we never get to the DP on the walnut table because while Freddie is still taking Camilla up the arse, and before Tony has had a chance to join in, there is a loud farting noise as all this lube and liquid comes out of Camilla's backside and on to the table.

'Jesus Christ!' she screams. 'What the hell was that?'

She is mortified. Freddie is horrified and the whole shoot collapses. Helen runs to throw up in Mitch and Laura's limestone bathroom and bang goes Kent's date. Not that it ever looked like it was on the cards. Kelly offers to wipe down the table but Camilla refuses. She gets back into her jodhpurs and sets to work on it. After a few minutes of polishing it is clear that there is a problem.

'It's come off,' she says, staring at the table. 'But there seems to be some sort of white stain.'

'It's not a stain,' I say, looking more closely. 'It's bleached the table.'

'What are we going to do?' she asks.

'I don't know,' I say. 'Maybe we should call some sort of cabinetmaker and get a French polish?'

'Or we could just fucking scarper,' suggests Kent. Which is the best idea I have heard all day.

Next morning I get an early wake up call. This time it is Mitch on the other end of the phone and it goes something like this:

'What the fuck have you done to my flat, you wanker? I asked you not to shag on the new sofas and by the looks of things you have shagged all over them. And what have you done to the bedroom? Don't tell me you had sex in our bed? The place is a tip. How could you fuck on our bed? I am going to have to burn the sheets. There's puke in the bathroom. A huge stain on the terrace and what the fuck happened to the dining table? Marco's hysterical. Can you hear him? Listen, he's hysterical, aren't you, Marco?' There is the sound of a grown man weeping in the background.

'Mister Mitch, Mister Mitch. It is very, very terrible.'

'Who the hell is Marco?' I ask.

'My Filipino houseboy, that's who,' shouts Mitch. 'And he is very, very unhappy. He's in tears.'

'I can hear.'

'Anyway, you better get your arse over here and clear up,' he shouts and then hangs up the phone.

Two hours later I am eating a lot of humble pie, apologising profusely and on my hands and knees cleaning vomit off Mitch's bathroom floor. Marco is scrubbing the sofas and Mitch is trying to rescue the balcony. He is more concerned about Laura's reaction than he is about losing his flat deposit. As part of the peace package I have brought over a large bottle of vodka, flowers and a box of chocolates. I give the chocolates to Marco and at about four in the afternoon Mitch and I crack open the vodka.

'I think we might just about get away with it,' he says, looking around the flat. 'She hardly ever goes out on to the balcony so I hope she won't notice the stain. What was it, by the way?'

'You don't want to know,' I say.

'But the table . . .' We both walk over to take a look. 'It's fucked.'

'It is.' I nod.

There is a large white stain in the middle that no amount of polishing or waxing can remove. It spreads out from the middle and measures about a foot across.

'What the hell did you do?' he asks, taking a sip of his vodka.

'Again, you don't want to know,' I reply.

We both stand and stare.

'I think it is something to do with the pendant light,' Mitch explains to Laura as we all gather around the table for lunch that Sunday.

'Are you sure?' she asks, running a manicured red finger-nail over the surface. 'It is all very odd. What do you think?' she asks me.

Someone down the other end of the table sniggers. Word on the stain has obviously got out. 'I am not sure,' I say. 'It wasn't anything to do with the party.'

Mitch has explained the persistent grey state of the post-dry-cleaned sofas by telling Laura that he and I invited some people back for a few drinks after the pub the other night and some glasses were spilt. He has, quite rightly, put me firmly back in the frame with his wife as far as flat damage is concerned. But so far she doesn't seem to know the truth. Although from the smirks and the winks and the questions about the stain in the middle of the dining table, I can more or less work out that about 70 per cent of the guests know about the porn shoot.

And some of the bastards are not very subtle about it. Some ask me what I've been up to this week. Others ask Mitch if he behaved while Laura was away and a total tosser called Mike asks to go out on to the terrace. He gets Laura to talk him through all the plants she has on the balcony, ensuring that she stands in the giant piss stain while she talks.

I pull Mitch over to one side.

'How many people have you told?' I ask.

'A few,' he smiles.

'It looks like everyone,' I hiss. 'It is like have a bloody great big elephant in the room and Laura is the only one not to notice.'

'Just so long as it stays that way,' he says.

'You'd better hope and pray no one talks.'

Despite all the tension and sniggering jokes, one good thing does come out of Mitch and Laura's lunch. An old friend of mine, Will, says that he and his business partner are moving offices next week and would I like to use theirs as a location. Just so long as he is allowed to watch, of course.

I take Will up on his offer and four days later Trisha Bigtits and Ray are preparing to have sex over Will's old desk. While Trisha and Ray are quite relaxed about the scene, which if I am being honest is quite hardcore and involves fisting and a few sex toys, my mate Will is finding it hard to cope. Which is weird as he has a porn collection to rival mine. But he is genuinely all over the place. He's smoked fifteen cigarettes in as many minutes and jumps every time anyone rings the doorbell. Just as I have finished talking Trisha and Ray through their scene he takes me over to one side.

'Are you sure?' he says all concerned. 'You know, about the fisting bit?' I nod. He is actually beginning to annoy me now. 'Trisha,' he says. 'Can you come over here?' Trisha walks over naked but for a pair of high heels. 'Do you want to put on some clothes?' he asks.

'I'm fine,' she says.

'You're not cold?'

'No.' She looks at him like he might be mad.

'Now this fisting thing, you don't have to if you don't want to,' he says.

'I am sorry?' she says.

'You know, if you don't feel like it?'

'Feel like it?' she laughs. 'I am a porn star. It's my job.'

'No one's forcing you to,' says Will, putting his arm around her shoulder.

'I know,' she smiles.

'So you're happy?' asks Will.

'I am fine,' she says. 'Shall we get on with it?'

Kent starts up the camera and Trisha bends over Will's desk. Ray takes her up the backside for about three or four minutes, pulls his cock out and is about to insert his hand between Trisha's parted buttocks when Will rushes into shot.

'Stop! Stop! Stop!' he shouts. Ray turns to look at him, his hand in the air.

'What?' he asks.

Trisha raises her head off the desk. 'What now?' she says.

'Are you sure about this?' asks Will, bending over her with concern. 'I mean, if you want to pull out now, you can. Can't she?' He looks at me.

'At any time,' I smile. 'Any time.'

'Good.' Will nods and looks her in the eye. 'Whenever—'

'Why don't you just fuck off,' says Trisha.

'Sorry?' Will is a little taken aback.

'Honestly,' she says, peeling herself off the desk. 'You come here with your liberal PC values. I am earning a living. Fucking leave me alone.'

'But—'

'I am not being exploited. I want to do this. It is a hell of a lot easier than working in a hairdresser's all day, which is what I used to do. It pays better. It's glamorous. I'm a star. If you can't handle that, you should leave.'

'I'm sorry. I'll shut up.' Will walks away with his hands in the air. 'I just—'

'Shut it,' she says.

'OK, I'm sorry,' he says. 'Sorry.' He looks at me. 'Sorry. Do carry on.'

The scene starts over again. Trisha is muttering something along the lines of Ray being a naughty big boy and that she should get out and do some surveying.

'I've got some hot property to see,' she says.

'I've got some hot property for you,' says Ray.

'Now that's hot,' she says, leaning over the desk. 'That's very, very hot.'

Kent leans in to get the close-up and just as Ray slips up Trisha's backside, there's a loud 'Ouch' sound from across the room. We all turn and look at Will who has his arms folded across his chest, engrossed.

'What?' he says, seeing us all staring at him.

'You said "ouch",' I say.

'I didn't,' he says.

'I think you should leave,' I add.

'D'you know,' he nods, 'I think you're probably right.'

With Will finally out of the way we speed up considerably. We do the anal, the fisting and a couple of other straight scenes and all the links before lunch. I can't believe it. I send everyone home early.

Back at the flat I have had some interest from the States about buying clips from *The Good Life*, although there seems to be a bit of a problem. I haven't got all the copies of all the IDs. Across the Atlantic the laws are even tougher than here. Well, I suppose it has something to do with their right-wing government but they are remarkably fuddy-duddy about porn. Everything has to be in order. They want two IDs as well as the health certificates and it seems I have mislaid the paperwork for either Ingrid or Krista. I knew that you were supposed to have two IDs and an STD/HIV certificate but I never thought to keep my filing in order and now I know I should. We have potentially lost thousands of pounds' worth of business. I realise that the guidelines were set up to prevent under-age girls getting into porn. But it seems that no guidelines can help if someone is determined to work in the industry anyway. I read a story recently about a girl who shot a porn film in Ireland and then went to the newspapers to complain that she was under age. Turns out her IDs were fake and yet the company's MD was sitting there saying he had two documents telling him she was eighteen. Luckily they found out about her fake IDs before the film was released. And she's not the only one. In the eighties there was a huge porn star called Traci Lords who was fabled and fêted until she finally admitted that her IDs had been fake and she had only been fifteen. Her films had to be removed from every sex shop in the world and it effectively meant that anyone who had ever watched a Traci Lords film had been watching kiddie porn and was actually a paedophile. In the end the industry tries to protect itself as much as it can, and the authorities usually end up going for the wrong people. They waste time going for those running the multi-million pound business who always do everything by the book. What they should be looking at are the unscrupulous pornographer scum at the bottom of the pool.

I call up the agency to see if they have any records of the girls. They are, I think, the people who should be in charge of all this paperwork. Some bloke answers who I haven't spoken to before. He says they don't keep very many records but he says he'll have a look.

'Although,' he adds, 'you try to track down a Polish girl who came here last year to work. She was in and out in two weeks with eight grand in her bag. She's probably halfway up a mountain by now with her five kids.'

'I appreciate it will be hard,' I say. 'But you know it is important. And I do do lots of business with you.'

'That's true,' he says. 'I'll see what I can dig up.'

I thank him and hang up. That is the last time I am going to be slack about paperwork. The clip market is huge and we are not going to have our revenue jeopardised by some bloody photocopies. I sit down and plan tomorrow's shoot. It is the finale of *The Surveyor* and we are shooting back in my mate Florien's flat in Wandsworth. The only thing is that he has half-moved out of the place and it is sorely lacking in furniture. Kent is supposed to be on the case, trying to source some stuff from Peter Jones, Heal's or Habitat, or at least that's what he's told me he is doing this afternoon. I am going through the shots when Ana comes tumbling through the front door. She is red-faced and sweating and giggling her head off.

'Oh my God!' she says. 'I have just been chased down the street by some old bloke!' She is grinning and smiling. 'I nearly got myself arrested.'

'What?'

'I know! I was taking photos of houses for the DVD cover and some bloke came out of his house to ask what I was doing. I told him I was an estate agent. He told me his house was not on the market and he told me to piss off. I didn't piss off quickly enough and he started to chase me down the road.'

'You naughty girl,' I say.

'Aren't I?' Ana smiles. 'Very naughty indeed.'

Next day Ray and I meet for an early breakfast before the shoot. He would normally have stayed last night with us but he wanted to see a mate out in Theydon Bois, so he's come in across town on the Tube. When I arrive at the café he is already at the table, tucking into a large plate of scrambled eggs. He is in a tight T-shirt, even tighter jeans and is the colour of mahogany. Carrying a rucksack of research porn DVDs, which I am planning to give Kent at the shoot, I make my way over to him. His mouth full of egg, he smiles at me as I take the seat opposite. I plonk the rucksack on the seat next to me and as I turn back to Ray the bloody

thing rolls over and pitches its contents on to the floor. Oh
shit. There are about forty DVDs all over the floor in among
the tables and chairs. Each of them has a filthy cover depict-
ing cocks and cunts in various positions. The titles yell *Anal
Butt Fuck* and *Spanking School Girl Sluts*. Several people in
the café get down on their knees to help retrieve them. One
old lady screams as she picks hers up. Another just drops it
back on the floor. There are waitresses with contorted faces.
There are mothers looking at us like we are the devil. They
all think we are foul. Ray suddenly stands up with arms out.

'It's all right, ladies,' he shouts. 'Don't panic, we're in the
business!'

Fortunately I am on my hands and knees under some
chairs so no one can see the embarrassment on my face.
God, I wish I'd not come to my local café with Ray. I won't
be able to show my face in here for a while. I leave a tenner
on the table for breakfast and we make the sharpest of exits.
We get into the car and head for the bank.

While Ray waits outside, I go in to withdraw some cash.
Once inside, they refuse to let me take out £10,000. They
tell me that I need to make an appointment and that there
isn't enough cash in the place. I take it on the chin and we go
and try somewhere else. The same thing happens. This has
ceased to be amusing. I need the cash, I have people to pay.
Porn just isn't the sort of business where you can write out an
IOU. I am beginning to get agitated. We try one more bank
and the answer is still the same. I am afraid I blow my top.

'What?' I shout at the top of my voice. 'Has this place run
out of money? I've broken the bank? With one request?'

The woman behind the cash desk starts to get anxious.
'Can you keep your voice down, please?'

I turn around to see the queue behind me shift uncomfortably. I am not sure if it is the fact that I am making a

scene and they are suffering a touch of British embarrassment or that they are genuinely worried about their own funds. Either way, no one's enjoying the situation, least of all the bank.

'Are you telling me I can't get at my own money? I ask. 'Or that you simply don't have it in the bank?'

'What do you need it for, sir?' she asks.

'Why is that any business of yours? It is my money, I can do what I want with it.'

'But—'

'Just get me the cash.'

'Could you wait here, sir,' she says. 'I am going to call the manager.'

While I am standing around staring at various dull posters advertising various dull services, my mobile goes. It's Kent.

'We've got a problem,' he says.

'What sort of problem?'

'We don't have any furniture.'

'I know that. That's what you were supposed to be sorting yesterday.'

'But the thing is, no one can deliver on time. It takes six weeks.'

'Can't you go and get a display sofa?' I ask.

'I've tried that. No one will sell one. Or if they do they can only deliver next week.'

'Shit.'

'Yeah,' he agrees. 'Double shit.'

'So we can't film?'

'Well, it won't look good,' he says. 'They could shag on the floor.'

'Shag on the floor!' I say a little too loudly. Half the bank turns and looks at me. 'No, they can't.'

'Unless . . .'

'Go on,' I say.

'I did see a purple sofa in the street three or four days ago in Shepherd's Bush.'

'Get it.'

Finally the bank manager comes downstairs and after only about ten minutes of me refusing to leave the bank does he give me the money. He asks what the money is for and I tell him it is to pay porn stars. He tells me off for being rude. I tell him it is the truth and I think he coughs up just to get rid of me. As I walk out of the bank, my pockets bulging with notes, Kent calls again.

'It's here!' he says, sounding triumphant. 'And I have bargained the bloke down to fifty quid.'

'Well done!'

'Except I don't have the cash.'

'What?' This has to be one of the more shitty mornings of my life.

I drive to Shepherd's Bush Road to find Kent parked outside some cruddy old shop. Behind him on the pavement is the most enormous purple velvet sofa. It is huge. It is the sort of thing you could find yourself sitting on while waiting for a takeaway in an Indian restaurant. Kent has managed to save the day and complicate it even further in one fell swoop.

'How the fuck are we going to get that to Wandsworth?' I ask.

'Don't look at me,' he says. 'I drive a Smart car.'

In the end we manage to hire a Rasta with a van and we drive in convoy down to Wandsworth. The bloke parks up and Kent and I try to work out how to move the bastard sofa.

Question: how many porn stars does it take to move a purple velvet sofa up three flights of stairs? The answer is three. Plus an elderly Rasta.

Florien is furious when he comes back at lunchtime and sees what we have done to his flat. The purple velvet offends his Aryan sensibilities. He tells us he has a date arriving for the weekend and he wants us to get out of there sharpish when we have finished.

'Well, at least she'll have something to sit on,' says Kent.

'I wouldn't let my dog lie on that,' Florien replies.

'You don't have one,' says Kent.

'Fuck off,' he says.

As he storms out of the flat, he warns us on pain of death that no one is allowed to use the bath, though he doesn't say why. We all decide to ignore him, of course. Well, we want to do a pissing scene and the only place for it is the bath. I think it can't be that much of a problem. Trisha pees. I tell everyone I'll clear it up. But as I leave the flat to take a phone call, I hear some bright spark turning on the taps in the bath. I rush back but the water has drained away nicely. It seems that Florien was just being pedantic and German after all.

Trisha, Ray, Alexa and Tony are just getting down to some straight B-G sex on the purple sofa when there's a knock on the door. I open it to find a very attractive thirty-something woman flanked by two little blonde-haired girls in boaters standing at the door.

'There's water coming through my ceiling,' she says. 'My whole apartment is flooded.'

'It can't be,' I say.

'What the hell?' shouts Kent coming to the door.

'Are you filming?' asks the woman

'Yes,' says Kent.

'No,' I reply.

'The plumbers are on their way,' she says. 'To fix the leak.'

'It's stopped,' I say.

'No, it hasn't,' she says. 'All this filthy water is coming through into my kitchen.'

If she only knew, I think. 'I'm sure it will stop soon,' I say.

'It had better,' she says. 'Will you come and tell me as soon as the plumber arrives?'

We end up having the most extraordinarily tense afternoon trying to shoot a foursome as quietly as we can, all the time aware that the plumber could turn up at any minute, or the yummy mummy neighbour could knock on the door. Still, I am determined to finish. This is our last scene for the film and it has been a hell of a day to get to this point. I am not going to let a little leak hold up the film.

After about an hour of quiet sex the plumber finally arrives. It takes him all of two seconds to work out what is going on. There are four orange people sitting on a purple sofa pretending to be up to nothing. There's also a skinny blonde with a pile of make-up on, a yeti dressed as a schoolboy, a monosyllabic assistant and a pile of wet wipes on the floor.

'Um,' he stutters, his cheeks turning red, 'where did you say the problem was?'

It takes him another hour to attach the waste pipe back on to the bath, explaining it all to the yummy mummy who keeps coming and going in and out of the flat. At last at about 6.30 p.m. we manage to get rid of everyone and try to start the shoot again. The boys get pumped up for the fifth or sixth time that afternoon and Trisha prepares to walk into the flat and bust Alexa, Ray and Tony in some sort of spit roast on the purple sofa. I leave them to get on with it and sit in the corner, leaning against the wall and propped up by one of the make-up boxes.

Some fifteen or possibly twenty minutes later I am woken by Kent kicking my legs.

'Will you stop fucking snoring?' he says. 'I can hear you on the audio.'

'I'm sorry,' I say. 'I took a painkiller earlier this afternoon for my back. It was moving the sofa, I think.'

'I don't give a shit,' he shouts. 'I've got a difficult foursome to shoot. We have been here for fucking hours and now you are snoring all over the soundtrack. It doesn't exactly make us feel that we are shooting anything very sexy or interesting if the bloody director's asleep!'

'I'm sorry,' I say. 'It's been a long day.'

'It's just so unprofessional,' he shouts. 'You're so unprofessional. This whole thing is so unprofessional. Do you know what?'

'What,' I say, with a huge yawn.

'You are so bloody amateur. I can't work with you any more. I resign!' He turns around and huffs off in the direction of the door, only to stop and turn around. 'Um, Pavel,' he says to the skinny assistant, 'can you pass me my bag?'

Nine

Although we have apparently reached the point of irre-trievable breakdown, Kent still does actually sit down and edit *The Surveyor*. Maybe he needs the money, or perhaps he is just doing the decent thing and fulfilling his contract. Not that we have anything written down, of course. Whatever his reasons, we sit in his edit suite for the best part of a week and cut and paste in silence. There is almost no to-and-fro between us. Just a few nods and coughs and we get the thing done.

I send it off to the BBFC and for the first time in my porn career it does not get sent back. I am so delighted. Saying that, I am not sure if Kent would have re-edited it or if I could have coped with having to ask him to do it or indeed to have sat next to him throughout the whole process.

I do think he and I just need a little bit of time apart. He is one of the more tricky people I have had to deal with and that includes all the coked-up idiots I knew in the music business. But I do have a certain fondness for him. He is temperamental and argumentative and sometimes just as difficult to deal with as the porn stars but at least he is good at his job. There are times when he shoots his own feet; they peek in at the bottom of the shot. It doesn't happen enough, though, to ruin the film. I am sure things will work out eventually. They have to, really. I am his main employer. I mean, who the hell else is going to give him a job?

My phone goes.

'Right, that's it!' It's Kent.

'What is?' I ask. He always seems to start a telephone conversation halfway through or as if he'd just hung up.

'I am fucking off and leaving you,' he says.

'Right.'

'I don't need you any more.'

'OK.'

'I am off to Eastern Europe.'

'Really?'

'Yes, really, you patronising piece of shit. I have a new job, with a new boss who has a lot more money than you.'

'Sounds great.'

'Great? It is fucking brilliant. I am off to Budapest for two months, maybe three. In fact I don't think I am ever coming back. It's the future. Budapest's the future. The girls are beautiful. The place is beautiful. The locations are amazing. And they fuck like rabbits. It is the new fucking Camelot. And you heard it here first!'

'Well, good luck,' I say.

'Luck? I won't need luck. I have this Russian backer who has so much fucking money, luck doesn't come into it.'

'Ah, I hope you have a good time,' I say,

'Yeah, well,' he replies. I think he is a little disappointed not to get a rise out of me. 'See you around . . . maybe,' he adds.

'Let's hope so,' I say. 'When are you off?'

'In a couple of weeks,' he says. 'They've booked me into the Four Seasons.'

'Perfect.'

'Yeah, it is.'

'OK, well, bye, then.'

'Bye.'

With Kent confirming his resignation by pissing off to Budapest, I am now in a bit of a quandary. Do I go looking for another cameraman? A bloke who can shoot and edit? Or do I wait and see what happens to Kent in Budapest? Or do I just go on holiday and think about what to do on a nice hot beach somewhere? Ana's been asking for a while about taking a break and going away together somewhere, so this seems like the perfect opportunity. Our cash-flow situation is not great but it has certainly picked up since Christmas. The sex shops in Manchester and Birmingham have reordered more copies of *The Good Life* and *The Painter* and they are all waiting for *The Surveyor*. So we can just about afford to go away. All I need is to get *The Surveyor* on DVD and we are one step closer to the plane.

I call Susie-Anne at Film Stuff. Some people might think me stupid for using them a third time, but I have a bit of a plan. I still haven't paid their invoice for *The Painter* and I have no intention of doing so until the end of June or July. They messed up my order, my life and nearly took me under, so I figure they can wait. I feel they owe me and if I can per- suade them to press *The Surveyor* without me giving them half the money upfront, then it would help my cash flow no end.

I spend five minutes on the phone to Susie-Anne and she is so shocked that I have decided to use her crappy company again that not only does she agree to my terms, but she promises the quickest job in the world. Ana and I get on the plane to St Lucia.

On our first night sitting between the Piton Mountains and tucking into our first rum cocktail, I get a call from Seb.

'Guess what?' he says.

'What?'

'Have you heard about what's happened to Kent?'

Although Seb and I don't work together any more, we still keep in touch. Seb is always good for gossip. This time he does not disappoint. It transpires that all is not rosy in Kent's world. Apparently he packed all his equipment up into a mate's Mercedes, along with a make-up artist, intending to drive to Budapest. His Russian backer was supposed to be following on behind in a gold stretch limo. The stretch couldn't fit on the ferry so the guy had to take it across on the Eurostar. Kent meanwhile drove down a hole on the Hungarian border and got stuck in a metre of snow.

'Can you believe it?' says Seb. 'They stayed freezing their nuts off for twenty-four hours waiting to be rescued?'

'That's so typical of Kent, thinking he can drive to Budapest in a matchbox, not realising that it is the middle of winter and the whole fucking country is under six feet of snow.'

'I know,' laughs Seb. 'But it gets worse.'

Kent's Russian backer was arrested on the Hungarian border. He'd been laundering money and now he's languishing behinds bars somewhere outside Budapest. Astoundingly the Four Seasons has also not materialised and Kent is currently staying in a rundown bedsit in the middle of the city.

'He is still insisting that things are going well,' says Seb, who is now wheezing down the phone he's laughed so much. 'I will promise to keep you in the loop,' he says 'Enjoy your holiday.'

Poor old Kent, I think, looking out to sea and taking a sip of my cocktail. One of the first rules of business is that you should never be too keen to take the deal. Kent was so bloody desperate to get to Budapest he would have gone there on his bicycle. I suspect the Russian knew that. All this talk about rooms at the Four Seasons was clearly bullshit. I can't believe he fell for it. I decide to send him a good luck text message on my phone. I am still very fond of the stupid fool. Even if he is a tosser. Ten seconds later I get a reply: 'Budapest is fantastic. Having the time of my life. 3 Course meal – 4 quid.' God, I wonder, why the hell did I bother?

Ana and I spend the next week more or less entirely horizontal. We are either lying on the beach, relaxing on a lounger by the pool or in bed. It is pure heaven. Kent on the other hand seems to be having quite a rotten time. Having rattled his chain with my text message, he now can't seem to leave me alone. He keeps texting, telling me what a fantastic time of it he is having. At least twice a day I get to find out what he is eating and how much his meals are costing. He sends photos of the beers he is drinking and shots of the girls he is hanging out with. 'Bet you wish you were here?' he keeps texting, like he is trying to prove something. Trouble is, I know the truth. Seb tells me that the Russian is still in jail and he might not be coming out for a week and in the meantime Kent has not been paid. He is larging it up in Budapest entirely at his own expense.

'He is out every night,' says Seb, 'throwing money around like it is going out of fashion. But he hasn't earned a penny since he has been there. Sounds like hell to me. Oh, also there's no heating in the flat.'

'What?' I say, rubbing oil into my legs. 'He's cold?'

'Freezing,' says Seb. 'I checked on the internet this morning. It's minus-nine there at the moment.'

'Thank God he's a hairy bastard.'

'I know,' agrees Seb. 'Who would have thought that back hair would have been so useful?'

I can understand Kent's reason for going out to Budapest. The porn industry is very well established there. The girls are stunning and they are well regulated and very professional. If you are not happy with the star the agency sent, there is another one along in a matter of half an hour. The place is awash with pretty girls who all seem to have a very matter of fact attitude towards sex. It is that Eastern European or Slav thing, where there is nothing particularly interesting or exciting about the naked body. I'm sure it is born from a culture of municipal saunas, communal flats with shared bathrooms and kitchens and grinding poverty. Only the rich can afford to be prudish. The rest of us just have to get on with it. So Kent is right in a way to think that Eastern Europe is the future of porn. And money obviously talks. It is the sort of place where the nightwatchman would open a metro station to you for a few hundred pounds. Nowhere is off-limits, it is just a question of crossing the right palms with the right amount of silver. But I have learned over the last couple of months that porn is an extremely unpredictable business: you are dependent on the whim of other people, so why make it even more difficult for yourself by adding foreign locations and local bureaucrats into the mix? There are so many little rules and regulations to break without messing with the cultural mores of another country.

I remember being told about Pierre Woodman, one of the biggest porn directors in the world, being arrested in Bali. He was on some £0.5 million shoot and had been bribing his way out of trouble for a week or so, when on the last day of filming he found a machine gun in his face and was asked to pay ten grand and told to leave the country. He ended up offering a small amount of cash on the basis that he would be coming back to shoot some more films. The offer was accepted. But he left the country and never went back. I think the problem was, he is a larger than life character who, instead of entering the country quietly and going about his porno business, arrived with dollies and girls and porn stars, and the Indonesian authorities didn't find it amusing at all.

The same is true of the Australian customs officers who arrested a whole load of porn stars on their way to New Zealand to shoot a film. They arrived in Sydney and they were orange and had been sampling the contents of the trolley bar most of the way. They were stopped and when their bags were opened officers found dildos, whips, lube, transparent plastic heels and a huge amount of porn paraphernalia. Asked what they were doing, the porn stars said they were on their way to film. The customs people asked for their work permits. To which they all replied: 'Work permits? But this is porno?' Needless to say, they were all popped on to the next plane home.

Ana and I spend the next few days enjoying the sunshine and wonder exactly how cold Kent must be. He, of course, continues to send text messages about how much his sumptuous meals are costing him, as well as snaps of the sexy girls that he is hanging with. And one thing is certain: the food is cheap and the girls are lovely. Thankfully, Seb keeps calling with updates.

The Russian backer is eventually released from the cells but he crashes his golden stretch and a few days later is rearrested. He manages to pay his way out of trouble and then goes on a three-day drink and whore binge to celebrate. Kent is apparently beside himself. He has been in Budapest for ten days and has yet to shoot a frame. However, all is not

lost because he gets to meet and hang out with the huge
Italian porn star called Rocco, who has one of the largest
cocks I have ever seen on film. The man is such an enormous star in Europe that he has his own brand of film,
where he gets through quite a lot of girls in a very short
space of time. His team had apparently hired a castle where
there were some fifty extras. Seb says Rocco was playing a
priest who arrives at a monastery and shags all the nuns.
And I have seen enough of his films to know that he will
shag them all in the same way. He'll go from blowjob to
going down on her, to her taking her top off; then he'll fuck
her, before they move to anal; then they'll do three different
positions, and then doggy and they turn her around and he'll
come on her face. He does the same to everyone. But then
again if I had a penis that size I might not feel the need to
mix things up.

'Well, he sounds like he is having a laugh out there now
anyway,' I say to Seb, while I stretch out on my sun lounger.

'I know,' says Seb. 'I have to say I don't know why any of
them are filming in Budapest at the moment.'

'Why's that?'

'It's far too early in the year. It's February.'

'So?'

'You're supposed to wait until at least April or at best May,'
he claims.

'What for?'

'All the stars are a little fatter in winter than they are in
the spring or summer,' he says. 'They've got some extra lag-
ging against the cold. It is only a question of a couple of
pounds here and there. But you can tell the difference.'

'Right,' I say, looking down at my own gut thinking it is
going to take more than a few warm spring nights to shift
this.

'I am only repeating what a photographer mate of mine once told me,' he admits.

'I'm sure it kind of makes sense.'

It is extremely nice to hear about the machinations of the Eastern European porn industry from the delights of the Caribbean. This is the first holiday that Ana and I have been on together for nearly four years. I suppose a lack of holidays is one of the many downsides of being freelance. I know I didn't work that hard when I was in the music industry, but I expended a lot of energy hanging around waiting for a call, any call, from anyone who would give me some work – Steps reunion tours included. Now I am my own boss, a two-week holiday in the winter sun is one of the upsides of working in porn. At least that is what I keep saying to Ana every time she looks the tiniest bit unhappy. To which she keeps responding:

'I am very happy that you are your own boss and things are beginning to get a little better. I just wish it wasn't porn.'

We are standing in the airport contemplating a shelf of rum in the duty free when I get a call from Kent.

'Hi there,' I say trying to sound consolatory. After all, the bloke's having rather a bad time.

'Just calling to tell you I did the best shoot of my life today,' he boasts.

'Good,' I say, picking up a bottle of something I have never heard of, but it is 45 per cent proof so I put it in my basket.

'I did an orgy in the back of a golden stretch limo overlooking the Danube,' he says. 'It was fucking fantastic.'

'Excellent.'

'We've got Didier over here.'

'What, French Didier?'

'That's the one. He's flown in from Tenerife.'

'He is very good.'

'Yeah,' agrees Kent. 'He's the only bloke I know who can keep an erection going in minus-three.'

'Minus-three? It's thirty-two degrees here.'

'Thirty-two?' I can hear him sneer from here. 'You poor bastards, that's far too hot.'

'Isn't it?' I agree. 'Thank God for cool cocktails.'

'Yeah, well, you can get a litre of beer here for less than a pound.'

'Who else is out there with you?'

'A load of people you don't know. Anton. That sort of thing.'

'What, Anton the art director?'

'How do you know him?' asks Kent, getting defensive.

'We work in the same industry,' I say.

'Well, him.'

'That the same Anton who is also a fisherman in the East End?' I ask.

'Might be,' says Kent. 'Anyway I've got to go, a porn star wants to buy me a drink.'

'Isn't it about ten in the morning with you?' I query.

'We start early here,' he says and hangs up the phone.

We come back to the UK to find that Film Stuff has for once been true to its word and there are six thousand copies of *The Surveyor* waiting for us in their warehouse. I get on the phone to the sex shops straight away. My plan has been to try to call as many of them in the country as I can in person. I think if they get to talk to me and hear what we are about, then they are more likely to order. And so far so good. I have nearly worked my way right down to the bottom of the list of 280 and the ones at the top have already begun to reorder. Even the one sex shop in Essex, which originally said it wouldn't take any stock as there has never been any call for upmarket porn, has been on the phone. Apparently he has had a few customers coming in asking for Touch Wood's stuff, so maybe he'll take a few copies of each of the films and see how they do. I offer him ten of each and he turns me down. So I send five. He's one hell of a tight bastard.

I have also been handing a few copies of *The Surveyor* out to mates. Will takes a few. He wants to see what his office looks like. He says he enjoys watching the film much more than watching it being made.

'Somehow you never expect it to be so goddamn bestial,' he says. 'It is the difference between watching a boxing match on the telly and sitting right next to the ring. In the flesh you can see, hear and smell every body blow. Somehow it is a whole less exciting and a hell of a lot more disturbing. It is actually quite weird watching people have sex.'

There are some who would disagree but I know what he means. Still, it seems he is not the only one to enjoy *The Surveyor*. Judging by the number of people who want to go and inspect Mitch's table at Laura's birthday drinks this evening, the DVD has clearly done the rounds. People who I don't know keep coming up and whispering in my ear:

'Is that the one?'

'The one what?'

'The one the girl has an accident over in the film?'

Some of them have seen the film; others have merely heard of it by reputation but are keen to get their hands on a copy. Poor Laura is very confused. She can't understand why her guests keep hanging around the table or wanting to have a look at the stain. There is also something else going on that is worrying her. Most of her guests seem to know their way around the flat, which is odd considering the majority of them have never been there before.

'I just don't get it,' she says to me in the corner of the kitchen. 'No one's asked me where the loo is? Someone else walked straight into my bedroom and told me how they've always liked this room, yet I know he hasn't been here before. Everyone wants to talk about the table. There are loads of people who want to take a look at the terrace even though it is freezing outside. Do you have any idea what is going on?'

'Why are you asking me?' I say in a manner that I hope is not too defensive.

'Because you are always at the epicentre of trouble,' she says.

'Me?'

'Yes, you?' She takes a sip of her drink. 'Now look me in the eye.'

'What?'

'And promise to tell me the truth?'

'OK,' I nod, preparing to fib with some sort of conviction.

'Just how big was the party that you and Mitch had while I was away?'

'Ah.'

'Yes, ah, that?' she smiles.

'Probably a little bigger than Mitch has let on,' I say.

'I knew it!' she says. She spins on her stiletto and marches across the room in the direction of her husband.

Ana berates me all the way home in the cab for my lack of respect. She says that she feels sorry for Laura. How awful it must be to have everyone in on the joke and to be the only one not to know.

'People were coming up to me all night giggling in my ear and I had no idea what they were talking about,' she says.

'I'm sorry,' I say, realising the real reason that she is so cross has little to do with Laura's embarrassment and more her own. 'I hate lying. I hate covering for you. God, I wish you didn't do porn.'

That night I lie there staring at the ceiling, being treated to the cold buttocks. I was hoping she'd be a little more reasonable by now. After all she's had nine, well, actually eight, months to get used to the porn idea. And it's just paid for a luxury holiday.

My mobile goes. It is one in the morning. Ana rolls over and puts a pillow on her head. I debate whether to answer it. But I can see that it is Kent. Why is he calling at this time of night?

'Hello?' I ask. 'You OK?'

'No,' he whispers. 'I am fucking shitting it.'

'What? Why? Why are you whispering?'

'I am hiding in a cupboard.'

'Why? What's going on? What's the matter?'

'Jesus Christ, you won't believe what's happened.'

'Try me.'

'I am in the cupboard in my room, sitting on all my camera equipment and there's a fight going on outside.'

'Really?'

'Yeah. Some gangsters have broken into the apartment. Yuri owes some guys some money and they have come to collect. And I'm fucking bricking it, stuck in here with ten grand's worth of equipment and meanwhile Didier is doing his stuff outside.'

'Eh? Didier is doing what outside?'

'He's fighting them.'

'He's fighting them?'

'Yeah. He's ex-legion.'

'What do you mean, ex-legion?'

'The French Foreign Legion, you twat, what else?'

'Didier's ex-French Foreign Legion?'

'Yes!' he shouts. 'Shit!' he whispers. 'Do you think they heard that?'

'Can you still hear fighting?'

'No, it's gone quiet.'

'Where are the others?'

'Anton's fucked off with the make-up artist and Yuri is out with some hookers doing coke.'

'Oh.'

'Yeah, meanwhile I am stuck here with my stuff hoping some tangoed porn star can save the day. What should I do?'

'Like I have been in that situation before?'

'Don't get smart with me,' he whispers. 'I can't stay in here for ever.'

'How about till morning?'

'OK,' he says.

'Are there coats to lie on?'

'Where the hell do you think I am, fucking Narnia? There's nothing. Just my equipment . . . shhh . . . did you hear that?'

'No, I'm in London.'

'Call you back.'

Kent doesn't call me back. I lie in bed worrying for a good while, thinking that he's been beheaded or something terrible. I have visions of him being dragged through the snow by his enormous Y-fronts, still clutching on to his camera equipment, shitting himself that he might lose his hiring deposit. I try calling him several times but he doesn't answer.

He doesn't call me when he gets back from Budapest either, which I gather was pretty soon after spending the night in the cupboard. Didier, or so I heard, really did save the day. He took on four gangsters single-handed while dressed only in his underwear. Apparently he was asleep on the sofa bed in the sitting room when they burst in, and he sent them all packing with a few well-timed kicks and karate chops. He broke one of the bloke's arms. He told Kent the coast was clear a few times but Kent wouldn't leave the confines of the cupboard until daybreak. Or least that's what Seb tells me over a few cold beers.

The next I hear is that Kent is working as a news camera-man for some cable TV station and he is doing shifts in the studio. I don't know why he doesn't call me. Perhaps he can't bear to hear the crow in my voice as he admits that Budapest was a total unmitigated disaster.

In the meantime I have another potential problem loom-ing on the horizon: Ana's parents are coming to stay. And Ana is in a tizz to say the least. They come over once a year from Norway. We take in a few shows and eat out in a few restaurants and they stay with their daughter. Or at least they have done for the past three or four years. It is usually fine. Her parents are charming. Her mother is a teacher and her dad is a doctor. I like having them around. Or I would do normally. Except this year I have become a porn director and the house is full of the stuff. There are boxes of porn in the hall. DVDs in the sitting room. Sexy toys in the spare room and industrial amounts of lube in the loo. All this would be fine and dandy if Ana's parents were liberal types who shagged around and smoked dope in the seventies. But they're not. They are nice people who would be horrified to check into a hotel if there was a porn channel on the TV. You may think I am joking but I'm not. It is her mother's first or second question when booking over the phone. So you can kind of understand Ana's sweat.

She rushes around vacuuming the place, tidying up and putting flowers in their room. The things she finds under Toby's bed actually don't bear repeating, safe to say there were a lot of old, hard tissues. Eventually the place looks fabulous. The best it's looked in a year, since the last time they came. But the one big problem is: what to do with all the porn? All in all there are about fifteen boxes of the stuff. They are mostly of *The Surveyor*, which is beginning to shift quite nicely. But there are boxes of *The Good Life* as well as *The Painter*. I mean, where else am I supposed to keep them? Space costs money and we are always trying to keep our overheads down. So in the end we come up with a plan. We cover the boxes in sheets and try to ignore them as much as possible. And when questioned we will say that they are a delivery from IKEA. I just hope and pray we get away with it. If her parents find out, as Ana has repeatedly told me, she will kill me. And I have to say, I believe her.

Sven and Angela are all suited and booted when they arrive and I am on my best behaviour. Ana cooks something meaty and full of pickled cabbage, something of a Norwegian delicacy, and everyone but me seems to enjoy it. Her parents mention the boxes a couple of times, mainly because they had to squeeze their suitcases past them, and Sven suggests that it is my general incompetence that means we have so much flat-packed furniture in our hall. He offers to help us put it all together over the weekend. I can see the panic rise in Ana's face.

'Oh, don't worry about that,' I say, trying to top up his already full drink.

'Someone has to,' he says. 'How long has it been sitting there?'

'A month,' I say.

'A week,' says Ana at the same time.

'Well, there seems to be something of a difference in opinion,' says her mother.

Oh God, I smile, I can hear the cogs of her brain turning from here. One of us is lying and the other is in denial. It would probably suit her down to the ground if our relationship didn't work. She has always wanted Ana to settle down with a nice hard-working Norwegian with IT skills and a nice pine house somewhere. They have never been that interested or impressed by my music career. Even when I was playing Wembley, all they managed to talk about and find interesting was some neighbour from the local choir who'd cut a record in Norway. He was apparently the nice sort of man their daughter should marry. I know I haven't helped my case by not popping the question. Ana and I have been living together for some eight and a half years now and I can see those little looks of expectation as soon as they come through the door. They check out her hand and then her belly. One straight after the other. The hand? No, she is not engaged. Phew! Thank God she isn't pregnant, either. Just my luck to have the straightest couple in Scandinavia as my potential parents-in-law.

Fortunately, we seem to get away with the pile of porn in the hall. I also manage to put Sven off the DIY by sending both him and Angela off to various exhibitions around town. But the worst moment in the whole stay happens on the day before they leave. We all meet up with some friends of theirs, plus children, in a gastropub off the King's Road. For some stupid reason I drink a little too much red wine. I think it's because I know they are leaving the following day and I have nearly made it to the end with my porn career intact. I go to the toilet and leave my mobile phone on the table. When I come back I find two of the kids have got hold of it. As I walk towards the table, a fixed smile on my shit-scared face, I am wondering how much they have seen. There are photos of cocks, cunts and cunnilingus in the gallery and that's only the start. There are phone numbers for Trisha Bigtits et al. DP stills from shoots. There's Camilla with an arse full of sex toys. There is so much incriminating stuff on that thing, perhaps I should just walk straight out of the pub right now. My potato wedges can wait, as can my fishcakes and sticky toffee pudding. I could just save face and go.

'What are you guys doing with my phone, then?' I ask in a measured voice.

'Oh?' says the older boy from beneath his mop of white blond hair. 'It is yours?'

'Yes, it's mine,' I say.

'Sorry,' says the younger little boy. 'We were just playing games.'

'Oh,' I say. My pounding heart begins to slow a little. 'Have you looked at anything else on there?'

'No,' says the eldest. 'That would be rude.'

'Quite right,' I say. 'Very rude.'

'We would never look through anyone's phone.'

'Of course not,' I say, sitting down and picking up a wedge. Thank God for well-mannered Scandinavians.

To say I put out the bunting as I waved Ana's parents off in a taxi to Heathrow is a bit of an understatement. I got so totally and utterly drunk that I actually lost two whole days of my life. It's the sort of bender that would do Toby proud. He is, I gather, still living with his parents, otherwise I might have asked him to join me. Instead I manage to meet up with Seb who fills me in on the latest with Kent.

'Poor Kent,' he says shaking his head. 'It's not going terribly well for him.'

'Oh really?' I say, not feeling too sorry for him as he does bring it all on himself, mainly because he is such a belliger-ent old bastard.

'Thing is,' says Seb, 'I don't think he's that good at taking orders from other people.'

'Really? You do surprise me.'

'Really?' he asks.

'God, you must be pissed. Can't you tell when I am being sarcastic?'

Seb goes on to tell me that Kent lasted all of two days in the newsroom. The first day he turned up early, which is surely a first, and because there was no one there, he started to rearrange the lights, the seats and the microphones.

'I mean, he sort of dismantled the set,' says Seb.

'Has he ever been in a newsroom before?'

'No, and that is where the problem is.'

'Right.'

'He had no idea that the place was so unionised. That everyone has their place and that his was not coming in front of the camera and reorganising everything.'

'Ah, I see.'

'The editor did not find it amusing. Neither did any of the other lighting or sound guys. In fact they were bloody furi-ous. But because he had not been in a studio before and because it was his first day on the job they let it go.'

'Thank God.'

'I know,' agrees Seb. 'But d'you know what the stupid bas-tard did the next day when he came in?'

'What?' I say, as I wait to hear the inevitable.

'Only the same old shit again,' he says. 'Can you believe it?'

'Does he never learn?'

'Doesn't look like it.'

'You're right,' I say.

'The bloke's a twat,' nods Seb. 'Do you think you'll give him his job back?'

'I shouldn't think so for a minute,' I say. 'I mean, he pisses off and leaves me high and dry without a replacement. Every time he's called, he's been aggressive. Every time he's texted me, it was only to tell me how cheap his grub was or how stunning the girl was sitting next to him.'

'I wouldn't,' says Seb.

'No, I won't,' I say. 'I mean, why the hell should I?'

'I agree,' he says. 'But you know he'll call.'

'Well, I can't wait.'

I lie in bed for the whole of the next morning with my phone switched off. Even if Kent did call I wouldn't know. Ana is irritated by my behaviour but she is so pleased we've had her parents to stay, and done the whole family thing until this time next year without them realising what I do for a living, that I get away with having got so plastered. I think she is hoping that in twelve months' time things will be different. That I might have managed to give up porn. Either that or I'll be so goddamn rich that no one will care by then anyway.

I turn my phone back on, half expecting to get a message from Kent. Instead there is one from an old friend of mine called Jeremy, who I haven't seen for ages. He is now a foreign exchange dealer who works out of the City. An incredibly busy bloke, he keeps very different hours from me. Normally he's up early and rarely goes out beyond 10 p.m. But he is occasionally prone to the odd £800 blow-out dinner and once or twice a year I get the call. I ring him right back.

'So are you on?' he asks, the excitement very much audible in his voice.

'Absolutely,' I enthuse. 'I can't wait. You know it is just

me?' I add. 'Ana has had to go on a shoot on the Norfolk Broads.'

'The Norfolk Broads?' he queries.

'I know, and who said fashion was glamorous?'

We arrange to meet at the Ivy. Jeremy says that he has fallen in love and he is desperate for me to meet her. And she does sound fantastic. She is studying philosophy at one of the London universities and she is so bright and clever and perfect, he confides, that he is thinking of proposing.

He is already at a table near the bar when I arrive. He looks plumper and pinker than when I last saw him. Some people pork up when they are in love, others lose weight. Like me, he is clearly one of nature's porkers.

'I am on the vodkas,' he says as I sit down. He runs his finger around the tight pink collar of his shirt. I am feeling a little uncomfortable in my own shirt and tie, so I am heartened to see that he is bursting out of his.

'I'll have the same,' I say to the hovering waiter who rapidly disappears. 'So where's your girlfriend? I can't wait to meet her.'

'She is on her way and will join us a little later,' he smiles, taking a sip of his drink.

Jeremy and I are halfway through our caviar starter when this long-legged blonde walks into the room.

'Ah, there you are,' says Jeremy, getting out of his seat and walking towards her. He gives her a very passionate, very public embrace in the middle of the room. He has the biggest beaming smile on his face. 'Here she is,' he says to me. 'Here's Irena.'

'Hi,' I say, getting out of my seat. She is absolutely gorgeous. Large eyes, marshmallow lips, a pretty nose, she is one of the best-looking women I have seen in years.

'This is the friend I was telling you about,' says Jeremy. 'He's the one who makes porn!' he chortles. 'Do you remember?'

'Of course,' she says. Her plump lips part into a smile.

'I am just off to the loo,' says Jeremy. 'You two should talk and get to know each other. Back in a minute.'

Irena sits down and takes a sip of the immediately poured glass of cold Chablis. She looks at me. I look back at her. Her face is unmistakable.

'Where have you been?' I ask. 'I have sent so many emails to your website but you never reply. I have been trying to book you for months.'

'Oh,' she says, without a flicker of emotion crossing her beautiful face. 'I have changed my email address. Let me give you my card. Call me and make a booking.'

Ten

All it takes is one phone call from Kent and he is back on the payroll. He doesn't apologise for leaving me in the lurch. He doesn't even admit that he was wrong about Budapest. He just calls on a rainy Tuesday morning and asks if I need a cameraman. We end up having one of those stilted conversations where nothing gets said. We are both waiting for the other to admit to making a mistake or to gloat. In the end we do neither. I simply arrange to meet him two days later at a pier beside the Thames.

'All right?' he sniffs, as I walk along the wooden planks towards him, the rain pelting down again. He looks fatter and hairier than I remember. He is still dressed in his signature khaki shorts and looks like he needs dunking in DDT. He holds out a hirsute hand. I take it. We shake, and I suppose this is the closest Kent will ever come to an apology. 'So,' he says, shifting from one long leg to the other, 'what are we shooting today?'

I explain to him that we are borrowing my accountant's barge for the day and that it is moored in the middle of the Thames. I can see he is on the verge of saying something along the lines of him not 'doing water' but thinks better of it. My accountant is six foot two of mad Scot, who loves rugby, cigarettes and alcohol. He is quite a character and the boat is something else. I point across the water at the 110ft barge and say that the boat can only be reached by the small dinghy moored below. Kent's face blanches.

'It can't be that difficult to get there,' I say. 'Patrick does when totally arseholed. Although the other day he did set off at full throttle having forgotten to untie the boat. It reached the end of its tether and he went flying over the top into the Thames. I think he is very lucky he didn't drown. The currents are terrible in there and he'd had at least half a bottle of malt.'

Kent looks at me and then at the water. I think he's about to bolt but the arrival of Ray, Trisha Bigtits and Luella calls his bluff. Luella is one of the new stars on the block. Slim with long dark hair and the most fantastic tits, she could cut it as a model in the real world if her boobs weren't so goddamn big. And they're real. Kent's tongue is touching his bottom lip.

We are also joined on the jetty by make-up artist Kelly, plus Kent's assistant Roger and a photographer and a journalist from *DVD* magazine. The magazine rang up last week and asked if they could come and photograph us on a shoot. They tell me they have heard of us through the grapevine, that they've been told our stuff is good, and they would like to do some sort of location report. Would I mind if they come along? Would I mind? I am so bloody delighted that I greet Dan and Len with open arms.

'Nice to meet you both.' I shake their hands. 'Welcome to the set of *West End Girls*. I hope you have a great day, we are very excited to have you here.'

They look a little taken aback. I don't think porn directors are usually pleasant to them. But as far as I am concerned all publicity is good and anything that helps raise the profile of Touch Wood Films is fine by me. There is, however, one thing that is bothering me: how are we all going to get to Patrick's barge when the Thames is this choppy looking, the weather so wet and the girls are wearing next to nothing and teetering about in transparent plastic high heels?

The thing is not to lose one's nerve, I think, as everyone bundles aboard the dinghy. I am grinning on the outside, and sweating like a rapist, all the time praying that none of these bastards falls in or slips over, as I have absolutely no public liability insurance. It would be the end of everything if someone were to fall arse over surgically enhanced tit and break their back. Fortunately Ray seems to be loving it. The whoops and high fives he makes every time we hit a wave seem to make everyone feel that they should be enjoying the adventure as well.

Once on-board, the boat is much more spacious than I was expecting. It has three fat sofas, a large widescreen telly and a relatively attractive kitchen, bearing in mind that the owner is a single bloke who loves figures more than fruit. Kelly immediately starts to unpack her suitcases and Trisha and Luella do the same. Ray sets about pumping himself up and Kent takes me to one side in the kitchen.

'So,' he says, 'can I have a look at the script?'

'The script?' I say.

'Yeah.'

'There isn't one,' I say. 'It's in my head.'

'In Budapest I got used to working with a script.'

'Fat lot of good that did when you were stuck in a fucking cupboard while your porn star was beating the shit out of the Russian mafia.'

'I need to know what to shoot, scene by scene,' he says, ignoring the cupboard comment. 'I want to know, say, is Luella going to come down the stairs of the boat?'

'Honestly.' I shake my head. You would have thought he might be grateful for getting his old job back. But apparently not. He's walking around with his hands in front making a square and looking through it like he is a cinematographer.

'I need to know shot by shot,' he says, looking at me earnestly through all his facial hair.

'Look,' I say, 'Trisha comes down the stairs – shot. She discovers Ray tossing on the sofa – shot. She says, "Ooh you are a naughty flatmate, sorry to have disturbed you" – shot. He says, "You aren't disturbing me. Do you want to join in?" – shot. She says, "Oh, er, yes please" – and they fuck – shot, shot, shot.'

'Thank you,' he says, running his hands through his hair like he's David fucking Lean. 'That's all I needed to know.'

Fifteen minutes later Kent is choreographing the shagging. He is now showing off, using terms like 'cowgirl' and 'reverse cowgirl', which basically just mean on top and on top from behind. We all know that and we have never really bothered to use them. But he's just telling me and the journalists present that he knows what he is doing. I also hear him saying to Len that he's just come back from Budapest. He drops Rocco's name a few times, even though I know he only met him in a bar. You would have thought he'd been shooting the bloke for months, the way he is going on. But actually I don't really care, he can talk as much as he wants – all I want is for us to shoot three scenes as quickly as we can without anyone falling overboard.

Trisha is bouncing around doing a reverse cowgirl on Ray's cock when I hear footsteps on-deck, which is quite a feat considering how much she is shouting her head off. I look around the boat and realise that everyone is accounted for. Oh fuck. This is all we bloody need.

When he handed over the keys to the barge, Patrick's only

word of warning had been to beware of Colonel Bufton-Tufton-Smythe.

'He's a nosy bastard with fuck all else to do except spy,' said Patrick. 'But don't let him find out. He chairs the mooring association and I could be chucked off my spot.'

Kent's moving in for the money shot. I can hear Colonel B-T-S approaching.

'Get a move on,' I hiss. Ray looks over Trisha's shoulder, his eyes bulging. The poor bloke is trying as hard as he can. I run over to the door of the boat trying to head the colonel off at the pass.

'Hello? Hello? Anyone in there?' come clipped Sandhurst tones.

'Good morning!' I shove my breezy face in his way.

'YES!' I hear Ray shout in ecstatic release.

'Can I help you?' I ask.

'Who are you?' asks the colonel. His red weathered face looks confused.

I explain that we are friends of Patrick's and that we are rehearsing a play and that I am terribly sorry for the noise. He says he likes the arts, he goes to the theatre all the time but that he hasn't come about that. Someone has parked in his spot.

'I think they're towing your car away,' he points. 'I'd shift it if I were you. They're very vicious around here.'

The colonel offers to ferry me over. I leap into his dinghy and we head off at speed. We both run up the jetty to find out that it is actually his car that is being towed because Trisha's is in his space. He blows a gasket and I grab the roll of cash from my back pocket and start paying our way out of trouble. The colonel gets fifty. The traffic wardens get a hundred each. I make my apologies.

By the time I get back to the boat there is only really time for one G-G scene before we shoot under the bridge, which is something I would like to do before it grows too dark.

The idea behind the G-G scene is for Luella to come back to the boat to find her brother and his new flatmate at it and for her to suggest that Trisha comes into her room for a bit of girl action.

It's all going well. Trisha and Luella are getting it on. Luella gets out her hairbrush and asks Trisha to smack her bottom. She bends over and Trisha thwacks away. Luella then grabs hold of the hairbrush and starts putting it up her own bottom. Trish then fucks her with the hairbrush and then just when we think that is the end of the scene, she puts her legs behind her head and says to Trisha:

'I want you to fuck me with your foot.'

I look at Ray. He looks back at me, a puzzled expression on his face. Clearly he hasn't heard of this, either. We both stand and stare. Trisha's foot slowly disappears up Luella's arse. Right the way up past the ankle. My mouth falls open. Kent mutters something like 'Jesus Christ'. He didn't see that in Budapest. The journalists are totally silent. In fact we are all mute as we watch Trisha apparently waggle her toes and Luella moan with what appears to be utter delight.

'Cut!' I shout. Trisha pulls her foot slowly out and Luella sits up.

'Well done,' she says to Trisha. 'I really enjoyed that.'

The rest of the barge just stands there, slack-jawed. We are all too shocked to speak.

Later that afternoon we manage to do a quick scene by Albert Bridge. Trisha Bigtits gives Ray a rapid blowjob under the arches. And I do mean rapid. We have to get it in the can before any dog-walking do-gooder comes up and busts us.

Next we head up to the Water Rat. The pub is not open yet but Steve, my mate who runs it, lets us in. I think Dan and Len have really had enough by now. They look cold and wet and exhausted. I don't think they expected to have to hang around on a barge or under a bridge on such a wet and miserable day. They are only too delighted to toast their backsides by Steve's real fire and knock back complimentary ale. Meanwhile the rest of us sneak upstairs to the dining room. Steve's missus has just had a baby and she is half asleep in the next-door room.

I am hoping this is going to be a quick scene, where Trisha comes into the upstairs room with a couple of pints in each hand pretending to be serving in the pub and she gives Ray, Luella and Tony, who has arrived for a half-day shoot, their drinks before they all have sex. She says something along the lines of 'Do you want nuts with that' and Tony says, 'You can have my nuts for nothing', and she says, 'Ooh, you are naughty', and then sucks his knob before the orgy kicks off.

'All I ask is that you try and keep it quiet,' I say. 'Steve's wife is asleep next door with a brand new baby.'

And for once they listen to me. It is the quietest orgy we have ever filmed and also one of the best. It's slick, it is sexy and they all do exactly what they are supposed to do. I think Luella is great. She is certainly the sort of girl I will work with again. That's if she doesn't burn out first.

One of the weird things that I have learned in my short time in the porn business is how quick the turnaround of girls is. Just as you start to hear about one, her career is over. We have tried to work with established stars. Trisha Bigtits and Jenny Saint have been around for a while, and they have a fan-base and website to prove it, but the others come and go so quickly. It normally takes about three months for a girl to be exhausted. I think it is because they can and do work every day that they burn out so fast. Plenty of people don't believe me but it is extremely hard work being a porn star. It sounds easy but being shagged every which way, every day of the week, for five or six hours at a time, takes it out of you. And it can't be that good for the body. They are bruised and battered, ripped and torn. I'm sure some of the less professional guys are not that gentle. The guys get paid less but they hang around longer. I suppose it's because no one is really looking at them. It is all about the girl, which is why she gets the wad. But also why punters get bored of seeing the same girls over and over and why the male porn stars get bored of fucking them.

As we are clearing up even Kent looks pleased. I'm not sure if it is the quality of the scene or the proximity of a watering hole that tickles him. The place is now open and he looks ready for a beer.

'Tell you what,' he sniffs, 'there is something very sexy about filming porn while listening to the pub slowly filling up underneath your feet. And they are all blissfully unaware of what is going on above their heads.'

'Right,' I smile.

'I find that a right turn on.'

'Good,' I say. I didn't need to know that.

Back downstairs in the pub Len and Dan are getting really quite pissed and as we all walk in from behind the bar there is a gentle ripple of applause. So much for Kent's furtive sex fantasy. It seems the whole bar is aware of what has been going on and they all want to buy us drinks to celebrate.

'That must be right old thirsty work,' says one old boy as he buys Trisha a drink.

The porn stars are in their element. Natural show-offs

and exhibitionists, they flit from table to table collecting drinks and compliments from their captive and alcoholically challenged audience. I am only thankful that Ana is away for the night on a shoot in Paris. I have rather overstepped the mark by inviting a troupe of porn stars to our local. I have to admit I didn't really think the whole thing through. I had hoped to be in and out of the pub before the punters started pouring in. What a great big fat mistake.

Still, as I sit here nursing my second pint, I can relax in the knowledge that I haven't got far to walk home. Seb's on his way in, so I haven't got to entertain Kent all on my own. At the moment he has got Len and Dan pinned against the wall, and is regaling them with his fascinating Budapest anecdotes. I am just about to light a fag when Steve comes and taps me on the shoulder.

'You'd better get your arse over here,' he says, looking a little concerned.

'What,' I say, following him around the corner.

'Look!' He points to the queue for the loo. There are five people stood in a line.

'So?' I shrug.

'Your porn stars have been in there having sex for the past twenty minutes.'

'And?'

'You get them out.'

'Don't look at me,' I say. 'I am off duty. What am I supposed to do?'

'They're your porn stars.'

'It's your pub. Who is it anyway?'

'I don't know,' says Steve. 'The orange bloke and the dark-haired girl.'

'What? Ray and Luella?'

'That's them.'

'But they've been shagging each other all day.'

'Well, they clearly haven't had enough,' he says.

I bang on the door and try to get them to stop. Steve bangs on the door and they still carry on. The woman in the queue does the same. Two blokes leave the pub and piss in the street. Steve's getting really rather annoyed. Finally, another ten minutes later, and after four other people have tried to disturb them, Ray and Luella come out of the toilet. There is a ripple of applause, plus some loud booing, as they walk back into the bar. I decide to make a sharp exit out the back. I don't need the hassle and I think these porn stars can look after themselves. I am going to go home, watch *EastEnders* and call my girlfriend, which might give both of us a pleasant surprise.

The next morning I meet everyone again in a café near South Kensington Tube. They are all looking hungover, tired and well slept in. I am a bit irritated. They all knew we were supposed to be shooting today. I have put everyone up in various hotels, hostels and B&Bs across the capital. If I knew they were all going to go back to Kent's for an impromptu rave and possible orgy, I could have saved myself about five hundred quid. And hotel rooms are at a premium at the moment. I know because I spent all of last week trying to find one for today. There is some travel conference on and most of London's quality places are booked up with reps. I have tried the Ritz, Grosvenor House, Claridge's, everywhere I can think of. I turned down a suite at the Travelodge in Woodford thinking I would be able to find somewhere better.

The hotel-room option is a last resort anyway because it costs money and gives you added grief. After our last experience, I am not keen to repeat the episode. The only thing is, I am low on friends with user-friendly apartments to shoot in. I was tempted to call Mitch and Laura to see if the Thames-side view was available. But Laura is still angry about the stains on her table and terrace and I feel I might be pushing my luck. Will is so traumatised by the scenes he witnessed in his office that he turned me down point blank, and Florien isn't talking to me. Well, he is. Just not very nicely. He keeps leaving threatening messages on all my voicemails, complaining about the huge purple sofa that I have left in his plush sitting room. He has decided not to move out after all and he wants me to collect it. He says that it is cramping his style and if I don't come and collect it soon, he'll dump it outside my neighbour's flat with a note telling them it's from me. I smile every time I hear his angry Germanic voice on my machine because I know his threats are empty – it took three porn stars and a Rasta to get the thing into his flat in the first place.

So anyway I have shelled out nearly five hundred quid and found a suite just around the corner from the café. Everyone gets the usual lecture about being subtle but they are hungover and deaf. I don't know why I am wasting my breath. Although if I am being honest I have muddied the waters a bit already. I rather aroused suspicion last week when I asked to see the room.

'What?' said the girl on reception. 'You want to see it before booking? Why?'

I made up some excuse about having very fussy clients. I said that we were interviewing for a position in a company and that we would also be videoing the interviewees. I kept on asking about the power supply to the room. The last thing I want is for Kent's lights to blow their fuses during a critical moment in a foursome.

As I escort the very orange, very tall Ray through the

lobby and upstairs to the first-floor suite, people's antennae are already on full alert. The girl on the front desk is all twitchy and I am sure I see her phone through to tell someone that we have arrived. But then again I could be paranoid. All I want to do is get everybody out of the café and into the room as quickly as I can. Trisha has been going on all morning asking questions about what we are shooting and what I want her to do. She has mentioned the name of the hotel twice. When I go back to collect her I can see the waitress frowning and trying to work out what is going on.

I get Trisha into the suite pronto but just as I am coming back with Luella, I find Trisha hanging around in the bar. I know it's spring but her white mini and knee-length boots and her Playboy bunny T-shirt kind of give the game away somewhat.

'What are you doing?' I hiss.

'I just want a coffee,' she complains.

'There are facilities in the room. And anyway I told you to stay in the room.'

Corralling porn stars is like trying to control a wilful group of schoolchildren on a trip. No matter how many times you leave instructions or tell them what to do, no one ever bloody listens.

'Please get back upstairs,' I say as slowly as I can. 'And do not come out.'

Kent is just as bad. He arrives with all his equipment, dumps it on reception and asks, 'Where's the set?' I have already walked through with six suitcases, the majority of which were vulva pink. The girl keeps looking at us as more and more baggage arrives, obviously odd for a room that is being vacated at 7 p.m. Luckily just as Kent is about to blow everything with his lights and grouchy, pierced assistant

Pavel, a French TV crew turns up and provides the best cover for us to sneak in the rest of our stuff.

Once upstairs in the fantastically plush suite, we crack on with a quick G-G. Within about half an hour of filming the limitations of the suite are obvious. Not only can we hear the traffic outside but almost every creak and bang in the hotel. The staff can also hear us using the shower, which I imagine is also not terribly in keeping with a corporate interview situation. We ask for extra towels, club sandwiches without anything green and more sugar for our teas, and we cane the hot water. In the end I give in and resort to obscene tipping. It is the only way. The girl who delivers our food gets twenty quid. The guy who comes with towels gets another twenty. The daytime manager gets another fifty. I have done almost a hundred pounds on smoothing things out by lunch. Come 3 p.m. and the big bang scene, I have already knocked back a couple of vodkas. My nerves are shot and Kent is annoying everyone. For a start he keeps trying to speak in Hungarian to his assistant. Now he's the sort of bloke whose language skills don't go beyond 'Two beers and a blowjob please', so it is something of a feat that he is trying. He also keeps trying to experiment when filming. Early today I caught him whipping the camera in and out and spinning slightly to the left and right.

'What are you doing?' I said

'Going gonzo,' he replied.

'Not on my time you're not.'

'It's what everyone's doing in Budapest.'

For a man who spent most of his time in a cupboard or in a bar, Kent claims to have done an awful lot in Budapest. What he forgets when he is bullshitting in front of everyone is that I have seen some of the stuff he shot while over there and it's not great. It is all badly lit. Trying far too hard. It is clear from the red backgrounds and the weird clothes that Anton should probably ditch the porn and stick to fishing in the East End. But what is really annoying is that he now thinks his ideas are better than anyone else's. He showed me the script that they used in Budapest and it had directions in it like: 'Car pulls up. Door opens. Shot of hand. Shot of hand opening car door. Shot of door opening. Shot of smile.' It was a load of old bollocks. Now he is seriously suggesting that we start messing around with the Touch Wood format. He thinks we should economise. He thinks all we need is five scenes and some gonzo stuff shoved on the end. As we sit eating overpriced sandwiches, he tells me that cutting back is the future.

'Are you telling me that just as the brand is making a mark for itself, just as we have managed to market ourselves as quality and something a bit different, we should chuck it all in and go for the cheap seats like everyone else?'

'You'd save money,' he sniffs.

'I would listen to you,' I smile, 'if I didn't know that you were so bloody incompetent.'

'I am not incompetent,' he says.

'Yes, you are,' I sigh. 'You can't sell any of the footage that you shot in Budapest because you forgot to ask the girls to sign release forms.'

'How do you know that?' he asks, defensively scratching his balls.

'Because you told Seb the other night when you were pissed.'

'Oh, right,' he nods.

Back to the foursome and things aren't going too badly. Ray, I think, is just delighted to be having a rematch with Luella and Tony has always got on well with Trisha. They have yet to reach that 'brother-sister' stage. We've managed a double cowgirl and reverse cowgirl manoeuvre. We have had both the girls being taken up the arse while playing with each other's tits. We have had spanking and sex toys and Luella did agree to a spit roast while Trisha stood and watched. There is just one final scene, with doggy and a cream pie, before we finish off. Kelly has mixed some more of her cum solution and is sitting next to me on a lighting box. She asks whether she should buy a dog.

'I mean, what sort of life is it for a dog to go from porn shoot to porn shoot every day. It could quite well get trau- matised,' she says, chewing gum and shaking her bottle of cum. 'It can't be healthy, can it?'

'I wouldn't have thought that it would make that much difference,' I say.

'I don't know,' she says. 'My mate has a dog called Love Sausage who was brought up on porn shoots and all he does is dry hump your leg all day.'

'Maybe the dog was always like that,' I suggest, as Luella and Trisha get up on to the bed on all fours. Ray and Tony are standing by the edge of bed, both pumping away.

'I've got cum here,' announces Kelly, giving her plastic bottle another shake. 'Should you need it.'

'Fuck off,' says Ray. 'We're professional.'

'I was only saying.' She pauses and snaps her gum. 'No, I think you're right.' She turns to look at me.

'What?' I say.

'I think Love Sausage would have been a sex maniac with or without the porn.'

'I think the clue is probably in the name,' I suggest.

'What makes you say that?'

Before I can explain myself, Kent calls for quiet and the doggy scene begins. The only thing is, there's someone styling their hair with a hairdryer next door. As the moans and groans increase in the suite, the dryer goes off for a second and then goes back on again accompanied by a very loud reading of the headlines on the six o'clock news.

'Go and tell them to turn it down,' orders Kent from the foot of the bed.

'And say what?' I ask. 'Can you turn the TV down please, we're shooting a porn film?'

Kent huffs and sighs while everyone else gets on with it. We've got to be out of the place in an hour. Better that we get the cream pie in the can quickly, than we have the management at the door asking us to hurry up.

I ask Kent to concentrate on Ray first. He has one of the most reliable money shots in the business and it doesn't take long for him to oblige. He withdraws rapidly, leaving Kent to move in for a close-up of Luella's labia as she straddles Ray's huge orange thighs. We are all quiet as we sit and wait for the cream pie to emerge.

'You've had a child, right?' says Kent. 'Use your bloody muscles.'

'I haven't had a fucking baby,' Luella replies.

'Well, use your muscles anyway,' says Kent. 'Push! Push! Push!'

Amazingly Luella obliges and after a few seconds Ray's sperm slowly begins to seep down.

'Good girl,' says Kent, his face closer to Luella's vagina than any gynaecologist's. 'That's it That's it. Excellent.' He stands up. 'Great stuff,' he says. 'Fucking legend.'

Trisha, bless her, is a bit less successful. All she manages is a litany of fanny farts before we resort to Kelly's cum bottle. It is brilliant stuff. It seeps and weeps like the best-quality sperm and we rap with twenty minutes to spare.

Everyone is delighted. We pack up the equipment and get everything downstairs. I tip the staff all over again, including the rather wily looking night manager. Fresh on duty, he looks me in the eye as he takes fifty quid and I know that he knows exactly what we have been doing. He has been around too long to have anyone as amateur as I am pull the wool over his eyes. The stars retire to the bar while Kent and I pack up his car. We come back in for a much-needed vodka and tonic and find Luella and Trisha sitting with Kelly and Pavel. The boys are nowhere to be seen.

'I think they're both out the back,' says Luella, taking a sip of her Malibu and pineapple.

'What?'

'Yeah,' she says. 'They picked up two women in business suits and briefcases.'

'But we've only been gone about five minutes.'

'That's thirty-somethings for you,' says Trisha. 'They're bloody desperate.'

'They've both been shagging all afternoon,' I say, thinking quite how knackered I would be after that much sex.

'Yeah,' agrees Trisha. 'But you know what they're like.'

'Two bloody stallions. They're bred for shagging.'

'Mmm,' both the girls agree.

'Well, two career girls are going to have the time of their lives tonight,' I say.

'I think they said they were lawyers,' adds Luella.

Standing outside in the cool evening air, I finally exhale and relax. No one fell in the river yesterday and today was not too bad.

'Good day?' asks the Australian doorman standing next to me.

'Yeah, great, thanks.'

'Making a film?' he asks.

'What makes you say that?'

'A porno,' he says.

'Absolutely not,' I say, sticking my arm out for a cab.

'Are you Ben Dover?' he asks.

'No, I am not fucking Ben Dover,' I say, opening the cab door as it pulls up outside the hotel. 'Fuck off.'

Three days later, it is 9 o'clock on Monday morning and just before I head off to start editing *West End Girls* with Kent, I give the BBFC a quick call.

'Hi there,' I say. 'Is Madeline about?'

'No, I'm afraid not. You've just got me, Nigel.'

'Hi there, Nigel, I was just wondering, what's the story with feet?'

'What do you mean, feet?'

'I have a scene in my film where a girl has a foot up her bottom.'

'What?'

'The foot is up her bottom,' I say again.

'What, right inside?'

'Right inside.'

He starts to laugh. 'I'm sorry, I've got to put the phone down.' He is really laughing now. 'Give me your number and I'll call you back.'

After about ten minutes he calls back. 'I'm so sorry,' he says, clearing his throat and trying to control himself. 'I have never lost the plot in my entire career at the BBFC. The idea just made me hysterical. In the end I had to go to the chief examiner on this one, as I have never encountered this question before.'

'Right,' I say. 'I am sorry to have caused you such a problem.'

'Problem?' he laughs. 'It is the best question we've had this year. Or possibly ever.' He chuckles. 'So, OK then.' He pulls himself together. 'The same rules apply with the foot as they do with the fist. You need to be able to see the end of the toes.'

'Ah,' I say. 'Well, this one is in up to the ankle.'

'The ankle?'

'It's amazing what you can do with a bottom.'

'Clearly.'

'So the answer is no?'

'Yes,' he sighs. 'I am afraid so. Although I can imagine it might be very interesting to see.'

Kent and I go on to edit the film in his grubby subterranean flat. We cut the foot scene and send it off, only to have it returned a couple of weeks later. There are problems with the scene under Albert Bridge. Firstly I have to deny that it is Albert Bridge, in case anyone saw us and was offended, and secondly there is something wrong with the dialogue. Trisha says something along the lines of 'Let me go, you mean and horrible cousin, I don't want to come and see your boat', which of course implies that she is giving a blowjob against her will. We delete the sound and hard-cut her against the boat sex and the BBFC seems to think that it is fine.

In the meantime Ana sets about trying to find a suitable image for the DVD cover. She settles on the idea of an extremely sexy pair of red shoes. After scouring most of the shoe shops up and down Bond Street, she buys a pair of tiny size threes. She checks with the assistant that she can bring them back if they don't fit.

'Why don't you try them on?' asks the assistant.

'I can't,' says Ana

'But they won't fit,' says the assistant. 'You must be at least a size six.'

'But I can bring them back if they don't fit?' asks Ana again.

'Yes, but they won't.'

We shoot them using a digital camera against a white duvet at home and bring them back to the shop the next day.

'I am so sorry,' says Ana, 'but they didn't fit.'

The assistant just sighs.

Finally all the artwork is done and the film is passed by the BBFC. We have also found a new place to have the DVDs made. It is a little company out beyond Hackney Marshes where they print and press on site. They are happy to do porn. They check everything with you first and say they can do it in a week. I am shifting all the business over to them. Film Stuff can kiss my arse. It costs a little more but at least they deliver on time with everything shrink-wrapped and there are DVDs actually in the boxes. Life is looking up. My porn career is really beginning to work. What could go wrong?

The phone goes. It's Kent.

'You are a wanker,' he says.

My heart sinks. What now?

'I am standing here in Heathrow on my way to a mini break in France and I buy *DVD* magazine and guess what I see?'

'I have no idea.'

'Photos of me on a porn shoot,' he shouts at the top of his voice.

'Well, you do work in the business,' I say.

'Yeah, but I don't expect to be photographed on fucking one, do I?' he yells.

'Ah.'

'My girlfriend is so shocked.' So am I. I didn't know he had one.

'You shouldn't have shown her the shots then,' I say. That really pisses him off and he shouts and swears some more, before adding:

'And do you know what is even more fucking insulting?'

'What, than being in a porn mag?' I say.

'They have put little high heels over my eyes so you don't
know it's me.'

I start to laugh. 'So you can't tell that it is you anyway?'

'Don't fucking laugh at me.' He is now sounding very
angry.

'I am not.' I am.

'I am going to sue you and the DVD mag,' he shouts.

'What for?'

'For breach of contract.'

'We don't have one.'

'For abuse then. For abusing me. For abusing my human
rights. In fact . . .' He inhales. I can hear him trying to think.
'I am taking all you cunts to the European Court of Human
Rights!'

Eleven

Kent seems to forget all about his human rights the moment he comes back from his holiday in France. Instead of suing me and/or *DVD* magazine he calls up to see if there are any plans for another shoot. To be honest, I had thought of taking a breather. The idea of making and releasing a film a month is proving to be a lot harder work than I thought. Not only does it take a lot out of me in terms of organisation and nervous tension, it is also quite difficult cashflow-wise. The fact is that in order to keep the money flowing, I need to make the films but to make the films I need the cash.

Luckily sales are really picking up. The sex shops are calling up all day every day asking for more and more stock. And there is nothing that puts a smile on Ana's face like sending out an invoice. Still, I think in order to hit the big time, to get the boat, the bunnies and the flash pad in Ibiza, I need to start exporting the arse off the product and flog some clips.

The clips market is chugging along nicely. We are doing between six and eight a week to the US at the moment. Which at one thousand pounds a go isn't bad for a company that was a mere germ of an idea in a sex shop in Pigalle less than a year ago. It is the exporting that we really need to work on.

So when a French magazine calls up and asks to come on a shoot with us for a six-page feature in their publication and a small DVD package attached to the front, I decide to make a film just for them. If I schmooze them and give them the time of their lives, it can only be good publicity for me and a chance to break into the French market, which is huge. Although their tastes are a little different from ours. The plots might not change much but I think you'd be surprised how different nations are when it comes to porn peculiarities. The French are a little more arse-orientated than we are. And they love the young girl and older man scenario, a touch of the Serge Gainsbourg, with a bit of pissing thrown in. The Germans like shitting and hitting, nipple clamps and pins and rubber gloves and black latex. The Italians love shagging nuns – it's all that Catholic guilt. Us Brits are all about spanking and the girl next door, the more real and out of shape she is the better. The US is all about artifice, anal and a totally shaved quim. They like their tits as fake as their sets. The Dutch love an animal any which way they can. Spain is about Barcelona and an eighties demi-wave. The Japanese love a schoolgirl in a hello-sailor uniform, white pants and shitting. But you are still not allowed to see any pubic hair. Which all makes me wonder how well we are going to go down in France. Then again a six-page feature in one of the best-selling dirty magazines in France has got to help.

I decide, in order to look like the huge player they clearly think I am, I should hire an international porn star. Summer Sun is a blonde bombshell from Denmark and one of the biggest stars to come out of northern Europe. She has large tits and a small arse, which is a perfect porn combination.

She is the most expensive star we've ever hired and I have to pay her airfare from Germany and put her up in a four-star hotel into the bargain. In fact she was quite specific about the amount of stars, so she is clearly a girl who knows her quality.

We have come up with an easy idea for the film. Called *The Tourist*, the story is that Summer Sun arrives in the capital and travels around taking in the sights. As she visits the various London landmarks, she gets herself into all sorts of trouble with various bus conductors and ticket touts.

It is not hard to spot Summer Sun when I collect her from Heathrow Airport. Her hair is big and blonde and she is so tanned she looks like she sleeps every night on a sunbed, like a slice of bread in a sandwich toaster. Unlike most porn stars, who wear hardly anything and leave little to the imagination, she is dressed in a full-length black coat and black leg warmers underneath a surprisingly long (knee-length) skirt. I know our summers are notoriously bad but I can't quite help thinking that she is taking the piss. She lets me carry her suitcase to the car and as she sits in the passenger seat she says, 'People are often amazed at how intelligent I am.'

My heart sinks. This is going to be hell. There are few things worse than porn stars who think they have a brain. Porn stars with actual brains are fine, of course. In fact, like Camilla, they tend to be witty and very good fun to hang out with. But one with intellectual illusions is going to be a nightmare.

On our way into London she tells me about her little allergies and intolerances. No alcohol. No bread. No milk. Her temple can't cope with toxic substances. Two cocks up her arse are fine. But no bread and jam with that, otherwise she might be terribly, terribly sick. As I pull up outside her four-star hotel in Bayswater, I realise that she is the first porn star in my whole year in the business that I dislike. Already. And we haven't shot a frame. There have been plenty I wouldn't work with again. But this piece of work has got shirty already and I haven't asked her to do anything other than sit in the car. I am getting nervous about how this shoot is going to pan out.

I wait for her to check in and then we drive straight to the jetty outside the Tate, where we are to meet up with the rest of the team and the French camera crew to take the ferry across the Thames to the London Eye – our first shoot of the day.

As we pull up in front of the jetty, a sudden wave of panic hits me. I see Kent, Kelly, Pavel, Ray, Tony and Camilla, plus the four French guys, and then I see the boat. It is fucking tiny. There is a whole queue of people waiting to get on-board. My idea of us casually shooting Camilla and Summer having a quick snog on the boat as we cross the river is looking unlikely. Our first shoot with the French crew and I am going to look like a rank amateur who doesn't know his arse from his anal.

'Hello there, I am Philippe,' says a handsome short bloke with neat brown hair and a long straight nose. 'I am the director of the DVD and this here is Jean François. He will be shooting the stills. Xavier is writing the article.' He points to a dark man with round glasses and a black shirt. I smile. He nods. 'And this is Andre, who is helping us with sound.' Andre has his back to me but is wearing a pair of earphones and is already wielding a large boom.

'It is delightful to meet you all,' I say.

'We have already introduced ourselves to your team,' he says, turning to look at my orange friends and Kent. 'So what is the plan?' He smiles and rubs his hands together. He looks excited.

'Well, we shoot a bit here on the boat and at the London Eye,' I say, pointing across the river.

'Cool,' he says. 'We will follow you.'

I have to say this is not quite what I had envisaged. Firstly I had not expected there to be four French and secondly the boat that usually makes this crossing is much larger and covered in Damien Hirst spots.

'Hi,' I say to the young student selling tickets at the bottom of the gangplank. 'What has happened to the other boat?'

'Oh,' he shrugs. 'The big one has gone to Greenland to be refitted. We are having to make do with the small one at the moment.'

We all trot on-board, followed by a Spanish family of six, a group from Bolton and four youths from Ireland. It is a tight squeeze and there is almost no way we can film. But I am desperate not to look like a fool in front of the French and Kent always says that he can film anywhere. He gets his camera out and lines Camilla and Summer up for a shot. No sooner does he turn the camera on than the Spanish squeeze grinning and waving into the frame. Kent moves to the left and the Irish youths join in with their thumbs up, gurning down the lens. This is a total fucking disaster. I am smiling and sweating and trying to distract the French by pointing out the splendid view of the Houses of Parliament. Just as I have run out of elegant vistas, the captain's assistant taps me on the shoulder.

'Hi,' he says. 'Are you making a movie?'

'Well . . .' I'm not sure what to say.

'We were just wondering if we could do anything to help?'

'I am sorry?' I'm a little shocked. This the first time someone has tried to make my life easier on a shoot.

'Well, you know, like slowing the boat down?'

'Hello there!' shouts the captain, poking his head out of the cabin window. 'If you want some embarking and boarding shots, we're happy to oblige the other side.'

I can't believe it. The crew have saved our bacon and my future export career in France. When we reach the other bank, the Spanish, the Irish and the northerners leave and we are given the run of the boat. We get the girls going onboard in their perspex platforms; we get them to snog on deck; we get some good shots of Ray. We dock and launch the boat a couple of times. The French shoot us shooting them and everyone is delighted. As we stand on the side of the river waving our new friends off and promising them copies of the film, two rather burly security guards and a fierce-looking woman come walking towards us. Kent notices them first.

'Fuck,' he says. 'Security at twelve o'clock. You keep them talking and I'll carry on filming.'

Kent takes his camera off his shoulder but keeps it running, pointing it at the Eye. Meanwhile the bouncers and the PR have me in their sights.

'Good morning,' says the woman. 'I am head of PR for the British Airways London Eye and I was wondering if I could see your permit?'

'Permit?' I say, trying to sound as innocent as I can. 'Why do we need a permit?'

'Because you are filming and this is private land,' she says, pursing her lips.

'Is it?' Over her left shoulder I can see Kent shoving a map into Summer's hands, telling her to wander around like a lost tourist. 'I never knew that!'

'So I would like to see your permit, otherwise I will have to stop you filming.'

'Filming? Us?' I say. 'What makes you say that?'

'We've just watched you film right here,' she says.

'Oh, right,' I smile. 'But we have stopped.'

'Oh,' she says, looking around trying to catch us out. Kent's camera slips to film the floor and the French look as innocent as schoolboys. 'Well . . . if we catch you, you will be arrested.'

'Of course,' I nod. 'Quite right too.'

For the next forty minutes we play a game of cat and mouse. Ray walks around chatting to an ice cream seller and handing out leaflets like he is a tour operator and Summer slinks around flicking her hair and tweaking her big tits, trying to look like a horny tourist who is lost and up for it at the same time. Kent films them in cheeky little bursts and the French team slip in a few shots while no one else is looking. Then eventually it becomes too much for the battle-axe and she releases her rottweilers. I am afraid I make a run for it. I am not the bravest of men in the first place. But to be chased down by four security guards at the same time is enough to put the wind up anyone. The French also scatter to the four corners. The rottweilers leave Ray, Camilla, Summer and the rest of the group alone and head after Kent. Amazingly he stands his ground. As I stop on the corner halfway towards the South Bank, my lungs burning in my chest, I turn back to watch him somehow manage to talk himself out of trouble. I don't know what he says or how he explains things but I see them write something down and then leave him and I watch him walk slowly towards the others. They hail two black cabs and I watch them all get in. My mobile goes. It's Kent.

'Where the fuck are you?' he shouts. 'Trust you to fuck off along with those garlic-munching surrender monkeys.'

'I can't believe they let you go,' I say, trying to be jovial.

'Well, I blamed the whole thing on you,' he says, in a manner that makes me realise that he is not joking.

'Right,' I say.

'I gave them your name and address and they let me go.'

'Oh,' I say.

'Where are we meeting up?' he asks.

'Parliament Square.'

'Are you going to tell the frogs or am I?'

I call the French and we arrange to meet near Churchill. Kent has collected his car and has parked it opposite the House of Commons. He is already filming out of the back by the time we catch up with him. He has Summer walking back and forth outside the main gate and Big Ben all lined up in the background. Ray is standing on the street corner, pretending to be a tour guide again, when Summer approaches. The idea is that she asks him where Big Ben is and he says that he knows of a bigger Ben and would she like to see it. She then goes back to his flat for some DP that I am planning to film tomorrow with Tony and Ray.

I have chosen this location to impress the French. This afternoon we are also going to film outside the Tower of London and Buckingham Palace. I am hoping that after the morning's debacle I can rescue my reputation a bit and make them think that we are cool and organised.

'I am terribly sorry about earlier,' I say to Philippe as we watch Summer teetering towards Ray in high heels.

'That's OK,' he says. 'It was very energising.'

'Good,' I say. 'I am not normally this disorganised.'

'Don't worry about it,' he says.

Why is it that porn stars always seem to wear the same cheap shoes? And why is it they can never walk in the damn things either? While I am pondering these questions I don't notice the approaching sound of police sirens, or the speedy arrival of a white van. It is only when it screeches to a halt in front of us and four coppers burst out of the back that I realise what is going on. Two of them pull Kent from his car and hurl him to the floor, while another grabs hold of his camera and the other shouts over at Ray and Summer. Kent is rolling around on the pavement, shouting and screaming and only making the situation worse.

'I am not a fucking terrorist,' he shouts. 'Get your hands off me. I am not a terrorist. I drive a fucking Smart car. Have you ever seen a fundamentalist in a Smart car?'

I start to panic. The last thing I bloody need is for my cameraman to be arrested. The French will think we are totally incompetent and the six-page feature with DVD will go out the window. I have the most expensive porn star I have ever hired wandering around the streets of London and we have yet to see her without her clothes on. This is more than a disaster. It is the mother of all fuck-ups. Kent flails around some more on the pavement. Please God, don't be abusive, I think, as I run towards him. Please don't hit an officer. I need you to work, you bastard. Don't blow it all now.

'Officer! Officer!' I say. 'Can I be of any assistance? Would you like to talk to me, Kent?' I shout.

'What?' he yells out from underneath a uniformed armpit.

'Will you calm down?'

'Calm down? Calm down? You're not the one being sat on by two police officers.'

In the end I send the French and the porn stars, plus Kelly and Pavel, to the Trocadero to get some lunch. I sit with Kent in the back of the police van, trying to talk our way out of a potentially tight situation. It takes them a while to believe our story. I think the idea of shooting a porn movie outside the Houses of Parliament is so absurd, they can't quite believe how stupid we are.

'You do know that you could have been shot?' asks one officer.

'Do I look like a terrorist?' asks Kent, pulling his shorts out of his arse crack. 'I know I have a lot of facial hair, but really.'

They keep us in the van for an hour and a half waiting to see if our story checks out. I don't know who they talk to or where they check but they seem satisfied enough to let us go with a small talking to. Either that or they get so bored and pissed off with Kent's endless chatting and complaining that they just want to see the back of us. They shove us out of the back of the van in Parliament Square and hand us back our camera, before speeding off to arrest some real criminals.

The rest of the day is spent trying to film outside the Tower of London, only to be frogmarched out by some Beefeaters, and getting away with all the filming we like outside Buckingham Palace. We manage to shoot Summer lifting her skirt outside the Palace. We manage to get her lost and horny by the Victoria Memorial. I don't know if it's because the guards couldn't care less, or because there are so many tourists that Summer's short skirt and large knockers are lost in the crowd. Anyway by the time we tip up at the Water Rat, I am ready to sink my bodyweight in drink.

I have booked a table for Kent, the French and me in the back of the pub. The food is quite tasty and I thought it might be a good way to entertain them and keep the schmooze going. Although I have a feeling that it is going to take more than a nice piece of belly pork and a glass of Shiraz to convince them that we are the players they thought we were at the beginning of the day.

As we all pack up outside Buckingham Palace, Kent invites everyone down to the pub. I have to say I am a bit pissed off with him. Last time Ray went to the Water Rat he blocked the loo for half an hour with his marathon sex session and I am not sure that Steve would really want him back in the place.

Ray sets the tone and the pace of the evening by ordering a double tequila shot and the French follow suit. My heart sinks. This was supposed to be a posh night out but it now looks like the beginning of a pub crawl. Kent has a pint. Camilla orders a G&T but she says that she can't stay long.

'I'm working tonight,' she adds, as I hand over her drink.

'Really?' I ask.

I haven't seen Camilla for a while but she does look different from the girl I once photographed with her legs apart in the grass. It sounds weird but she just isn't as fresh-looking as she was. She looks jaded. Hard around the edges. Or maybe I just have a rather romantic idea of what she looks like. I've always had a bit of a soft spot for her.

'I'm escorting,' she says.

'Escorting?'

'Yup, and before that I've got a quick bukkake party in north London.'

'Bukkake?' What the hell is she talking about?

'Yeah, you know . . .'

'Bukkake?' Kent interrupts. 'Are you into that now?'

'That's right,' she grins. 'It's such a laugh. I've been booked for some party with fourteen blokes and I think it's me and just one other girl.'

'Sounds fantastic,' says Kent, taking a swig of his drink. 'Maybe I should come?'

'I think it's booked up,' says Camilla. 'They all booked online a while back, I think. I'm on the 8 p.m.–10 p.m. shift.'

'I'm sorry,' I say, 'I've never heard of bukkake. What is it?'

'How long have you been working in this industry?' asks Camilla, taking a step back in shock.

'Nearly a year.'

'And you don't what bukkake is?' She is incredulous.

'No!' I'm a little annoyed.

'It's when a group of men pay to wank on a girl's face,' says Kent.

'They can do it one at a time or all at once,' says Camilla. 'Basically you lie there and everyone wanks on you and you end up covered in spunk. It's hilarious. It's my new thing,' she grins. 'I love it! And I get about eighty pounds into the bargain.'

'Eighty quid, is that all?' I ask.

'You know me, I'm into everything.'

'Right,' I nod.

'I am trying to get myself invited to a shitting party next week. I have been to one where some bloke shits and you lie down underneath a glass table,' she says.

'Where's the pleasure in that?' I ask.

'Isn't there some actor famous for it?' asks Kent.

'That's right,' says Camilla, clicking her fingers. 'Damn it. I can't remember his name.'

'So shitting?' I say.

'Absolutely,' she nods, sipping her G&T. 'I want to experience everything. Absolutely everything. I would love to fuck a dog.'

'Isn't that illegal?'

'Is it?' she says.

'I think so.'

'Shame,' she shrugs.

'Drink?'

'I'm sorry, I can't,' she says. 'I can't hang around too long.'

'Of course, wouldn't want to be late for the party.'

'How many blokes did you say were going?' asks Kent.

'Around fourteen,' she says.

'And what are you doing? Snowballs?' he asks.

'Is that when the blokes come into your mouth and then you snog the other girl and you pass the spunk from one mouth to another?' she asks. Somehow it doesn't sound quite so bad in a cut-glass boarding school accent.

'That's it,' nods Kent.

'No, I haven't managed to find a girl who would do that with me.'

'Or a summit?' asks Kent.

'What's that?'

'When all the leftover sperm that has missed the girl's mouth is collected in a glass and she drinks it?'

I spit my beer across the room. 'Jesus Christ!'

'Oh, I've done that!' claims Camilla, her finger in the air. 'Hilarious! And I have done a dream shower – you know, where you shag one of the blokes and all the others take it in turns to wank on your face while you're having sex.'

'Have you ever thought that you were just rebelling against your parents?' I ask.

'What?' she says, looking at me as if I were mad. 'Rebelling?' she repeats. 'Don't be stupid. I just love sex. Why do you think I am escorting?'

'All the girls in porn are escorting at the moment,' says Kent.

Kent appears to be right. I hadn't really thought about it but I have noticed it more and more. Maybe it is because you can earn four or five times in one night what you would earn from a day's shoot. There are also guys who are willing to pay a premium if they get to spend the night with a porn star. The internet has made the whole thing much more easy to organise. You don't have to put cards up anywhere or even be part of an agency. You post up your ad on the net and see the offers pour in. And you can kind of see the appeal. Why bother to do porn shoots when you can do two or three escorting jobs a week and earn the same amount of money? Why bother to take the cold early-morning train into town from Halifax to shag someone you may not like all day? To argue about your travel money? To eat a Somerfield sandwich and take the long train journey back again? When all you need to do is turn up to a hotel room, sleep with a businessman and go home again. These porn stars' goalposts are always moving. Some of them go from G-G to B-G to DP in a matter of months. It is normally only a matter of time before they think about escorting.

Kent thinks that half of London is at it. He keeps saying that the only way any of these girls could afford their flats, their handbags and their cosmopolitan cocktails on their office salary is if they are on the game. I think he is just obsessed because the rest of the world is having more sex than him. Everyone's doing it, except for him – now that he's been dumped. And actually me – now that I'm a porn director. I'll tell you one thing: filming sex all day makes you much less inclined to have any yourself. I often wonder if I am a little intimidated by the huge cocks I see or is it because I know I am never going to be able to do anything that hard and vigorous and gymnastic? Or am I just another sad bloke in his forties who is simply exhausted after a hard day's work? Half the world is doing it and the other half is downloading it. And the rest of them are escorting. I can't help thinking as I kiss the lovely Camilla goodbye and thank her for her work today that escorting is just a nice way of saying prostitute.

Summer comes over and asks for a sambuca, which is an odd drink to choose at the best of times, particularly when you've told everyone that you're teetotal. I buy her one with Coke, which makes me gag even to order it. But anything to keep the talent happy, as they say. I ask Steve to make our table larger and invite everyone for dinner.

By 10 p.m. the long table is littered with bottles of sambuca and tequila and most of the porn crew are tucking in to their well-done steak and chips without salad, and all I am thinking is how much this is going to cost me. Dinner for twelve was not something I had budgeted for. But at least the French guys seem to be enjoying themselves. They all have red faces and appear to have abandoned some of their Gallic sophistication. Philippe is entertaining Summer and Jean François is doing tequila shots with Ray. They are both going to regret their behaviour in the morning. However, not as much I do, when I pick up the bill. I can't believe that some meat, potatoes and a few cheap shots can come to a grand, but apparently they do.

Drunk and fleeced, I finally get to bed at 1 a.m., only to be woken at 6.30 a.m. by Kent.

'This is going to be shit,' he says. 'I bet you haven't seen the set and checked out the new girl.'

'Oh, shut up, will you,' I yawn. 'You always do this on an important shoot. You call up paranoid and berate me for something or other and it always turns out fine in the end.'

'Fuck off,' he barks

'Fuck you,' I reply. He hangs up And now I am too pissed off to go back to sleep.

The French team, Ray, Tony, Summer, Kent, Pavel and I all meet at a rather nice flat in central London that I have managed to blag off a mate. He is on holiday in Italy. In a white stucco-fronted building, it is a stunning piece of real estate with views over Regent's Park. We are waiting for Kelly to turn up. She has phoned to say that she has to pick something up on the way over. The new Brazilian girl who I have never used before is also late. I'm rather nervous about her as all I know about her is what is on the agency website. But when she walks through the door some twenty minutes later I know I have done well. She is stunning. Bronzed and lithe, with dark curly hair and an arse you just want to sink you teeth into, the whole room falls silent as she walks in.

'Hello?' she purrs. 'I am Pica. Sorry I am late.'

'Hi everyone,' breezes Kelly, rushing in behind Pica, holding a very small yapping dog. 'This is Foxy.'

You can say that again, I think, and the dog's not that bad either.

It is Foxy and Pica's first porn shoot and they both take to it like lap dancers to a pole. Foxy dry humps everyone and everything from Kent's leg to the lighting pole. While Pica is unstoppable.

We have a few issues at the beginning with her health certificates, which are so amateur I could have written them myself. They say something like: 'She's been tested for everything and she is fine.' Summer looks at them long and hard. Ray and Tony scarcely give them a second glance they are so excited at the prospect of someone new and nubile. They are hard as rocks and gagging for it. Just to make sure and put everyone's mind, mainly Summer's, at rest, I call up the clinic where Pica says she got her tests. I get through to Dr Joyce and Dr Joyce says she is fine. Which is the good news that everyone, bar Summer, is desperate to hear.

We start with some gentle B-G. The story, such as it is, means that Summer comes back to the flat with Ray to find Tony, his flatmate, already at it and then as if by magic they join in. Kent starts up the camera and Tony and Pica start to have sex. The room is hushed. Even Foxy is still. We are all staring at Pica, who has to be the most sensual shag I have ever seen. She writhes and moans with pleasure. Philippe's mouth is hanging open. Jean François is getting a little agitated. I'm afraid I have to leave the room and get some air. This is the first time I have ever felt a little fresh on a shoot. I have one of those inconvenient stiffies that make it uncomfortable to walk. I try to ease my way out of the room as naturally as possible. It is not a good look for the director to get a lob on while shooting his own film. But it is hard not to. She is so goddamn gorgeous and she appears to be loving it. She has a great big grin on her face and overwhelming enthusiasm in her hips.

Once outside in the fresh air I spark up a cigarette and walk briskly round the block trying to get the air to circulate around my balls. I think of ice, cold showers, sprouts and my mother, anything to take the edge off the horn. My mother seems to clinch it and I walk back into the room to hear Kent shout, 'Cut!' Pica and Tony carry on for another three minutes until she reaches this loud, expansive, shuddering climax. One of the French team starts to applaud. Philippe takes out his handkerchief and mops his brow and Jean François just can't stop taking photos.

The rest of the afternoon is a nightmare, though. As a reaction to Pica's glorious scene and subsequent attention, Summer releases her inner, not terribly well-hidden diva. She complains about the food on set. She says that she can't eat anything that isn't handmade, so the pile of Boot's sandwiches we provide at lunchtime aren't good enough for her. She won't touch the foul chocolate that everyone else is eating. And she is not happy with her hair and make-up. But a bit more mascara won't get her into Pica's league. In a fit of pique she swans off set for a break and takes a large swig from a bottle of mineral water.

'Oh, no,' says Pica, running towards her stark naked. 'Don't drink that.'

'Why on earth not?' says Summer, taking another swig.

'Because', she says, 'I have just drunk from it and my mouth has been around Ray's cock and his cock has been up my arse.'

Summer spits the water out of her mouth and runs screaming and spitting to the bathroom. I can hear her running the tap, coughing and making herself retch. It couldn't have happened to a nicer girl.

The rest of the afternoon is spent with Summer going through the motions, Foxy the dog getting into most of the shots and everyone trying to think up more reasons to include Pica in the film.

At around three Summer starts to ask about getting a plane home. She bangs on and on about taxis and her flight and when she can leave. Eventually I take her to one side.

'Listen,' I say, 'I have flown you over here, put you up in a hotel, taken you out to dinner, paid you double the rate of everyone else and still you want to leave?'

'Yeah,' she says, looking at me like a defiant teenager.

'Oh, grow up and stop it,' I say. 'You've got one more scene. Why don't you do it with good grace and then you can go?'

Summer does as she is asked for the first time that day and I even catch her slipping down a quick Boot's chicken sandwich when she thinks my back is turned. Her body is not such a truculent temple after all.

As I shove her well-worked arse into a taxi at 6.30 p.m., hoping she makes the 8 p.m. flight, I am very glad to see her go. It makes me wonder if expensive stars are worth it when there is so much untapped natural talent out there.

Philippe shakes my hand to leave.

'That is the best couple of days I have ever had,' he says. 'I like very much the gonzo style that you shoot in. I like very much the locations. I like the dinner. But most of all I like that Brazilian girl.'

'I think we all like the Brazilian,' I wink.

'Ah, bloody hell, fuck yes,' he says. 'I shall put you on my cover two months in a row.'

'Really?' I say.

'Of course,' he smiles. 'We have a circulation of a quarter of a million readers. Welcome to the French market, my friend.'

Twelve

We have just got our first order of ten thousand DVDs through from France. Some very on-the-ball distributor has heard about our cover story on the French porn mag and is stocking up in advance. Ana is ecstatic and I am over the moon. This month it looks like we might clear about £20k through our account. It is almost exactly a year since I started in the porn industry. Things are really beginning to happen.

Kent and I edited *The Tourist* without too much argument and we are waiting for it to come back from the BBFC. We don't envisage too many problems with it as we didn't go too overboard – most of our shooting time was spent either in the care of the authorities or trying to escape from them. All the best scenes have nothing to do with Summer Sun and all to do with that firecracker of a Brazilian, Pica. I would use her again at the drop of a lens cap, if anyone knew how to get hold of her. Her agency says that she has disappeared and her mobile no longer responds. I can't help but think some lucky man found her one night and is never going to let her go. In the year that I have been in this business she is the best girl I have come across.

Ana and I are sitting at the kitchen table drinking cups of

tea and sending out invoices when the phone goes. I am initially reluctant to pick up as Kent has already called me a couple of times this morning to tell me that he has someone sitting outside his house stalking him.

'It's the VAT man,' he whispered down the phone. 'He is waiting for me to come out of the house so he can get in and confiscate my stuff.'

'Why doesn't he ring the doorbell?' I asked.

'He's after me,' he said. 'He wants to take my money and my things.'

'He has a legal right to enter any property,' I said. 'If he wanted to come in he would.'

'That's not his style, he's sneaky,' replied Kent. 'I am not moving from the house for anyone.'

'OK then,' I said. 'Call me later.'

'Oh, I might come and see you later for a drink.'

'But I thought you couldn't leave the house?'

'He'll clock off at six,' he said. 'He always does.'

Honestly there are times when I think Kent must be taking LSD. Either that or he took so much in the past he is having flashbacks.

I inhale and steal myself for some more insanity.

'Hello?'

'Hello,' comes a female voice down the line. 'It's Elaine here from *ETO* magazine.'

'Hello?'

'Is that Touch Wood Films?'

'Yes?'

'Oh, good,' she says, a smile sounding in her voice. 'I am ringing to tell you that you have been nominated for an *ETO* award.'

'I have? We have?'

'That's correct,' she says.

'Really? This isn't a wind-up?'

'No,' she replies, a little put out. 'Why would it be a wind-up?'

I can't believe it. My heart is racing and I'm smiling so hard I look like some nutter who's put his knife down a toaster.

'We've been nominated for an award!' I tell Ana opposite me, a quizzical expression on her face.

'Congratulations!' she exclaims, getting out of her chair and putting her arms around me. She kisses my neck and gives me a tight hug. 'What for?'

'Oh, yes, um, sorry, Elaine, you still there?'

'Yes.'

'What's the award for?'

'Best British R18 DVD,' she says.

'That's amazing,' I say. 'Which film?'

'*The Surveyor.*'

'Cool,' I reply. Mitch and Laura had their flat trashed for a reason, then.

'You're up against six other films,' she continues. 'Which include *Roxy Jezel's Fuck Me*, *Sexpose Dogging*, *The Little Shoe Box* and *Whoops, I've Wet My Panties*.'

'I can't believe it,' I say, shaking my head.

'The ceremony is in a few weeks' time at the NEC in Birmingham,' she says.

She talks me through the whole thing. From the names of the other nominees to the price of the tickets, to the hotel we should stay in and the possible trains we can take. There's a trade exhibition first, followed by a black-tie dinner. The tickets are a hundred pounds each and she suggests I take a table of ten, seeing as I am a nominee.

I hang up and do a small dance around the kitchen, punching the air and kicking my legs. From zero to *ETO* nominee in a year. That's not bad going. I am overjoyed. Not only does it justify my decision to go into this industry in the first place, it also means that I must be quite good at it.

'I am so happy for you,' says Ana. 'I am so, so pleased. I wish we could phone my parents and tell them. Or call your dad and celebrate.' She shakes her head. 'It is such a shame you are doing porn.'

Shit. Ana has just reminded me that I am supposed to be having lunch today with my dad. I arranged to collect him off the Paddington train and then go for lunch in his club in the West End. The only thing is, I have several porn deliveries to make beforehand. I have to visit three or four sex shops to drop off some DVDs. I wonder if I dare kill two birds with one stone?

Half an hour later I have my dad in the car and 175 copies of hard pornography on the back seat. I've collected him from the station and we are taking the scenic Soho route to Pall Mall. Fortunately he doesn't come up to town very often so he is not too sure of his way around. But even he is beginning to shift a little uncomfortably as we wend our way through Soho Square.

'Are you sure this is the way?' asks my father, his white bushy eyebrows curling into a frown.

'It's Ken Livingstone,' I say.

'Ah,' he says, nodding knowledgeably like the old Tory voter he is. 'Of course, Red Ken.'

On the pretext of dropping off a few bits and collecting a few bobs that have something non specific to do with my internet business, I manage to pull over four times and deliver about 120 of the DVDs. Thankfully my father is so transfixed by the sight of leather-clad men holding hands that I am able to go about my business without too many questions while he searches, in vain, for some Christian inclusivity. By the time we get to his club he is so culturally shocked and exhausted he orders a glass of sherry. I have to say the last time I saw him drink at lunchtime was back in 1997 when Tony Blair was elected and he needed something strong to steady his nerves.

We spend most of the time over our lunch of poached salmon and summer pudding discussing my younger brother. My father is worried about him. He doesn't seem to be happy.

'Have you noticed anything odd?' he asks, pouring more cream over his berries.

'Not really,' I say. 'I spoke to him a couple of weeks ago and he seemed fine.'

'I wonder,' he says, 'if James shouldn't come and work for you?'

'For me!'

'Don't sound so surprised,' says my father. 'I mean, you are doing well.'

'Yes,' I say slowly.

'I'm sure he would fit in.'

'You are?'

'Yes, well, the computer thing can't be that hard,' he says, taking a sip of mineral water. 'James was always very good at maths.'

'I don't think maths has a lot to do with it these days,' I say.

'He has a head for figures.'

'You'll need that,' I joke.

'Well, what do you think?'

I am in half a mind to tell my father that to have one son working in the hardcore porn industry is probably enough for any vicar, without him forcing the other down that turbulent and some might say diabolical path as well. But I don't. The cosy panelled confines of a Pall Mall gentleman's club are no place to break a father's heart, no matter how far apart you've grown or how little his opinion of you matters any more. I do, however, allow myself to smile. If he only knew what he was suggesting – it would take more than a thimble of sherry to steady his nerves.

So I sit and gently persuade him that James is fine. That perhaps all he needs is a holiday or a rest. What he doesn't want is another desk-bound job like mine, typing away all day. Maybe what is required is a total change of direction?

'I mean,' I say, 'have you ever thought that he might want to have a chat with you?'

'Me?'

'Yes,' I say. 'I can't help but think that he might be interested in the church.'

'Really?' asks my father, his cheeks pinking slightly.

'Yes, really,' I say. 'He was always much more religious than me.'

'That's certainly true,' laughs my father. 'You were always very irreverent. To tell you the truth,' he smiles, 'I always thought that you might well come to a sticky end!'

'Really?' I laugh. 'Whatever gave you that idea?'

'I know,' he giggles. 'So very silly of me!'

On the way back to the station with my father my mobile goes in the car. I answer on speakerphone.

'Hello there, Kent.'

'All right.'

'Just to say that my dad's in the car,' I say, dropping as loud a hint as I can.

'All right, Dad,' he says.

'Hello there,' says my father, leaning over on to my lap.

He doesn't quite understand the concept of the speaker-phone.

'So we've been nominated for an award?' says Kent.

'You have?' says my father turning to look at me. 'What for?'

'Well . . .' Oh shit, I think.

'Best hardco—' I hang up before Kent can finish.

'Oh dear,' I say. 'He got cut off.'

'You've been nominated for an award?' says my father again. 'Why on earth didn't you tell me?'

'You know,' I shrug.

'What for?' he asks.

'Best . . . hard . . . drive,' I say.

'Best hard drive? What does that mean?'

'I'm not sure really.' I smile. 'Some sort of computer thing.'

'Right,' he says, nodding away.

We arrive at the station and I pull up outside.

'Here you go,' I say. 'Are you sure you'll be all right?'

'Of course,' he says, running his finger around the edge of his dog collar. 'The Lord looks after his own.'

'I thought that was the Devil,' I reply.

'Him too,' says my father. 'Good luck with the best hard award.'

'Thanks.'

'I mustn't forget to tell your mother, she'll be very excited. Be sure to phone and tell us if you win and then you can bring it home to show us.'

'Absolutely,' I lie.

'See you,' he says and leans across to shake my hand. 'Thank you for a lovely lunch.'

'Thank you,' I smile back.

I wait until he is safely inside the train station before I call Kent.

'You are a total cunt!' I bark as soon as he picks up. 'I told you my father was in the car and you couldn't resist, could you?'

'It's not my fault if you lie to your parents, is it?' he says. 'Isn't it time you grew up and told them what you were doing?'

'No!' I shout. 'And you can fuck off!'

By the time Kent and I are both trying to squeeze into our black tie at the Marriott hotel before the *ETO* awards we are back on speaking terms. I wouldn't normally pick a fight with him, but there was something about his cavalier attitude towards my family that really got on my nerves. I have since learned that he hasn't spoken to his own father for about twenty years, so maybe in some way he was jealous? Or has he just forgotten how to talk to parents and doesn't know what things they should and should not be party to?

Still, we've had an amusing day together. We've been to the trade exhibition in a small hall next to the hotel. Somehow this morning I managed to persuade Kent to sneak past the VAT man parked outside his flat and get on the train with me to Birmingham. Perhaps it was the fact that I'd booked a table of ten at the awards and invited the Paul Raymond boys to join us that made him so brave. Or the possibility of meeting a few busty porn stars. Or the promise of copious amounts of alcohol. Whichever way, we sat opposite each other in the train knocking back the vodkas at 10.30 a.m. It was a beautiful sunny Sunday morning. If I weren't for Kent chugging back the booze and tucking into the salt and vinegar crisps in front of me, I could almost swear I was going to visit my old granny in Solihull.

We arrived at the NEC raring to go and, I have to say, as we walked into the exhibition hall I was a little disappointed. In comparison to the Erotica at Olympia, the show was tiny.

There were only something like forty to fifty stands and most of them were for sex toys. There were more dildos and lube than you could shake a stick at. But nothing much else. Kent and I walked up and down the aisles, looking out for a friendly face, but didn't see anyone we knew. The ID Glide girls were sexy and pally enough. All blonde hair and big boobs: we hung out on their stand for a while, listening to all the gossip about a new sex toy, the Cone. Apparently it was going down a storm at the show. It can vibrate in ten different ways and one of the girls had already tried it out and had a large grin across her face to prove it. I was on the verge of buying a couple for my mates but then I remembered how many of those Just Perfect bastards I still have hanging around at home.

On the way out Kent spotted the bar. We couldn't believe we'd missed it on the way in. After all Kent can sniff out alcohol and a scratching at forty paces. Through the smoke, the silicone and the chat, I managed to pick out the spiked blond hair of, yes, Ben Dover. Sporting a leather jacket with tight jeans and a sleeveless T-shirt, he looked surprisingly normal for a bloke who is supposed to have the biggest cock in the business. I don't know what I was expecting. Maybe some sort of larger than life character who is so well endowed he needs an extra bar stool for his penis? Instead he looked like the spare bass guitarist for Dire Straits. So much so in fact that I spent a quick few seconds looking for the piano keyboard tie. Despite this he was surrounded by women, all hanging off his every word.

But then he's famous for being nice to the ladies in his films. The conceit is that he takes out his handicam and lures the 'girl next-door' off the street and persuades her to take off her clothes. She then blows him and someone else comes in and shags her. All Ben does is film, he doesn't really get that involved with the girls at all. No wonder then that they were all over him like a cheap suit. I could hear his cheeky-chappie cockney tones and their giggles right down the other end of the bar.

Kent and I ordered ourselves a couple of vodkas and started to do the rounds. We bumped into Wedding Video Dave sitting on his own drinking what looked like his eighth or ninth pint of the day. His face just managed to light up as we approached. Things weren't going so well. Apparently his baby was due any second but his porn star girlfriend had done a runner back to Poland and no longer wanted anything to do with him. She'd been making good money knocking out pregnant and milking porn but had now booked herself on the plane home.

'So I'm back on me own,' he told us. 'Still doing the weddings and the porn. You should come down and see us sometime,' he said. 'But I imagine you're a little busy these days. You know, being so big and that.'

We bought him another pint, agreed to go and see him and moved on, next bumping into Freddie who was looking toned and tanned with a couple of birds on each arm. He looked very pleased to see us. He shook our hands and shook off the girls and asked if there was any work going.

'You guys are doing so well at the moment,' he smiled. 'A film a month. You must be needing many people.'

'Sure,' I said. 'Whenever you want.'

'Do you mean that?' he asked, grabbing hold of my arm.

'Yes, of course, why not?'

'The thing is, man,' he whispered, 'I know you've heard some things about me recently.'

'No?' I said.

'Well, there's been some bitching.'

'Right, has there?' I really hadn't heard anything.

'Yeah, well, ignore it. It's not true.' His eyes narrowed. 'They are all just jealous bastards.'

'OK then,' I nodded.

'So we're cool?'

'We're cool.'

We shook hands and I told him I would certainly use him again. I didn't know he had been having a hard time. I imagine some people don't take too kindly to getting a dose. But perhaps it was more complicated than that.

Kent and I nodded at a few other familiar faces and decided to make our way back to the hotel room to change. The awards were due to start before too long and we both had to get into our suits.

'D'you know what?' I said to Kent as we walked across the car park in the glare of bright sunshine.

'What?'

'I think people are taking us seriously.'

'Fuck off.'

'No, they are,' I said. 'D'you think it is the award?'

'Maybe,' he shrugged. 'If that's what happens when you've only got a nomination, imagine what will happen if you win.'

Hot and sweaty with a tight seam parting my balls, I am suited and booted and standing by the downstairs bar in the hotel, waiting for the Paul Raymond boys to show. Kent is still in the room struggling with his black tie. He has already ditched the waistcoat on the pretext that it is high summer, only we both know he can't button it over his gut. Now he is trying to work out how to do up his fly. There seems to be an inch or so of cloth missing on his waistband, so he is putting together some sort of Heath Robinson contraption using elastic bands and string. I have simply inhaled, pulled it all in and am crossing my fingers that the strained stitching is going to last the night.

'Mate!' says Adam as he saunters across the lobby towards me, looking slick and slim in his black tie. He points at me with his cigarette. 'How the very hell are you?'

'Hello there!' adds Sean, following along in his wake. He is looking lean and rather chipper. He has a spring in his stride and a grin from ear to ear. 'I'm on a pink ticket,' he winks as he shakes my hand. 'The missus has let me out for the night.'

'Better make the most of it,' laughs Adam, slapping his colleague on the back. 'This only happens once a year!'

Following along behind Adam and Sean are a very dishevelled looking Kent and another three lads from Paul Raymond. Having shelled out for the table of ten, I decided that in the spirit of networking I should pass on the majority of the tickets to Adam and Sean.

I was going to ask the people who had made Touch Wood possible. The key figures who got the company up and running in the past year. But Toby is not really allowed out after dark, Ana would rather pluck her own eyes out than spend a night with porn people and that grey Andrew the bank manager would probably not be the best of company. Most of the others who had all lent their various flats, houses, boats and gin palace villas are still not really on speaking terms with me. Florien remains cross about the sofa. Mitch is continually having to come up with little white lies to Laura about the state of the terrace and/or table. It is whispered that Simon and Claire are the porn kings of Oxfordshire. And Will is seeking therapy for nightmares he keeps having after we shot in his office. All in all it would perhaps not be the most jolly of tables.

'Have you seen the cop cars outside the hotel?' asks Adam, sparking up another cigarette.

'D'you think they've come for me?' asks Kent, his eyes bulging over the top of his vodka, his trousers held together with string. I seem to have brought a tramp to the party.

'Nah,' says Adam, looking him curiously up and down. 'Why? What have you done?'

'Nothing,' I say. 'Ignore him, he's paranoid these days.'

'It's my VAT,' says Kent. 'I'm sure they're after me.'

'They don't look like VAT cops to me,' says Sean.

'No,' agrees Adam. 'I think they're here to keep an eye on us porn types. I have no idea what they're expecting.'

'A spontaneous orgy?' I suggest.

'A sudden outbreak of group sex?' says Adam.

'A bloody great gang bang,' adds Sean.

'I'm up for one of those,' says someone else.

'Only problem is,' says Adam, 'there are no girls.'

I look around the bar and realise he's right. For a major porn event, there seem to be very few lady stars present. Well, actually, none. All the people crowded around the hotel bar, stuffed in their black tie, are blokes. And they're nearly all middle-aged to boot.

'Where are all the porn stars?' I ask Adam.

'It's only the second time they've done this,' he says. 'So I suppose it is going to be all industry types.'

'There are a few over there,' says Kent, pointing to three girls coming out of the ladies lavatories, all dressed in floor-length apricot satin dresses.

'Afraid not,' says Sean, shaking his head. 'Those are bridesmaids.'

'Bridesmaids?' I ask.

'Yeah,' he says. 'There's a wedding going on downstairs.'

'What?' I say. 'There is a wedding downstairs and a porn convention upstairs?'

'Yup,' smiles Adam. 'I have a feeling the hotel's on double bubble.'

'Christ!' I say shaking my head. 'What's going to happen later?'

'Well, I'm looking forward to getting my hands on a bridesmaid,' sniggers Kent. 'There's plenty of Babycham and Malibu and pineapple in my minibar.'

'Our minibar,' I say, shooting him a look. I am beginning to regret sharing a room with him already.

We finish up our drinks and make our way across the road to the hall for the awards. Walking inside the smallish room, it is obvious that this is not going to be a patch on the *Adult Video News* Awards that are held in Las Vegas every year. The biggest event in the world of porn, the *AVN* Awards are the adult entertainment industry's Oscars and they are accompanied by hordes of screaming fans, huge porn stars lining up to sign autographs and more stretch limos, surgically enhanced bunnies and naughty impresarios than you can shake a dildo at. They have gongs for Best Blowjob, Best Anal, Best Threesome, Foursome, Cum Shots and Gang Bang. This, by total contrast, looks like one of the best-behaved evenings I have ever attended. Looking around at the suits sipping champagne and the few middle-aged women chatting, I'm sure I've had larger parties in my flat.

I help myself to a large glass of champagne and a cocktail sausage and start to circulate. The first person I bump into is Susie-Anne from Film Stuff. Dolled up in a strapless dress with a black ribbon around her neck, she is sweating through her make-up.

'Good evening,' I say.

'Oh, hello,' she coughs. A peanut fragment shoots out of her mouth on to my shoulder. She frantically brushes it off, while blushing to the roots of her stiff, sprayed hair. 'Wow, gosh, wow, you. Ha ha ha,' she giggles. 'What are you doing here?'

'I know,' I say. 'Unbelievable, isn't it, that I'm still in business?'

'Yes!' She laughs a little hysterically, before taking a large sip of her champagne. 'I mean, no. I mean, yes. I mean, what are you doing? Here? Are you on a table? Who's invited you?'

'I know, who would invite me?'

'No, I didn't mean that.' She is now so flustered that she looks like she is going to cry.

'I have been nominated for an award.'

'Have you?' Her nose falls forward.

'Yes.'

'Wow!'

'I know. Not for anything that you did.'

'No,' she says. Her head rocks from side to side as she gurns slightly and inhales through the back of her teeth. 'Sorry about that.'

'Yes, well,' I say. 'So who are you here with?'

She launches into a two-minute, blow-by-blow account of exactly who is on her simply fantastic table. They are all terribly important people within the porn industry and she is doing so, so well and they're brilliant. And she is brilliant for asking them along and everything is going really, really well. I nod along to all her marvellousness.

'Anyway,' she says, 'can you believe the Paul Raymond boys are here? I mean, they are such big players in the market. Everyone wants to work with them. I was saying just the other day that I should try and set up a meeting with them. All I need is someone to put a good word in. Oh, look,' she says, tapping me on my shoulder, 'don't look now, one of them is coming this way.'

'All right there, mate?' asks Adam, giving me a small slap on the back. 'I think I have found your table. We're somewhere near the front of the stage. Which bodes well for the award, don't you think?' He slaps me on the back again. 'See you down there in a second?'

'I'm coming with you.'

'Sorry to interrupt,' says Adam, nodding politely at Susie-Anne.

'Don't worry,' I say, smiling directly at her, 'you weren't interrupting anything.'

As we weave our way through the golden chairs and pink tablecloths towards the front, I turn back to look at her. She is standing rooted to the spot, holding her glass of champagne and looking from me to Adam and back again. Her jaw is hanging open. For once she is silent.

We all settle down at our tables and tuck into our seafood salad starter, followed by roast beef. Looking around the room, I can't really believe how respectable and well behaved everyone is. I think I could have bought grey Andrew along after all; he would have fitted right in. The only table that seems to have a whiff of decadence about it belongs to an internet company. Most of them are covered in studs and piercings. In fact three of them appear to be chained together and now that I look more closely they have forked tongues.

'Jesus Christ!' I say to Adam, sitting next to me. 'Have you seen the tongues on that lot over there?'

'Fucking hell,' he says, recoiling slightly.

'How do they get those, I wonder?'

'I imagine they cut their tongue very slowly and let it heal each time,' says the woman sitting next to me.

'Really?' I ask.

'We get that sort of kinky request quite often on the back pages,' she says.

It turns out that Sally, who is on the other side of me, sells phone line ads in the back of top-shelf magazines. Married with two young children, she is charming and attractive and could be working in any business except porn. But she knows her market and she knows it well. She tells me that a lot of the magazine's profits come from the ads pages at the back where 'Virgin Sluts' and 'Lonely Schoolgirls' are all prepared to talk on the phone for forty-five pence a minute.

'There are may be over a hundred telephone numbers on the page,' she explains, 'but they all go to one of two call centres, and then on to private homes, where the same girls pretend to be schoolgirls or dominatrixes. Or there are recorded stories that are played down the line.'

'That's amazing,' I say. 'I always thought they went to loads of different places. What is the most obvious kink?'

'The gay lines,' she says. 'Who would have thought that when we are on our own the majority of us become bi-curious? They call up the 'Home Alone Lesbian' or the 'Home Alone Gay Man'. She smiles. 'The "Naughty Twins" rarely get a look in.'

Just then the chocolate pudding arrives, the lights dim and amid very little fanfare the awards ceremony starts. The sound is a hit and miss, and the compère not the most charismatic of individuals. *Desire* wins Best Magazine and there are whoops and applause from one of the next-door tables. ID Glide takes Best Consumable and Rock-Chick Vibrating steals it from I Rub My Duckie and Rabbit Deluxe to win Best Adult Product.

'And the nominees for Best Overseas R18 DVD are . . .' says the man in the blue-frilled shirt and black tie on stage.

'You're up next,' says Adam.

'. . . *Lusty Bust Desires 1* (Bizarre), *Pirates* (Digital Playground), *Robinson Crusoe on Sin Island* (Private),

Chateau Episode 1 (Private), *Jenna Loves Pain* (Vivid) and *Sixty-Five-Guy Cream Pie* (Devil's Film),' continues the compère. 'And the winner is . . . *Jenna Loves Pain!*'

There's lots of shouting and screaming and clapping and whooping as a couple of blokes in bootlace ties weave their way to the front. I think they were hoping for something a little bit more glamorous than the piece of perspex they're given but they take it all with good grace.

'So now for the big one,' says the compère. 'Best British R18 DVD.'

'Good luck,' says Adam, giving my shoulder a squeeze.

I sit back in my seat. Kent is looking tense. I take a sip of my champagne. I can't believe this is happening. A year ago Touch Wood did not exist and now we are nominated for an award. Granted it is not the flashiest of events, there are hardly legions of fans and screaming press. This is a small piss-up in Birmingham. But it is as good as it gets in porn at the moment. Give it five years and it will all be different.

'And the nominees are . . . *Cabaret Bizarre* (Harmony Films), *Roxy Jezel's Fuck Me* (Harmony Films), *Sexpose Dogging* (Relish), *The Affair* (Pumpkin/Big Willy), *The Little Shoe Box* (Asphyxia), *The Surveyor* (Touch Wood Films)—' Adam, Sally, Kent and Sean all cheer, '— and *Whoops, I've Wet My Panties* (Rude Britannia).'

The whole room applauds the nominees. There are some big players on the list: Relish and Pumpkin/Big Willy have been around for a while, and Harmony and Rude Britannia are huge. We are the newest kids on the block and punching well above our weight. Kent and I hold our breaths. My heart is racing. My hands are clammy. My mouth is dry.

'And the winner is . . . *The Affair!* Pumpkin/Big Willy!'

Shit. I take a large swig of champagne, find my dignified loser's face and applaud another Cathy Barry success. Her warehouse outside Bristol is churning out the porn and she is raking in the cash. You have to admire her for it. I clap away, nodding left and right like it was a great decision. Inside I am gritting my teeth and swallowing my disappointment. It would have been the perfect end to a less than perfect year. It is only now that we have lost that I realise how much I wanted to win. I know I wouldn't have been able to tell anyone and the award would only have been put under the IKEA sheets in the hall or have kept the sexy toys company under the bed. But it would have been nice. I would have been able to share it with Ana. Hell, she might have been proud of me. I know what she'd have said. 'I am so pleased for you, but isn't it a shame that it's porn?' Or maybe she'd have stopped halfway through the sentence and paused at the word 'pleased'. Sadly I'll never know. I think about calling her to commiserate. But, I think, it's late, I'm quite drunk, so I'll bore her with my failure in the morning.

'Bad luck, mate,' says Adam, patting me on the back. 'D'you fancy a drink?'

Do I hell.

Adam, Sean, Kent and I get totally wankered. I remember little of the rest of the awards, except some important bloke called Clive is crowned Hero of the Year. Best Lingerie goes to GotLingerie and Dreamgirl wins Best Erotic Clothing. I only remember those clearly because a couple of sexy girls get up on stage. Oh, and Mantric Marketing gets Best Sex Toy Manufacturer and I am introduced to the bloke who owns it, an ex-Guards Officer, at the bar.

After sinking our bodyweight in bubbles, Adam, Sean, Kent and I retire to the hotel bar where we meet and mingle with a few stragglers from the wedding. Kent does manage to corner one of the apricot bridesmaids who gives him a blowjob in the gents, before she passes out, mouth open, on one of the sofas in the lobby. Meanwhile the forked-tongued group get a swimming party together and try to persuade us to join them in the lake.

I crawl upstairs to bed at about 5 a.m. As I tiptoe into my room I am met with the sight of Kent lying semi-naked on the bed. He has taken off his shirt but the string around his waist has evidently floored him. His trousers have been ripped in the struggle, his socks are still on and he is flat on his back, his arms and legs splayed out like a starfish. He is snoring his face off. Fortunately I am too drunk and tired to care. I curl up next to him on the bed and make a note to myself to book separate rooms next year.

The following morning there are roadworks going off in my head and my mouth is as dry as the Sahara. Kent is still snoring, so I leave him to it and head off down for some breakfast. As I get into the lift, I bump into the forked-tongued threesome. One of them is not wearing any trousers, but quite frankly that is the least of their worries. They don't appear to have slept and they are all covered in green slime.

'Good morning!' I say trying to be jolly.

'Hello,' says the bloke, staring me in the eyes.

'Had a good evening?' I say.

'Yes,' he nods, rather slowly. 'We've been in the lake.'

'Excellent,' I say as the lift reaches the lobby. The doors open and I look out of the windows at the thick green pea-soup of a lake below. It is like something out of a Chernobyl experiment. 'It looks very nice.'

The group head off in the direction of breakfast and I hang back. Better to given them a wide berth. I walk out to the car park to stretch my legs.

It is a beautiful morning, the sun is shining and the sky is a clear bright blue. I am still dressed in my black trousers and white shirt, but somehow the fresh air makes me feel a whole lot better. I inhale and raise my arms above my head. Things are going to be fine, I think, as I walk along. Touch Wood is going to work. I know it is.

I am staring out at the lake when I hear a voice behind me.

'Good morning,' says an American bloke.

'Hi,' I say.

'Are you the guy from Touch Wood?' he asks.

'That's right.'

'I have heard good things about you,' he says.

'Really?'

'Yeah,' he nods. 'I have heard you're exporting to France.'

'That's right. Germany's next.' I add.

'Good for you,' he says. 'Have you thought about the US?'

'Only the biggest market in the world,' I laugh.

'Well, I like your stuff, I like the way you work. I reckon you're the sort of man we are looking to do business with. My name is Len.' He smiles and touches the corner of his large-brimmed hat.

'I'm sorry, what did you say you were called again?'